CONTENTS

ABBREVIATIONS OF WORKS BY NABOKOV

Full details of the items listed will be found in the bibliography.
Unless otherwise indicated, translations are my own.

AL	*The Annotated Lolita*
BS	*Bend Sinister*
EO	*Eugene Onegin: A Novel in Verse by Aleksandr Pushkin*
IB	*Invitation to a Beheading*
KQK	*King, Queen, Knave*
LD	*Laughter in the Dark*
LL	*Lectures on Literature*
LRL	*Lectures on Russian Literature*
LATH	*Look at the Harlequins!*
NWL	*The Nabokov-Wilson Letters*
NG	*Nikolai Gogol*
PF	*Pale Fire*
PP	*Poems and Problems*
RLSK	*The Real Life of Sebastian Knight*
SL	*Selected Letters 1940–1977*
SM	*Speak, Memory*
SO	*Strong Opinions*
TT	*Transparent Things*

STYLE *Is* MATTER

INTRODUCTION

Lolita, and a Hitherto Little Remarked-upon Reader

SOMETIME IN LATE 1960 or early 1961 Adolf Eichmann, jailed and awaiting trial in Jerusalem, was given by his guard a copy of Vladimir Nabokov's recently published *Lolita*. Hannah Arendt recounts this curious incident as follows: "Eichmann's best opportunity to show this positive side of his character [which he insisted that he had] in Jerusalem came when the young police officer in charge of his mental and psychological well-being handed him *Lolita* for relaxation. After two days Eichmann returned it, visibly indignant: "Quite an unwholesome book"—'Das ist aber ein sehr unerfreuliches Buch'—he told his guard." (Arendt, 49). Though we are not privy to, nor does Arendt speculate upon, the intentions—if any—of this officer charged with Eichmann's "mental and psychological well-being," it is difficult to imagine that they were limited to procuring Eichmann a little "relaxation." The tale of a homicidal madman writing under observation and awaiting a trial that will consign him either to death or prolonged imprisonment—and which fate spares him by felling him with a heart attack—could hardly have been very relaxing for someone at that moment writing his own memoirs and himself awaiting a trial that would consign him either to death or prolonged imprisonment.

Might we not be justified in imagining other intentions on the part of Eichmann's guard? Is it not more likely that the intention behind the loaning of the book was an ironic one? Or that it was motivated by a dark curiosity—something of the order of an experiment? The sulphurous halo of Nabokov's book was still burning brightly in the popular consciousness of 1960.[1] Might Eichmann's guard have seen *Lolita* as a sort of litmus test for radical evil: to see whether the real-life villain—he who impassively organized the transport towards certain death of countless innocents—would coldly, or even gleefully, approve of the various and vile machinations of Nabokov's creation?

This is all, however, only speculation, and Arendt's account does not give occasion for further exploration of the question. After congratulating Eichmann on his indignation, she moves on to other matters.[2] In any event, given Eichmann's radical conventionality one could hardly imagine him liking—or even very well understanding—much of the book. As Eichmann himself avowed, during his adult life he had read only two books—one of them being Theodor Herzl's *The Jewish State*. Whatever the motivations of Eichmann's guard, whatever Eichmann's degree of comprehension might have been, and whatever congratulations Eichmann might have deserved for his disgust, the incident raises a question for the study of Nabokov's finest work that has yet to be answered. Before formulating this question, let us turn to the book that raised it.

Lolita

Lolita was written in large part in the summer, during the Nabokovs' yearly trips from Ithaca, New York, to various spots in the Rocky Mountains to butterfly-hunt. Its lighter and darker passages were written during moments of idleness or inspiration, during rainstorms, bouts of insomnia, or whenever else a new element of the story fit itself into the image Nabokov was patiently forming. As his tale of ardent love and aching loss took clearer shape, Nabokov read psychological case studies and rode around Ithaca in school buses to better render the tenor and tone he sought. This proved so difficult to achieve that at one point Nabokov ceremoniously carried the exacting and unfinished

1. Given Eichmann's nearly inexistent English, the copy in question was doubtless the German translation of the novel published the preceding year (1959).

2. Her task indeed lay elsewhere. It is perhaps, however, not irrelevant to note a circumstance involving the publication of Arendt's work. *Eichmann in Jerusalem* was first published as a series of articles in the *New Yorker*—the same magazine that not only harbored a number of Nabokov's most vocal American supporters, but also the one that had most frequently published his work and which had—up to the publication of *Lolita*—a contract with Nabokov whereby he was required to offer them first for publication any work (essay, poem, or story) before seeking to publish it in any other periodical. The magazine which had in some sense given Nabokov his American start (under the rough-feathered wing of Edmund Wilson) might have wished to minimize the shadow cast upon the work, and maximize the serious critical attention directed towards it. For this reason, we might imagine that the editorial staff of the magazine would not have been overeager for Arendt to explicitly present the book as a valid test for radical evil. But this is, after all, only speculation and our task too lies elsewhere.

manuscript to the incinerator behind his house so as to burn it. His wife caught him just in time.

The fifty-four-year-old Nabokov at last finished *Lolita* in 1953. It was his twelfth novel, his third in English, the finest he would ever write, and amongst the finest ever written. He promptly presented it to a friend and publisher and was told that the book was astounding, but that if he published it they would both go to jail.

As Nabokov hunted for a way to publish *Lolita* without risk of incarceration, he sent it to his editor at the *New Yorker*, Katharine White, stating in no uncertain terms that no one but her was to see it. Nabokov was understandably much consternated when he read in that same magazine a few months later a story by Dorothy Parker telling of a widow and her daughter competing for the affections of an older man—and which bore the title "Lolita." White assured Nabokov that this was pure coincidence.[3]

Despite these early frustrations, Nabokov kept up his resolve, and, having abandoned plans of anonymous publication (as he became more and more aware that nothing would be more likely to attract the attention of the censors), he searched farther afield for a courageous publisher. His European agent found one in the curious person of Maurice Girodias, director of the Paris-based English-language Olympia Press. Olympia had published the first English translations of Jean Genet, had published Samuel Beckett, Laurence Durrell, William Burroughs and Henry Miller, and though what little Nabokov knew of these writers did not lead him to hold them in high esteem, the publishing house seemed serious enough for him to entrust his wayward child to it.

Lolita appeared in the Olympia Press's Traveler's Companion series alongside, indeed, Durrell and Genet, as well as such vibrant titles as *The Whip Angels*, *The Enormous Bed*, and *I'm For Hire*. Relatively few readers took notice of it—until the end of the year. In the Christmas issue of the London *Sunday Times* Graham Greene declared the unknown novel, neither advertised nor reviewed in England, one of the three best books of the year. John Gordon, a Scottish journalist of no small conservatism and editor in chief of the *Sunday Express*, examined this unexpected entry in Greene's list and declared it, "the filthiest book I have ever read. Sheer unrestrained pornography" (*Sunday Express*, January 29, 1956). The difference in opinion did wonders for the book: sales soared, and after much editorial and legal preparation the work was published in America in 1958, and in England in 1959, without the much-feared opposition from the censors. It spent six months as number one on America's best-seller charts (only to

---

3. Parker's story appeared in the August 27, 1955 issue of the *New Yorker* (32–35). Parker expressed great admiration for Nabokov in an article which appeared in *Esquire* in 1958, "Sex—Without the Asterisks"; Nabokov expressed admiration for Parker in a private communication (*SL*, 352).

be displaced, much to Nabokov's disgust, by Boris Pasternak's *Dr. Zhivago*). Nabokov wrote a screenplay of the novel for Stanley Kubrick and James Harris in 1960 and by then having earned enough money from the book's various revenues he retired from teaching and moved with his wife Véra to Montreux, where they remained in gentle and productive seclusion until Nabokov's death seventeen happy years later.

Lolita has been read by millions and written about by thousands. It has been transformed for the stage and screen and been the subject of several court cases of note. Modern dance pieces and pop songs have found inspiration in it. Indie-rock bands have borrowed their names from its hero and its villain (who are both, in fact, villains). An Italian novelist has told the story from the young girl's perspective. An Iranian critic has credited it with helping her to teach women in her homeland to think courageously about their world. The *Oxford English Dictionary* has incorporated its inventions. Nearly every university in America offers classes teaching it. And yet, despite all this activity and adulation, the book has remained resolutely enigmatic. And what has remained enigmatic in it is nothing less than its nature: whether it is a sterile exercise of linguistic virtuosity or a deeply human account of love and loss, whether it is an incitement to vice or an encouragement to virtue, whether it is art for nothing but its own sake, or a work of rare moral force.

The Standpoint of Someone Else

Returning to the readers with whom we began, Arendt notes elsewhere in her account that it appeared to her that Eichmann was nearly "*aphasic.*" She observes that, "when he did succeed in constructing a sentence of his own, he repeated it until it became a *cliché,*" and suggests that "his inability to speak was closely connected with an inability to *think*, namely, to think from the standpoint of somebody else."[4] Arendt offers here nothing less than a definition of *thought* itself. "To *think*" is glossed ("namely") by Arendt as "*to think from the standpoint of someone else.*" Though as a definition of thought this is hardly impressive (evidenced by its very form: "to *think*, namely, to think"), it nevertheless expresses something essential about Arendt's conception of thought and thinking.

---

4. Arendt's italics. Arendt notes several instances of Eichmann's comical battle with the German language (his native and only language) as well as his remark to Judge Landau during his trial in Jerusalem that "Officialese [*Amtssprache*] is my only language." Her view of his difficulty in expressing himself is supported by Eyal Sivan and Rony Brauman's film *The Specialist* (1999), which shows archival footage from Eichmann's trial bearing witness to his less than silver tongue.

virtually all readers of the book have expressed in one fashion or another: an uncertainty as to how to read it. The goal of this study will be to clarify the terms of the question, and to offer an answer.

The Aesthetics of Judgment

Humbert is, as Nabokov himself once stressed, "a wretch," and yet he is a singularly engaging one and he is given an entrancing story to tell (*SO*, 94). As the reader glides into its deceptive depths, the second half of Ray Jr.'s sentence—the one bearing the clause of moral responsibility—is easily forgotten. This might seem inevitable. To be "entranced" is to abandon, or to be lured away, from one's normal state in favor of an exceptional one. Coleridge spoke of the "willing suspension of disbelief" as the good grace we are asked to bring to the experience of a work of art. In this justly famous description of the phenomenology of passionate reading, we do not quibble over probabilities and possibilities but instead give ourselves over to the singular and strange experiences the work of art offers us. In such a state, not only does our concern for petty plausibility recede, and not only do our daily cares seem to recede with it, but so too do many other conventional commonplaces and pragmatic maxims. The result is that the more we are "entranced" by a work of art the less inclined we are to perceive it as "abhorrent." And it is at this point that the two elements in John Ray Jr.'s instructions—being entranced and abhorring—begin to part company, and to compete for our attention.

This is a categorical difficulty and in its shadow we would do well to return to the question of judgment. Kant may have signaled out "thinking from the standpoint of another" as the maxim of judgment—but it was not his maxim of aesthetic judgment. As he carefully noted, art was to be seen from another standpoint: it should be experienced and judged in purely "*disinterested*" fashion, and this most fundamental article of aesthetic belief has held sway ever since. In this same *Critique of Judgment* where Arendt found the essence of thought as thinking from the standpoint of another, Kant defines the taste we should judge works of art with as follows: "*Taste* is the ability to judge an object, or a way of presenting it, by means of a liking or disliking *devoid of all interest* [Geschmack *ist das Beurteilungsvermögen eines Gegenstandes oder einer Vorstellungsart durch ein Wohl-gefallen, oder Mißfallen*, ohne alles Interesse]. The object of such a liking is called beautiful" (Kant, 53; 302; Kant's italics). As Kant's definition makes clear, what the modern spectator is expected to be is, before all else, *disinterested*. When this is not the case, the faculty of aesthetic judgment—or taste—is impaired. Plato felt the need to banish artists from his ideal republic because the "divine terror" they aroused in their spectators was a source of great instability; because, to cite the terms Kant would use to approach the same question, the *Wohlgefallen* or *Mißfallen* they aroused in the spectator was anything but *ohne alles Interesse*. By Kant's time, art had cooled. To be properly appreciated and to be properly judged in the dawning age of taste and aesthetics, art had to be seen with an eye discerning because it remained cold, and with a heart wise because kept within the bounds of reason. Perhaps no more compelling commentary on this aesthetic dictate is to be found than in Kant's own private reading—in a note he made to himself in the margins of his copy of Rousseau's *On the Beautiful and the Sublime*: "I must read and reread Rousseau until I am no longer distracted by the beauty of his formulations. Only then will I be able to reasonably examine the whole."[8] Nabokov's place in this tradition becomes clear when we look to his reading practices. In his lectures he tells his students to shun identification with fictional characters—the "worst" type of reading he knows of—and asks them instead to rely upon "impersonal imagination" (*LL*, 4). And what is that but *disinterested judgment*? "We ought to remain a little aloof," he says, "and take pleasure in this aloofness while at the same time we keenly enjoy . . . the inner weave of a given masterpiece" (ibid.).

Since the eighteenth century and the rise of a discourse about taste and a discipline called aesthetics, cultivated readers in the Western tradition have singled themselves out for their ability to read with measure and distance— something, as Kant told others and told himself, that required discipline. The advice Nabokov gives his students, like the that which he has John Ray Jr. voice follows in the footsteps of this tradition—and invites the reader to trip. To be truly entranced with a book, to be truly swept away by the enchanting story it relates, is not to remain a disinterested appreciator of a work's formal refinement and expertise, but instead to be brought into its world as into a magical and mystifying place. To be entranced is to be an *interested* reader—and not merely in the sense of being interested enough to continue reading, but passionately and personally interested in the work of art.

While Kant's criteria may seem too categorical, they are not easy to simply dismiss and his injunction was and remains eminently reasonable. If what is at stake is *judgment*—the judging of works of art—we should not let subjective criteria such as our degree of personal interest or involvement with the work's setting or theme interfere with our fair and balanced evaluation of it. I may love dogs and loathe cats but if I use this criterion to rate a work of art featuring a dog higher than one featuring a cat, and leave out of account questions of formal harmony and mastery, then I may be a passionate dilettante, but I am a poor judge of art and lack what centuries of aesthetic judgment have called

8. This bit of marginalia is noted by Ernst Cassirer in his *Kants Leben und Lehre* (Cassirer, 92).

taste. This matter becomes, of course, significantly more fraught when setting and theme are more incendiary than choice of pet: when suffering, crime, and punishment are the matter of a work that, following the dictates of aesthetic judgment, should be experienced in a "disinterested" fashion. It is here that the full complexity and difficulty of aesthetic judgment become clear. The ideal response to a work of art is one that is indeed disinterested—but only slightly. It is a "disinterest" that does not exclude understanding and empathy. The fine line between personal and partisan—between idiosyncratic reaction and the cold evaluation of nothing but the fineness of a work's form—is one that is often extraordinarily difficult to draw. And it is precisely this line that *Lolita*, from its very beginning, traces.

The Formal Challenge

While John Ray Jr. may tell us that we should be entranced with Humbert's memoir while at the same time abhorring him, and while, either intentionally or unintentionally, many critics have endeavored to follow this advice, Nabokov himself seems to have recommended something completely different. From the moment of the book's first publication he advocated a specific interest and distance for the reading of *Lolita*: the combinatorial interest and distance of a solver of puzzles and a player of games. As he tirelessly repeated in the years following the work's explosive publication, he wrote works of art for art's sake. *Lolita* is singularly rich in puzzles to solve and games to play and Nabokov was at no small pains to point these out, going so far as to compare the composition of the novel to the composition of a chess puzzle. "Chess problems," he informed his reader, "demand from the composer the same virtues that characterize all worthwhile art" (*PP*, 15). In such a light, moral outrage—contempt for the narrator or a sense that one is being seduced by his story—would make as much sense as our shedding tears at the lowly pawn cut down by a ruthless bishop. We might be moved by the concrete fate of the abstract pawn, but it would entail our having misunderstood the rules of engagement—and misunderstood that it is a game.

While Nabokov may be right that chess problems demand from their composers the same virtues found in all worthwhile art, the way these virtues are employed is different. Readers discussing their own ethical responses to *Lolita*, such as the ones we saw above, are not introducing foreign matter into the text. Instead, they are following the lines laid out for them therein. The novel may have the same compositional *virtues* as a complex chess problem, but it has different compositional *matter*. And this matter is unquestionably ethical. *Lolita* places moral questions at the center of its fiction and makes one of its central and explicit themes the line between acceptable and unacceptable behavior, between moral and immoral acts. A reader responsive to these elements is in no way reading into the novel private preferences or reading against its special grain—no matter how programmatic and peremptory Nabokov might have been in claiming, as he often did, that his novel had "no moral in tow" (*AL*, 314–315).

In an interview from 1962, Nabokov remarked that "*Lolita* is a special favorite of mine," and that "it was my most difficult book—the book that treated of a theme which was so distant, so remote, from my own emotional life that it gave me a special pleasure to use my combinatorial talent to make it real" (*SO*, 15). *Lolita* was thus an exercise in empathy—and a singularly "difficult" one because it demanded of the artist that he draw on that which was most foreign to him. In an interview for *Life* magazine two years later he noted that "of all my books *Lolita* has left me with the most pleasurable afterglow—perhaps because it is the purest of all, the most abstract and carefully contrived" (*SO*, 47). Nabokov treasured the formal (or "combinatorial") challenge the book presented and stresses how "carefully contrived" it was. We should not forget, however, that like Flaubert's in *Madame Bovary* this formal challenge is the challenge of empathy. Flaubert found the idea of writing *Madame Bovary* alluring because he found it repugnant—and his challenge lay in creating empathy for what might so easily have been repugnantly banal or immoral. In this respect, *Lolita* is in a perfectly analogous position to *Madame Bovary* (a work that also received its fair share of obscenity accusations and whose author doggedly insisted was nothing but *l'art pour l'art*). That *Lolita* was "carefully contrived" does not mean that it was meant to feel artificial—on the contrary, Nabokov stresses that the artifices of his art were to be marshaled so as "*to make it real.*" To make Humbert real to his readers, Nabokov needed to make the repugnant alluring. It would have been easy enough to portray his narrator as loathsome, if simply because of the loathsome things he does. To that end, no special "combinatorial talent" and no careful contrivance would have been required. What was difficult, what was challenging, and what Nabokov *did* was the opposite: he made Humbert engaging, amusing, appealing, and alluring: he made him "seductive."

To this end, what Nabokov presents us with is not the image of a child molester with which we are familiar, not the image found in newspaper accounts or handbooks of sexual pathology (both of which Nabokov abundantly consulted in his research for the novel).[9] When we read in the newspaper of

9. An exemplary instance of what Nabokov found therein can be seen in Krafft-Ebing's *Psychopathia Sexualis* (with which Nabokov was familiar). In the subsection "Violation of Individuals under the Age of Fourteen" under the heading of "Violation," we read: "The term violation, in the legal sense of the word,

a crime like the one committed against Sally Horner, to choose an example it appears Nabokov was familiar with (cf. Dolinin 2005), we are aghast. The digest form in which the crime is related to us is devoid of anything we could identify with, and anything we could understand. It seems bestial and cruel and we shudder at it—and turn the page. Our culture accustoms us to such stories of suffering and to not understanding their deeper and more complicated causes, not understanding what dark and winding roads led to them. We fail to understand these causes not because we are unwilling, although at times we may be, but because there is so much of this suffering and it is so difficult to understand its causes on such scant or schematic bases. Were one to reduce the story *Lolita* tells to such digest form, to a single column destined for a newspaper, or an entry in a work on sexual pathology, it would be rich in lurid details and, in all likelihood, essentially incomprehensible. We would be aghast, and we would understand little more than how much we long for a world in which such things do not happen.

It is against this background that the formal challenge Nabokov set himself in *Lolita* profiles itself. Instead of the familiar demonizing traits, *Lolita* sketches and shadows a criminal who presents himself in disarmingly human guise and who at no point corresponds to the template we have come to expect. The stereotypical image of the feeble-minded or feeble-bodied molester—the weak, insane, or semi-impotent figure drawn in such typological accounts as those of Krafft-Ebing or Havelock Ellis—is a far cry from what we find in *Lolita*. We find instead someone dressed in all the attributes of adult attractiveness and cultivation. Humbert is intelligent, eloquent, charming, and witty. He is handsome and robust and not plagued by fears that he is weaker or less potent than those around him. And while agreeable to listen to, he is difficult to read. At times he professes perfect indifference to his reader, and at others implores that same reader's careful attention and understanding. He often anticipates his reader's reactions and responds to them in varied and subtle fashion. At times he surpasses his reader's condemnations with his own and seems at such points to upbraid our slowness. On other occasions he points out the unthinking prejudices behind many commonsense or commonplace judgments. He

---

comprehends the most horrible perversions and acts, which are possible only to a man who is controlled by lust and morally weak, and, as is usually the case, lacking in sexual power. A common feature of these crimes, committed on persons that are more or less children, is that they are unmanly, childish, and often silly. It is a fact that such acts, with exceptions in pathological cases, like those of imbeciles, paretics, and senile dements, are almost exclusively committed by young men who lack courage or have no faith in their virility; or by *roués* who have, to some extent, lost their virility. It is psychologically incomprehensible that an adult of full virility, and mentally sound, should indulge in sexual abuses with children" (Krafft-Ebing, 402). Nabokov is clearly endeavoring to present a case that would not be "psychologically incomprehensible."

does not let his desires and acts pass behind closed doors but reveals them to the reader. And still more disturbing, those desires and those acts are not, for him, inexplicable incidents of bestial satisfaction—however much he might regret them. They are, for him, lyrical moments representing the pinnacle of earthly beauty and charged with all the poignancy, uncertainty, and passion of love.

In this sense, the formal challenge of *Lolita*, what needed to be so carefully contrived for the work to achieve its end, was a challenge by definition at once aesthetic and ethical. Humbert is a child molester and a murderer—crimes we are not in the least inclined to pardon. What Nabokov needed then so as to achieve his singular end was to shift, at least for a portion of the novel, the traditional poles of ethical response: the *categorical* and the *conditional*. The *categorical* response is that in taking ghastly advantage of a child Humbert commits a crime that is in no way, shape, or form, not for a year, a month, or a day to be countenanced. We are summoned to judge such acts categorically following maxims of ethical judgment necessary for maintaining a society with a claim to being just and that cares for and protects those most in need. The *conditional* response is that Humbert's person and circumstances are special and should be understood as such. Life is always more complicated than the maxims that endeavor to simplify it or to reduce it to manageable proportions and tidy distinctions. The conditional view reminds us that the life we live is never black and white and to understand it we need to see all its colorful exceptionality. To make Humbert real—and really compelling—Nabokov needed to make him an artist of the conditional. He had to carefully contrive the means through which the sensitive reader focuses on the conditions of Humbert's trespass, listens carefully to his explanations and exculpations, his dazzling array of mitigating facts and factors, his significant efforts to free himself from his obsessions, and his candor as to their success and failure. The reader has on the one side the maxim and on the other the individual case; on the one side the rule, and on the other the exception; on the one hand *judgment*, and on the other *empathy*. And it is from these elements that Nabokov crafts his story. In his own memoir Nabokov refers to "the writing of one of those incredible novels where the author, in a fit of lucid madness, has set himself certain unique rules that he observes, certain nightmare obstacles that he surmounts" (*SM*, 290). In the case of *Lolita*, the most nightmarish obstacle was to create a criminal who could evoke empathy *and* judgment.

In an article as insightful as it is vehement, Trevor McNeely notes that, "*Lolita* was written to prove a simple point in a complex way. The point is that style can do anything" (McNeely, 185). McNeely judges that "it is perhaps the cleverest of Nabokov's devices so to have structured his book that the reader is forced into a moral/aesthetic dilemma by it from which there is no escape—or rather there is only one possible escape, and that is . . . to reject totally both book and author for the frauds they are, even though one may still admire the author's language skill and intellect" (McNeely, 186). McNeely seems to take John Ray Jr.'s advice—and to apply it not to the narrator of the novel, but to its author. He says that we may indulge ourselves in a measure of disinterested entrancement, but we should not forget, if not to abhor the author, at least "to reject totally" his work. McNeely's article is entitled "Lo and Behold: Solving the *Lolita* Riddle." There is indeed a riddle in *Lolita* and there is also a solution—but it is not simple rejection.

Critics

André Gide once noted that "one of the admirable things about great authors is that they permit later generations to disagree" (Abercrombie 1951). If we take such disagreement as indexical of greatness, the dissensions of readers and critics of Nabokov in the past fifty years make an excellent case for his greatness (with an additional quotient added by the fact that the great author Nabokov found the great author Gide thoroughly mediocre).

This is best seen by following the generations. The unlikely best-seller *Lolita* enjoyed singularly good reviews in both the evaluative and qualitative sense of the term. The book's popular (and financial) fortune was made by the scandal Greene and Gordon set off. Shortly thereafter its critical fortune was made by a series of reviews remarkable for their intelligence, balance and perspicacity. Not only Trilling, but also John Hollander (the work's first reviewer), Kingsley Amis, Howard Nemerov, and many others showed themselves sensitive to the many shifting and shimmering levels the novel presents, and whatever their degree of enthusiasm, they were unanimous in stressing the serious achievement and the more than sensual subtlety of Nabokov's novel.

These reviews were soon succeeded by the first academic studies. They showed themselves powerfully influenced by the "strong opinions" Nabokov had been making in forewords, afterwords, and interviews during these same years, in which he strove to distinguish and distance his person from the cruel and unpleasant narrators to be found in his novels, early and late, as well as claiming that his work was not social commentary or political allegory but instead art for art's sake. The first book-length study of Nabokov's work, that of Page Stegner, dates from scarcely a decade after *Lolita*'s publication and bears the programmatic title *Escape into Aesthetics: The Art of Vladimir Nabokov* (1966). There is a historical irony in this title. Stegner's work is entirely unpolemical and lauds such an escape—seeing it as an escape not from ethics, or the world, but rather from the unethical worldviews of fascist political regimes—but the first generation of Nabokov's critics tended to take this descriptive title (*Escape into Aesthetics*) as an imperative one. Generally speaking, they either lauded Nabokov for having effected such an escape, or took him to task for the more or less craven flight it implied. This approach brought with it a widespread focus on the intricate artifices of Nabokov's deceptive fictions strengthened not only by Nabokov's imperative declarations on the matter, but also by a critical atmosphere wherein a postmodernism on the rise privileged such concepts as metafiction, unreliable narration and play.

The extremity of this first swing of the critical pendulum set in motion an equal and inverse movement, and the last three decades have seen ever more emphasis on the ethical underpinnings of Nabokov's densely patterned fictions. The initial *escape into aesthetics* has been followed by something tending towards an *escape into ethics*. Like its predecessor, this movement owes something of its impetus to the critical climate of its times in which ethical categories and questions returned from their brief exile and have come more and more to stand at the center of literary study. Like the first one, this second swing of the critical pendulum was also given an additional push by an ex cathedra pronouncement from the author—this time mediated through his widow. In a preface to a posthumous collection of Nabokov's Russian poetry published two years after his death, Véra Nabokov stresses the crucial role in all of her late husband's work of *potustoronnost* (a Russian word alternately translated as "transcendence," "reaching toward another world," or "the otherworld") (V. Nabokov, 1979). In a series of remarkable studies from this period, at the forefront of which stand those of D. Barton Johnson, Vladimir Alexandrov[10] and Brian Boyd,[11] the metafictional has been brought into close alignment with the metaphysical.

In recent years the pendulum seems to have begun a new arc. In *The Magician's Doubts* (1994) Michael Wood (following Wittgenstein) claims that "the ethical"

10. Cf. Alexandrov's *Nabokov's Otherworld* (1991) for the principle exposition of his views on this transcendent matter. As editor of the *Garland Companion to Vladimir Nabokov* (1995) Alexandrov himself wrote entries on the relation of nature to artifice and on "otherworld." In her review of this valuable reference work, Jane Grayson notes a remarkable attention (amply evidenced by the index to the volume) to "cosmic synchronization," "the hereafter," "the otherworld," "life after death," the "two-world theme," and other themes relating to this transcendent tendency. She observes that this tendency even extended to the visual presentation of the volume: "The face of Nabokov which Alexander has chosen to fill his cover is austere, the gaze directed away from the reader out beyond the spine into the steely cosmic blue of an 'otherworld'" (Grayson, 214).

11. Boyd's emphasis is clear in all of his works, from his critical study of *Ada, or Ardor* from 1985 (*Nabokov's Ada: The Place of Consciousness*) through his two-volume critical biography (*Vladimir Nabokov: The Russian Years* [1990]; *Vladimir Nabokov. The American Years* [1991]), to his study of *Pale Fire* (*Nabokov's Pale Fire: The Magic of Artistic Discovery* [1999]), as well as numerous reviews and essays. It should be noted that Boyd's conceptions are clearly distinct from those of Alexandrov, and that Boyd has himself noted in a recent essay: "I regard *Nabokov's Otherworld* as flawed, after its fine introduction" (Boyd 2005, 47–48).

in Nabokov is "the realm of the unspeakable," and goes on to wittily note that Nabokov "is neither the aesthete that he himself and his early readers kept making out he was, nor the plodding moralist that recent criticism, with an audible sigh of relief, has wheeled on to the page" (Wood, 7). More recently, the French critic and editor Maurice Couturier has expressed his objections to those who "have tried to prove the celestial level of [Nabokov's] moral standards, often counting upon his (and sometimes his wife's) pronouncements to introduce their demonstrations" (Couturier 1996, 215). Continuing in this vein in his introduction to the first volume of the French *Pléiade* edition of Nabokov's works, Couturier again objects to this "metaphysical" school of Nabokov criticism. He notes the weakness of an edifice that bases its interpretative approach on a remark made by the author's widow, as well as pointing out that this approach "is accompanied by a somewhat suspect erasure of everything in Nabokov's work that arises from pleasure or transgression" (cf. Couturier 1999, ix–l, xliv–xlv, xlvi.). Still more recently, D. Barton Johnson has remarked, "I am now entertaining the belated suspicion that the subsequent widespread adoption of the 'metaphysical' Nabokov with his multiple worlds was in part motivated by some of the same fear of social pressures that triggered the perceptual shift from the cold, calculating virtuoso to the warm, gooey moralist Nabokov" (Johnson 2002, 21).

It is the nature of critical studies—particularly when they focus on a single author—to accentuate the negative. One notes the points of disagreement for the logical reason that noting all the points of agreement would take up too much space (and be too presumptuous). Whatever contribution the following study might offer to a clearer understanding of Nabokov's ethics, aesthetics, and the relation between the two would not have been possible without a wealth of critical studies that will, of necessity, receive short shrift. Without the pioneering studies of critics from the ones named above to Julia Bader, Julian Connolly, Alexander Dolinin, Ellen Pifer, Carl Proffer, John Updike, Savely Senderovich, Dieter Zimmer, and a host of others, this one could never have been written.

In the interest of brevity and readability I have endeavored to keep the critical apparatus to a minimum. This means that much critical material has been lodged in the halfway houses of footnotes. In his introduction to *Bend Sinister*, Nabokov noted that "footnotes always seem amusing to a certain type of mind" (xviii). There are indeed more in this study than, strictly speaking, could be amusing. I have tried to pare and prune them as much as possible. Beyond this, I can only appeal to the reader's patience. Unless otherwise noted, all translations are my own.

PART ONE

READER AND RESPONSE

CHAPTER ONE

CRUELTY, OR NABOKOV'S READER

EVIL IS A WORD that rarely helps us understand—or limit—what we bring under its dark heading. More often than not it marks a boundary beyond which we are unwilling or unable to venture. Things stand differently, however, with *cruelty*. Once asked why he wrote *Lolita,* Nabokov answered with another question, "Why did I write any of my books, after all?" and gave as answer, "I like composing riddles with elegant solutions" (SO, 16). If we are to solve the at once aesthetic and ethical riddle *Lolita* presents, we might begin with what we know of the riddler who composed it. All readers are in agreement that *Lolita*'s narrator, Humbert Humbert, was cruel. But what of his creator? Did he share this trait with him? Was Vladimir Nabokov a cruel writer?

Few of Nabokov's readers have begrudged him their admiration, but many their affection. Asked in 1959 whether he felt that the novel was then traversing a "crisis," Italo Calvino, an author with an affection for formal challenges, responded that he thought it was not, and pointed to the recently published *Lolita* as proof (Calvino 1:1524). Many years later, Calvino was to restate his admiration, but this time accompanied by an aside. He remarked that Nabokov was "truly a genius, one of the greatest writers of the century and one of the people in whom I most recognize myself," and that "if I had to name the author whom I've preferred above all others . . . these last years I would answer: Vladimir Nabokov" (Calvino 2:2908). Calvino goes so far as to credit Nabokov with having "invented an English of extraordinary richness" (ibid.). Alongside of this highest of praise, however, he also added that, as a writer, Nabokov possesses "an extraordinary cynicism and a formidable *cruelty*" (ibid.; my italics).

Calvino was not the first and not the only reader to remark upon a cynicism and a cruelty in Nabokov's writing. Simon Karlinsky summarized the tenor of much of the Russian criticism of Nabokov's work in the European émigré communities of the 1930s by stating that Nabokov's "originality and novelty" were often seen as "a mask covering up his indifference to his fellow humans" (Karlinsky, 10). Much later, in Nabokov's country of adoption, Joyce Carol Oates wrote of him that he "exhibits the most amazing capacity for loathing that one is likely to find in serious literature" (Oates, 37). Even Nabokov's close friend and, later, bitter enemy, Edmund Wilson chimed in and diagnosed what he called Nabokov's "addiction to *Schadenfreude*" (Wilson 1971, 161).

This note of "cruelty," "indifference," "loathing," and "*Schadenfreude*" is heard with equal regularity from Nabokov's more academic critics. Carl Proffer calls Nabokov "a somewhat sadistic author" and William Carroll observed that, "being a character in one of the Vladimir Nabokov fictions is evidently not much fun" (Proffer, 4; Carroll, 203). Couturier gave his study of Nabokov's works the programmatic title *Nabokov, ou la tyrannie de l'auteur* ("Nabokov, or The Tyranny of the Author"), and followed it up eleven years later with *Nabokov ou la cruauté du désir* ("Nabokov, or The Cruelty of Desire"). In the first book-length study of Nabokov, Page Stegner separates Nabokov the person with faults he finds difficult to pardon from the good writer he likes very much (cf. Stegner, 133–135). Nabokov's most insightful and sensitive contemporary critic, Michael Wood, found himself similarly distressed—and without any recourse to the person of the author. He was so perplexed by Nabokov's literary character that in *The Magician's Doubts* he delimits four different and distinct facets of it, among them "Nabokov the mandarin," whom he does not like, as well as the private, diffident, sensitive, and highly observant Nabokov whom he likes very much (cf. Wood, 22ff.).

In one of the most discussed and debated essays on Nabokov, Richard Rorty contends that the "central topic" of Nabokov's books is "cruelty" (Rorty, 146). "Nabokov wrote about cruelty from the inside," says Rorty, "helping us see the way in which the private pursuit of aesthetic bliss produces cruelty" (Rorty, 146). In Rorty's view, not only did Nabokov concern himself with nothing so intensely as cruelty—he revealed its hidden connections to aesthetic pleasure. Martin Amis, true to form, was still more lapidary in his estimation that "Nabokov is the laureate of cruelty" (M. Amis, ix). Just as had Calvino, a host of Nabokov's most perceptive readers found a kernel of hard, bright cruelty at the heart of Nabokov's person and work—and were at something of a loss as to what to make of it.

This cruel streak did not escape Nabokov himself—on the contrary. While at work on *Pnin* in 1954, Nabokov wrote to his editor Katharine White, "let me say merely that the 'unpleasant' quality of Chapter 2 [of *Pnin*] is a special trait of my work in general" (*SL*, 150). Contrary to what White suggested, such unpleasantness was an integral part of his enterprise and could not be removed or altered. In an interview from 1962, Nabokov noted that for the early part of his career, he simply "saw the world as cruel" and in a novel from this period his narrator describes himself as "contemptuous of everything on earth but her" (*The Listener*, November 22, 1962, 68; *KQK*, 254; the "her" is his dancing partner). Nabokov's acknowledgment that there was a method to the madnesses of his characters does not, however, explain *why* he graced them with such. *Why* then did Nabokov paint—and with such strange relish—the portraits of such endlessly unpleasant characters as Humbert Humbert?

In an unsigned article entitled "Vladimir Nabokov-Sirin,[1] Lover of Life" from a 1931 issue of *Le Mois* (a Parisian periodical which also contained in that same issue an essay of Nabokov's), one finds a laudatory and artful essay on Nabokov. Amidst the praise therein is the following reserve: "It is a strange and paradoxical fact that this young man—healthy, balanced, active, and brimming with vitality, enjoys depicting perverse, sickly, even pathological figures. There is scarce a single likable character in any of his novels" (Anonymous, 141).[2] This insightful observation dates from years before the appearance of a new and dazzling generation of villains in such works as *Laughter in the Dark* (1938), where

---

1. "Sirin" was Nabokov's Russian pen-name. His principal reason for selecting a pen-name was that he shared his father's name and at the time of his first publications his father was a well-known and prolific political contributor to the same émigré periodicals in which Nabokov's poems and stories appeared. His reason for selecting this pseudonym, in addition to his professed affection for its sound and color, had to do with its meaning. A *sirin* is a mythical bird of partial human form (almost always feminine) which brings joy and success. Like the Sirens (also part-bird and part-woman and having a common origin with the Russian *sirin*), it entrances with its singing and in certain folk-beliefs its songs were thought to confer joy by expressing the divine word. In certain versions of the myth, only a happy—or, alternatively, lucky—person can hear its song. In *Strong Opinions*, Nabokov explains: "In modern times *sirin* is one of the popular Russian names of the Snowy Owl, the terror of tundra rodents, and is also applied to the handsome Hawk Owl, but in old Russian mythology it is a multicolored bird, with a woman's face and bust, no doubt identical with the 'siren,' a Greek deity, transporter of souls and teaser of sailors. In 1920, when casting about for a pseudonym and settling for that fabulous fowl, I still had not shaken off the false glamour of Byzantine imagery that attracted young Russian poets of the Blokian era" (*SO*, 161).

2. Given the general atmosphere of hoaxing with which Nabokov surrounded his literary self, all such artful and anonymous moments connected with the reception of his works excite suspicion. Though Alfred Appel Jr. is a flesh-and-blood critic, Gore Vidal was astute (and daring) in suggesting that he was Nabokov in disguise (cf. Vidal's review of *Strong Opinions*, "Professor V. Nabokov," *The Observer*, May 12, 1974, reprinted in Vidal's *United States*). As to this early essay, although it is possible that Nabokov wrote it himself, it is more likely that it was written by his close friend Gleb Struve (for circumstantial evidence to this effect, cf. Boyd 1990, 364).

the unjust are punished by nothing more than the loss of their cash cow, *Lolita* (1955), *Pale Fire* (1962) and *Ada, or Ardor* (1969). In all these cases, Nabokov's readers are confronted with a cruelty that is difficult to reconcile with the kindly, if mischievous, figure the author cut.

To understand what cruelty might lurk in his works, we should recall that Nabokov's characters were not just cruel to other characters—he was cruel to them. This begins with how he describes him. While many a character in his works lives and breathes with surprising life, they do so in absolute servitude. In his accounts of the process of his creation, he treats his characters with a tyrannical stringency recalling nothing so much as Michelangelo's boast that marble trembled when he approached. In a letter to his mother, the twenty-six-year-old Nabokov tells of how the characters in what would become his first novel, *Mary* (1926), had become "real people, not characters invented by me" (cited by Field 1977, 182). It seems, however, that after this first work Nabokov began to keep his characters more carefully in line and in the years to come he would boast: "my characters are galley slaves" (*SO*, 95). In response to a question about the experience of having "a character take hold of them and in a sense dictate the course of the action," Nabokov replied: "I have never experienced this. What a preposterous experience! Writers who have had it must be very minor or insane" (*SO*, 69).

Nabokov's description notwithstanding, novelists neither minor nor insane have, however, often recounted such experiences. Though one might find Balzac's calling on his deathbed for a doctor from his work rather than his life as beyond the bounds of a healthy relation to one's creations, it is not difficult to understand and appreciate the position of his countryman Gide some hundred years later declaring toward the end of his own life that "no sooner have I conceived of the work than I am completely at its mercy, and my every energy is dedicated to its composition. I then have no more personality than that which is appropriate to the work in question" (Gide's remark is from a journal entry dated July 1922, cited by Blanchot, 88, n. 1).[3] By his own description, such experiences were quite foreign to Nabokov and even in jest he never said anything like "Madame Bovary, c'est moi." In the preface to the first edition of *David Copperfield*, Dickens—one of the relatively few novelists in English (or any language) whom Nabokov genuinely treasured—writes that, "no one can ever believe this Narrative, in the reading, more than I have believed in the writing" (Dickens, iv). Though Nabokov will say, in the closing lines of a lecture on a different work of Dickens (*Bleak House*), that "a great writer's

---

3. It is reported that as Balzac lay on his deathbed in 1850, he cried wildly but in vain for a certain "Dr. Bianchon." His cries were in vain because Dr. Bianchon was not a real doctor but a character who recurs in a number of the works which make up *La Comédie humaine*.

world" is "a magic democracy," the writer himself, as Nabokov sees him, is an absolute monarch (*LL*, 124).

In relegating such experiences of characters taking control of the course of a book to the "minor" and "insane," Nabokov was perhaps thinking of an author whom he considered, in fact, to be both: Henry James. A few years earlier, Nabokov had debated with his choleric correspondent Edmund Wilson the value of James' writing and found James sorely wanting. (In another letter to Wilson, Nabokov concedes to James a certain "charm . . . but that's about all" [*NWL*, 53].) As the celebrated prefaces to the New York edition of James' works bear ample witness, James experienced, half-appalled, half-enthralled, what he called that "happiest season of surrender to the invoked muse and the projected fable," when his characters resolutely took the upper hand and dictated to him the rhythm of the work (James 1984, 1057).

Whether he was thinking of James or not, Nabokov's literary calendar knows no such season of happy surrender. To make sure his galley slaves are rowing in unison, he goes so far as to penetrate the confines of his fictional worlds, appearing as a cross between a character and a God in his fictions. In his Stanford lectures on drama, Nabokov found breaking the proscenium (the imaginary boundary between actors and audience) "freakish," and says that when it occurs, "then either the breaking is only a delusion, or the play stops being a play" (cf. *The Man from the USSR and Other Plays*, 316). And yet, he would employ its equivalent with much relish in other genres. In *King, Queen, Knave* Nabokov and his wife stop in for a dance. In a late addition to his screenplay for *Lolita* Nabokov appears, butterfly net in hand (Kubrick cut the scene from his shooting script).

In a passage omitted from the second edition of *Speak, Memory*, Nabokov says of Sirin (that is, of himself) that "his best works are those in which he condemns his people to the solitary confinement of their souls" (cited by Appel at *AL*, 453). The novels *Invitation to a Beheading* and *The Defense* are perfect instances of such and in both works the author—an "anthropomorphic deity impersonated by me" (*BS*, xviii), as Nabokov will later call himself—offers encoded tips as to how to break out of such confinement (Cincinnatus from *Invitation to a Beheading* succeeds, and Luzhin from *The Defense* tragically fails). Nabokov's early Russian novels and his remarks in the forewords to their translations often take up this theme of a character dimly aware of a creator, but powerless to gain a greater share of knowledge or control. In the foreword to *Glory*, Nabokov writes, "how cruel to prevent him [the novel's protagonist] from finding in art—not an 'escape' (which is only a cleaner cell on a quieter floor), but relief from the itch of being" (*Glory*, xiii). Nabokov may have found this cruel, but that did nothing to hinder him.

In the Foreword to Nabokov's second American novel, *Bend Sinister*, this itch of being is placed at the center of the fiction. And that itch is, at the book's close, relieved as the protagonist (a philosopher) "suddenly perceives the simple reality of things and knows but cannot express in the words of his world that he and his son and his wife and everybody else are merely my whims and megrims" (*BS*, xiv). In Edward Albee's theatrical adaptation of *Lolita* (the play, an unconditional flop, premiered in New York in 1981),[4] Albee aptly reflects this tendency by introducing a character named "A Certain Gentleman" who is none other than the Author himself, and, following the same intention but in better taste, W. G. Sebald's *The Emigrants* (1992) features a recurrent, mercurial figure of fate who is none other than Nabokov himself.

This vision of the role of the creator in creation is reflected not only in Nabokov's writing, but also in his reading. In a lecture on *Ulysses*, he claims to identify a minor figure in a brown mackintosh as "no other than the author himself. Bloom glimpses his maker!" (*LL*, 320). Coleridge once wrote, "When a man is attempting to describe another's character, he may be right or he may be wrong—but in one thing he will always succeed, in describing himself"—and a more apt motto for Nabokov's lectures would be difficult to find (Coleridge 1957, 3:73; entry 74 G.68). Nabokov's assertion about Bloom glimpsing his maker finds little support in Joyce's text, but much support in his own. Its principal interest is, however, in describing himself. As "anthropomorphic deity" stopping in to maintain order in his carefully patterned texts, Nabokov often seems to evince an indifference to whatever cruelty is inflicted upon his creations worthy of another of Joyce's texts, where, "the artist, like the God of the creation, remains within or behind or beyond or above his handiwork, invisible, refined out of existence, indifferent, paring his fingernails" (Joyce, 223).

This sovereign distance often led Nabokov to strong opinions about his readership. He was often frustrated by editorial changes made to his texts so as to accommodate what he contemptuously called the "average reader" (*NWL*, 154–155). In the margins of a notebook containing his lectures on playwriting

---

4. That Albee's play was a flop despite its celebrated cast and extremely talented author is not difficult to understand as the play is startlingly coarse and incongruous. Charlotte asks Humbert if he is a "fairy"; he refers to her as a "pig" (Albee, 27, 28). She tells him that she is a "one for one" woman: "*He* has an orgasm, I want one! He comes. None of this pile on, puff-puff, squirt, roll off and go to sleep" (Albee, 29). Of the scene where Humbert is surreptitiously masturbating while Lolita frolics nearby, he remarks to the audience: "And at that moment—the moment I would have had her in my lap, clothed, no danger, no damage, and I would have spilled into my trousers all my love for my Lolita, a wet run, so to speak, for my true heart's . . ." (Albee, 24–25). Humbert is prevented from attaining his joy by the maid, who "appears with a broom" and informs Humbert that he must "get up off [his] professorial ass" and kill an insect that is bothering her (Albee, 25).

Nabokov expresses his hidden agenda for the course: *"exploding the myth of the average audience"* (Boyd 1991, 30; my italics). Though this conviction was already visible in his earliest writings, it was reinforced and strengthened through his experiences with American academia, as seen in a letter from 1956 where he writes, "I . . . think that at a time when American readers are taught from high school on to seek in books 'general ideas' a critic's duty should be to draw their attention to the specific detail, to the unique image, without which . . . there can be no art, no genius, no Chekhov, no terror, no tenderness, and no surprise" (*NWL*, 298). We should be careful to understand that Nabokov's goal was not simply the snobbish one of dismissing the uncultivated reader and reducing that reader to a state of wide-eyed, wide-mouthed ineffectuality. It was, instead, that of combating the individual's tendency to merge into an undifferentiated group. But when the individual gave into that tendency, or social acceptance of that tendency was too great, his reaction sounded much like indifference.

Nabokov was not simply joking when he quoted, as he was fond of doing, Pushkin's dictum: "I write for pleasure and I publish for money."[5] Cicero relates the anecdote of a disconsolate young flautist told by his teacher after a cool response from a Roman audience to forget the masses and "play for me and the Muses" (Cicero xlix.187). For Nabokov, however, this would have been already too many. In *Strong Opinions* he states that, "I think that the audience an artist imagines, when he imagines that kind of thing, is a room filled with people wearing his own mask" (*SO*, 18). In Nabokov's Russian poem "Fame" he refers to the, "laughable . . . empty dream / about readers, and body, and glory" (*PP*, 102–103). It should come as no great surprise then that as a professor Nabokov appears not to have been overly concerned with student response. He blithely notes in *Strong Opinions* that, "my method of teaching precluded any genuine contact with my students" and Boyd cites Nabokov's remark regarding his lecture course at Cornell: "I had not much contact with the students. This is something I liked" (*SO*, 104; Boyd 1991, 172). In place of Gertrude Stein's "I write for myself . . . and for strangers," Nabokov writes, "for myself in multiplicate" (*SO*, 114–115). He includes his wife in this multiplicate: "She [Véra] and

---

5. Nabokov quotes this remark in a French documentary entitled *Vladimir Nabokov est un joueur d'échecs*, directed by Bernard Cwagenbaum. This little-discussed documentary consists of interview footage with Nabokov interspersed with footage of two very serious, very pre–May 1968 *Sorbonnards* discussing Nabokov's oeuvre. The last question posed in that dialogue is the interviewer's accomplice asking him, "*Nabokov, qu'est-ce que c'est, en fait, en définitif?*" ["Nabokov—what, ultimately, is he?"]. In his unauthorized biography, Field also quotes Nabokov's quoting of Pushkin's dictum (cf. Field 1977). The gifted and enigmatic Sebastian Knight expresses the pleasure-principle of his prose in similar, if more strident, terms: "no imminent punishment can be violent enough to make me abandon the pursuit of my pleasure" (*RLSK*, 53).

I are my best audience . . . I should say my main audience"—but the circle does not appear to extend much farther (cited by Schiff, 53).[6]

While on these few occasions Nabokov spoke of combating the "myth of the average reader," as a rule he seems at times to have seen himself in a very special relation vis-à-vis his readers: virtually no relation at all. In artistic matters, their opinion is not of the slightest importance to him and their problems and pleasures do not seem to concern him. Umberto Eco once claimed that "*L'autore dovrebbe morire dopo aver scritto. Per non disturbare il cammino del testo*" (So as not to disturb the text's travels, the author should die after having written it) (Eco 2000, 509). Like Eco, Nabokov disapproves of the author constantly coaxing and correcting his readers—not, however, because he wants to allow his text and its readers a maximum of freedom, as did Eco, but simply because their welfare is a point, if we take him at his word, of no importance. This is a position which Nabokov will hold until the end of his life—witnessed by his remarks in the final interview he gave where he reminded his readers that

> . . . the writer's task is the purely subjective one of reproducing as closely as possible the image of the book he has in his mind. The reader need not know, or, indeed, cannot know, what the image is, and so cannot tell how closely the book has conformed to the author's intentions, nor has the author any business trying to learn whether the consumer likes what he consumes . . . the author is perfectly indifferent to the capacity and condition of the reader's brain.[7]

This perfect indifference led directly to Nabokov's position on the extra-literary importance of his—and others'—works. As to questions of social, moral, or political utility, he was particularly pointed. This is all the more surprising in light of the fact that he actually wrote two works bearing all the earmarks of political novels: *Invitation to a Beheading* (1938) and *Bend Sinister* (1947). Given the atmosphere in which he wrote them, the totalitarian motifs than run through

---

6. Jorge Luis Borges' response to a question posed to him at the Cornell Nabokov Festival in 1983 as to whether he writes "for a particular public or a general public" bears noting in this regard: "I write because I have to write. I don't choose writing. I have to do it. It's a mysterious task imposed on me by somebody or something. It's a necessity" (Jorge Luis Borges. "Conversation with an Audience," in Gibian and Parker, 77–78).

7. Interview with Robert Robinson, 122. Nabokov's indifference to readers in general did not prevent him from remarking to Katharine White after the latter's rejection of what Nabokov felt to be his best short story, "The Vane Sisters," "what matters most is the fact that people whom I so much like and admire have completely failed me as *readers* in the present case" (*SL*, 117; Nabokov's emphasis). One hears a similar note in a letter to Edmund Wilson from 1955 regarding *Lolita*, where he notes that "I realize that *even* you neither understand nor wish to understand the texture of this intricate and unusual production" (*NWL*, 296; Nabokov's emphasis).

them come as no surprise. What *is* surprising are his accounts of those books. In a letter written by his wife Véra (who conducted the lion's share of his correspondence), but with his imprimatur ("at this point my husband thinks it essential to submit to you . . ."), that though one of the main "themes" of the book was "a rather vehement incrimination of a dictatorship," "the dictatorship actually represented in the book is imaginary, it deliberately displays features peculiar a) to Nazism, b) to communism, c) to any dictatorial trends in an otherwise non-dictatorial order" (*SL*, 80). More directly to the point, and more directly flowing from Nabokov's pen, in *Strong Opinions* Nabokov claims of *Invitation to a Beheading* and *Bend Sinister* that they offer "absolutely final indictments of Russian and German totalitarianism" (*SO*, 156). Nevertheless, in the foreword to the English edition of *Invitation to a Beheading* he states: "I composed the Russian original . . . some fifteen years after escaping from the Bolshevist regime, and just before the Nazi regime reached its full volume of welcome. The question whether or not my seeing both in terms of one dull beastly farce had any effect on this book, should concern the good reader as little as it does me"—thus making his wife's letter, and his own earlier statement, sound rather disingenuous (*IB*, 5).[8] In the introduction to *Bend Sinister*, he wrote with still more vehemence: "I am not 'sincere,' I am not 'provocative,' I am not 'satirical.' I am neither a didacticist nor an allegorizer. Politics and economics, atomic bombs[9], primitive and abstract art forms, the entire Orient,

8. It is interesting to note that the U.S. Government initially requested Nabokov's permission to publish a German translation of *Bend Sinister* as a part of the reeducation program after World War II (cf. Balestrini, 217).

As regards the aesthetic success of his work, Edmund Wilson dedicates perhaps the most intelligent letter he wrote to Nabokov during their long correspondence to precisely this question. After having read *Bend Sinister* (in 1947), Wilson caustically (caustic for an amiable letter) remarks: "You aren't good at this kind of subject, which involves questions of politics and social change, because you are totally uninterested in these matters and have never taken the trouble to understand them. For you, a dictator like the Toad [in *Bend Sinister*] is simply a vulgar and odious person who bullies serious and superior people like Krug. You have no idea why or how the Toad was able to put himself over, or what his revolution implies. And this makes your picture of such happenings rather unsatisfactory. Now don't tell me that the real artist has nothing to do with the issues of politics. An artist may not take politics seriously, but, if he deals with such matters at all, he ought to know what it is all about" (*NWL*, 183). Wilson goes on to make the even more acute observation that, "what you are left with on your hands is a satire on events so terrible that they really can't be satirized—because in order to satirize anything you have to make it worse than it is" (ibid.). This intuition, like that which Adorno was formulating in this same years, is a decisive one for literature which wishes to pose, present, or represent political problems. It is indeed Beckett, unmentioned in Wilson's correspondence with Nabokov, and hardly an international figure in 1947, will be the writer of his, and Nabokov's, generation best able to rise, or sink, to this occasion.

9. In an article from 1996 Anderson notes that though, "in *Lolita*, the political elements that make *Bend Sinister* so recognizably personal and historical seem almost completely absent," they are not on that account irrelevant, and he places particular stress on "genocidal and nuclear holocausts" for a full understanding of the novel (Anderson, 77).

symptoms of 'thaw' in Soviet Russia, the Future of Mankind, and so on, leave me supremely indifferent" (*BS*, xii).

For Nabokov, art that treats "Ideas," that concerns itself with *generalities*, was without importance or interest. He notes of Dickens' *Bleak House* that "the sociological side . . . is neither interesting nor important" (*LL*, 68). The biographical approach to literature is granted the same opprobrium. Again of *Bleak House*, Nabokov epigrammatically says, "so let us be thankful of the web and ignore the spider" (*LL*, 65). Of studying an author (qua something other than author) via the work Nabokov closes his circle with the announcement that "it is childish to study a work of fiction in order to gain information about a country or about a social class or about the author" (*AL*, 316). There is a certain measure of the histrionic in these statements and Nabokov is indeed, at times, amusing himself at his interviewers' expense. Nevertheless, these remarks are not limited to the interviews and Nabokov is not simply amusing himself. There is a common theme to his remarks: the rejection of utilitarian criteria for art. Nabokov's stance was so extreme that he claimed, at points, that anything *utilitarian* in the work of art endangered its essence. He tells his students to "remember that literature is of no practical value whatsoever, except in the very special case of somebody's wishing to become, of all things, a professor of literature" (*LL*, 125). As concerned his own works, he expressed the matter still more tersely: "I have no purpose at all when composing my stuff except to compose it" (*SO*, 114–115).

What Calvino, Oates, Carroll, Proffer, Rorty, Amis, and many others were responding to in Nabokov's work was in part an indifference verging on the cruel *within* his works—in the cruel fates dealt to kind figures. But they were also responding to an indifference verging on the cruel as concerns his relation to his audience and his stress that he was "perfectly indifferent," "supremely indifferent" to what they thought and felt. Writers haughtily unconcerned for who is to follow the intricacies of their works are not rare in twentieth century literature. One need only think of the dense arcana of Pound and Eliot, both of whom Nabokov detested, or the kaleidoscopic allusiveness of Joyce, whom Nabokov adored. James Mercanton recalled having once visited Joyce and having found him and Stuart Gilbert at work on the then *Work-in-Progress* (which became *Finnegans Wake*), "gleefully" inserting words taken from a Samoyed dictionary so as to make it more "obscure."[10] Nabokov never showed quite this level of insouciance as to who was to follow the forking paths of his subtleties, but he displayed, nevertheless, extraordinarily little concern for his readership.

10. Cf. Mercanton, 219. This anecdote is also cited in John Bishop's *Joyce's Book of the Dark*, 3.

Nabokov once conceded that, "some of my characters are, no doubt, pretty beastly, but I really don't care, they are outside my inner self like the mournful monsters of a cathedral facade—demons placed there merely to show they have been booted out. Actually, I'm a mild old gentleman who *loathes cruelty*" (*SO*, 19; my italics).[11] Readers have noted a cruelty in Nabokov's professed relation to his reader and a loathing in his work, and have been put off by it. But perhaps, young and old, Nabokov *was* in fact what he claimed to be—a gentleman who loathed cruelty, and when he portrayed it did so for a very specific reason. Nabokov's son Dmitri wrote that "the deepest, most important theme" in his father's writing was "contempt for cruelty—the cruelty of humans, the cruelty of fate" (*Stories*, xiv). Are not the "demons" and "mournful monsters" which Nabokov exiled to the façade of his art that which so often leaves his readers with a sense of his cruelty? And might it not be that these expulsed demons and monsters are meant as reminders of a special sort?

In the following I will examine the nature of Nabokov's cruelty, and will try to show what relation the most famous of the expulsed, Humbert Humbert, stands to art's cathedral, how he endeavors to enter therein, and why he stands as an example for later visitors.

11. Nabokov was doubtless aware of Proust's famous use of the metaphor of the cathedral to describe his work, and was quite possibly also familiar with Wordsworth's less well-known use of the metaphor in his declaration that the entirety of his work should be seen as the parts of a cathedral of which the poet's person is the unifying principle ("Preface to *The Excursion*," 754). Nabokov's friend and colleague at Cornell, M. H. Abrams, refers to the latter passage in a work that he published in 1953 during Nabokov's Cornell tenure—*The Mirror and the Lamp*, p. 99.

CHAPTER TWO

THE REALITY OF THE AUTHOR

Art for Art's Sake

THE *CRUELTY* seen in the last chapter pervades Nabokov's work—from the fates dealt his characters to his "supreme indifference" as to when and how readers were to follow his subtleties. To better understand the many facets of Nabokov's literary cruelty—and to which we will return at the close of this study—let us look more closely at his vision of the relation of author to reader, and art to reality.

In an interview with the Italian periodical *Il Giorno*, Nabokov once remarked that "the people I invite to my feasts must have stomachs as strong as wineskins, and not ask for a glass of Beaujolais when I offer them a barrel of Château Latour d'Ivoire" (cited by Schiff, 55). Such invitations were not frequent but they were always accompanied by the command to drink deeply. Elsewhere, Nabokov refers to the "mammoth-tusk tower" in which he works and couples that metaphor with another: "my mirage is produced in my private desert, an arid but ardent place, with the sign No Caravans Allowed on the trunk of a lone palm" (*SO*, 110, 112). In his first English novel, *The Real Life of Sebastian Knight*, we find the ivory tower in a letter from Sebastian to a publisher in which he writes: "you seem to wonder . . . why the hell I should take a nice porcelain blue contemporary . . . and let him drop from *the tower of my prose* to the gutter below" (*RLSK*, 52; my italics). Sebastian shares much with his creator, including the tower in which he composes his works. In *Lectures on Literature*, Nabokov told his students that though mixing with the crowd can on rare occasions be illuminating, "taken all in all, I should still recommend, not as a writer's prison but merely as a fixed address, the much abused ivory tower" (*LL*, 371). Abused as it may be by others, for the singularly itinerant Nabokov the ivory tower was where he felt most at home.

As we have seen, Nabokov does not profess much concern for the wishes or welfare of his readers. But what leads him to dismiss his reader's expectations as he does? Is this a personal idiosyncrasy or irascibility without further consequence for his idea of art—or does it touch upon its very essence? The beginning of an answer is to be found by looking at what his position most resembles: the idea of *art for art's sake*. In a letter from 1948, Edmund Wilson— then Nabokov's best American friend—wrote to him: "you simply took over in your youth the *fin de siècle art for art's sake* slogan and have never thought it out. I shall soon be sending you a book of mine which may help you to straighten out these problems" (*NWL*, 211). The book in question was Wilson's *The Triple Thinkers: Ten Essays in Literature* (it does not appear to have "straightened out these problems"). For Wilson, a singularly querulous correspondent, turnabout was always fair play, and he had received a letter from Nabokov earlier that year in which Nabokov explained Wilson's enthusiasm for Bolshevism in these same terms—as a naive and youthful enthusiasm fueled by an unreflective idealism. But there was more than one-upmanship at issue and the matter Wilson promises to clarify for his friend is that which, alongside of the love of family and the pursuit of butterflies, lay at the center of Nabokov's life—*art*.

Responding to Wilson's letter, Nabokov wrote: "'Art for art's sake' does not mean anything unless the term 'art' be defined. First give me your definition and then we can talk" (*NWL*, 214). Wilson chooses not to do so, and one can hardly blame him, not only because the term is so difficult to define, but also because Nabokov shows no greater eagerness to do so. While art may indeed be a thing fantastically difficult to define, to assert that Nabokov created his art for art's sake seems a simple paraphrase of his many remarks on the matter. What else is an art which proudly proclaims its independence from all social, moral, philosophical, and political tasks but an art for its own sake? Why then should Nabokov not simply accept a motto that so closely corresponds to his position?

To answer this question we need to look more carefully at what, precisely, the expression *art for art's sake* means. On the one hand, it is a (circular) statement of purpose; on the other, it traces a historical movement. The term's provenance in English letters is from the French—most notably through Gautier and Baudelaire. It first appeared under the pen of the obscure French journalist Hippolyte Fortoul, who, in 1833, was describing the new movement at whose head Gautier would soon stand. There is every reason to believe, however, that the term had gained an underground currency in Parisian literary circles years earlier, in or around 1818 when Victor Cousin first used it in his *Cours de Philosophie* for that year (first published in 1836). He claimed that "we need religion for religion's sake, morality for morality's sake, just as we need art for art's sake" (Cousin, 224).[1] By 1845, the term was a hotly debated one in France and in 1847 Gautier could justly refer to it as "that formula rendered famous by polemic"[2] It was some twenty-five years later that the English form "art for art's sake" entered into circulation (the *Oxford English Dictionary* notes its first usage in 1872, by Swinburne), where it became the rallying cry of British aestheticism.

Neither Cousin nor Fortoul nor even Gautier was, however, the true originator of the term. Surprisingly enough, *l'art pour l'art* is German. In 1804 the multitalented and multilingual French man of letters Benjamin Constant traveled with Madame de Staël to Weimar, drawn by the presence of such luminaries as Goethe, Wieland, and Schiller. He noted in his diary for February 11 of that year: ". . . I had a visit from a certain Robinson, a student of Schelling's. His ideas on Kant's aesthetics ingenious. Art for art's sake [*L'art pour l'art*], without purpose, as all purpose perverts art. But art reaches the goal it does not have [*Mais l'art atteint au but qu'il n'a pas*] (Constant, 58). That art should be created for its own sake, that an external purpose would "pervert" it, is an idea that we have no problem understanding. How art reaches "the goal it does not have" is, however, another matter. As John Wilcox has noted, "Constant's dominant concerns were four: women, politics, the history of religions, and gambling"—i.e., *not* philosophy, and he does not return to the matter in his diaries or elsewhere (Wilcox, 363). Nevertheless, it appears that he brought the term back with him from his travels, and, along with Madame de Staël, introduced it into Parisian salons it would come, decades later, to dominate.[3]

Edgar Wind has noted that the strangeness of the phrase Constant noted in his diary was less the effect of fatigue (from his travels and conversations) than translation, and was in all likelihood an attempt to render a famous formula that his interlocutor had employed. This was the epochal definition Kant

1. The immediate context of Cousin's declaration is an attack on utilitarian conceptions of life and art (cf. also "*L'art ne doit avoir pour but que d'exciter le sentiment du beau, il ne doit servir à aucune autre fin; il ne tient ni à la religion ni à la morale, mais comme elles il nous approche de l'infini, dont il nous manifeste une des formes*" [Cousin, 226]).

2. "Du beau dans l'art," *Revue des deux mondes* 19 (1847): 901. Cited by Wilcox at 376.

3. It was likely that it was in those salons that the young Victor Cousin, a great fan of de Staël's *De l'Allemagne*, first heard the term—or at least of the currents of thought which led to it (it is known that Cousin met August von Schlegel in de Staël's salon). Constant's remark was first noted by J. E. Spingarn (Egan, 10). For the tracing of the term as it crossed the Rhine, cf. Egan and Wilcox.

had given of the nature of aesthetic activity—"*Zweckmäßigkeit ohne Zweck*," "purposiveness without purpose" (cf. Wind, 118 n. 23).[4] What is often obscured by the phrase's geographical and semantic wanderings, is that *art for art's sake* is an attempt to reformulate what Kant defined and Nabokov championed: the autonomy of the work of art. A corollary of Kant's assertion that the work of art does not have the same types of *ends* or *goals* as other creations is Nabokov's contention that the work of art should have no social, moral, or political goals.

What then does Nabokov object to in the term? It seems that Nabokov's greatest problem with the expression *art for art's sake* was that it was not of his own crafting. In *Strong Opinions* he remarks:

> Although I do not care for the slogan "art for art's sake"—because unfortunately such promoters of it as, for instance, Oscar Wilde and various dainty poets, were in reality rank moralists and didacticists—there can be no question that what makes a work of fiction safe from larvae and rust is not its social importance but its art, only its art (*SO*, 33).

Nabokov thus adopts the phrase's conceptual outlines and rejects its historical connotations. For him, what is brightest and finest about a work of fiction is "its art, only its art." In 1929 Walter Benjamin observed that "*l'art pour l'art* is almost never to be taken literally and is almost always flown as a flag under which goods sail that one cannot declare because the name for them does not yet exist" (Benjamin 2:301). Nabokov's observation is of precisely this same nature. What Nabokov distances himself from is the phrase *art for art's sake* having been taken up as a rallying cry by individuals who did not live up to its high standards—who were, "in reality rank moralists and didacticists." For Nabokov, the problem with the banner *art for art's sake* seems to be that it was used to fight other battles, and to smuggle other goods than artistic ones.

Whether Nabokov was *right* in his assessment is another question. His objection, at least as concerns the only artist he names—Oscar Wilde—is not unfounded. Whether Wilde's witty proclamations corresponded to his deepest or final feelings is difficult to say. When Wilde wrote that "there is no such thing as a moral or an immoral book," that "vice and virtue are materials for art," and that, "all art is quite useless," he was speaking in terms kindred to the ones Nabokov will use (Wilde, 5, 7). However, essays such as "The Soul of Man

---

4. Wind does not note, but was surely aware, that Constant was nearly as fluent in German and English as in the language of his diary (French), and that as he sat down to write of his day he would in every likelihood be translating German conversation into French notes.

under Socialism," or his writings following his trial for homosexuality such as "De Profundis" or "The Ballad of Reading Gaol"[5] might have led Nabokov to conclude that, at least by the time that Wilde ended his days there was more in his art than just art. As regards D. G. Rossetti, A. C. Swinburne, Théophile Gautier, or James Whistler, Nabokov showed little interest. Because of his ribald eccentricity, Aubrey Beardsley finds a place in *Lolita*, both playfully half-evoked in the mysterious form of Aubrey McFate and in Humbert's pseudonym for the town to which he and Lolita move—Beardsley—but Nabokov nowhere evidences any deeper interest.[6]

There was one member of this school of thought whom Nabokov did attend to with more patience than Wilde: Walter Pater. He cites Pater's definition of Romanticism ("the addition of strangeness to beauty") in one of the most important entries in the monumental annotations he prepared for his critical edition of Pushkin's *Eugene Onegin* (the note in question is a mini-essay on Romanticism in and after the time of Pushkin) (cf. *EO* 3:33–34; Pater's remark is from the "Postscript" to his *Appreciations*). What is more, many of Pater's ideas and terms are echoed in Nabokov's writing. Pater observes that Michelangelo possessed "a wonderful strength verging, as in the things of the imagination great strength always does, on what is singular or strange," and in doing so anticipates the connection Nabokov will trace between imaginative "strength" and the "the singular or strange" (Pater, 57). As will Nabokov, Pater will often stress the importance of "the vision within" which the artist

5. It bears noting for an understanding of some of Nabokov's strong opinions regarding fellow writers that neither in his works nor in his life did he look with an especially understanding eye on homosexuality. As concerns Nabokov's personal life, his indirect account of the discovery of his brother Sergei's homosexuality in *Speak, Memory* amply reflects this. As concerns his art, Nabokov's egomaniacal critic Kinbote from *Pale Fire* is unable to perceive things in terms other than those couched by his desire and this trait is intimately linked in that novel to his homosexuality. The homosexual friend of Humbert Humbert's solitude, the lovably elephantine Professor Gaston Godin, is more gently presented, but nevertheless shares Kinbote's perceptual ailment in that he too only really sees what he desires. For instance, he is so little aware of Lolita's existence that because each time he sees her she wears a different outfit, he assumes each time she is a different person and, as a result, that Humbert has a whole bevy of teen daughters. Theodor W. Adorno once wrote that "homosexuals display a sort of color-blindness of experience [*Farbenblindheit der Erfahrung*], the inability to recognize the individualized; to them all women are in two senses indifferent [*gleich*]," and this is a position echoed in Nabokov's fictions (Adorno, 8:84). It is not to be ruled out that Nabokov's vocal dislike of such writers as Wilde, Thomas Mann, or André Gide was in part influenced by those artists' sexual inclinations. An account of the relation of Kinbote's narcissism to his sexual orientation is to be found in Kevin Ohi's "Narcissism and Queer Reading in *Pale Fire*."

6. Clare Quilty's misleading entry in a hotel registry, "Aubrey Beardsley, Quelquepart Island," consolidates the reference (*AL*, 264). Whether Nabokov was thinking of the robust priapism of Beardsley's drawings, or the ribaldry of his writings, such as the unfinished "The Story of Venus and Tannhäuser" (which offers a startling panoply of perversion), is uncertain.

should seek to meticulously reproduce, as well as the futility of trying to define beauty in general terms and that "to define beauty, not in the most abstract but in the most concrete terms possible, to find, not its universal formula, but the formula which expresses most adequately this or that special manifestation of it, is the aim of the true student of aesthetics" (Pater, xix). This focus on image and precision is one that prizes not only art for art's sake, but also the idea that art is not to be understood as an abstraction, but as strange and singularly concrete.

However, Nabokov's most kindred spirit among authors who at one point raised the flag of *l'art pour l'art* was no "dainty poet," but a stout prose writer: his much-loved Flaubert. The latter wrote that "As it possesses its own reason and rationale, art should not be considered as a mere means" (Flaubert 1963, 294). An art which has its Principle of Sufficient Reason in itself and which should not be considered as a *means* to another *end* is by definition *art for art's sake*. As a corollary to this position, what Nabokov shares with Flaubert is the idea that the purest art is made only for its own sake and should under no circumstance lead the author to link his or her efforts with other artists. In a letter to Louise Colet from 1853, Flaubert stated that "it seems to me that in this day *to belong to anything*, to enter into any convening body, brotherhood, or literary boutique . . . is to dishonor and debase oneself—so low has everything sunk" (Letter to Louise Colet, May 3–4, 1853; Flaubert 1973–1980, 2:665). The coda Flaubert attaches to his *profession de foi* ("so low has everything sunk"), with its tragicomical sigh, calls to mind Beckett far more than Nabokov, but it is Nabokov who is the most vocal modern inheritor of Flaubert's refusal to join a literary group, school, club, or movement. In a letter to Jason Epstein criticizing a statement made by W. H. Auden, Nabokov wrote: "the slogan 'highbrows and lowbrows, unite!' which [Auden] . . . spouted . . . is all wrong since true highbrows are highbrows because they do *not* unite" (*SL*, 217).

What is at issue here is not only the definition of art's nature, but also of its *purpose*. Kant claimed that artistic activity is "purposiveness without purpose" and Nabokov's stance is its worthy inheritor. In this light, Wilde's remark that "all art is quite useless" can be understood less as brash charm and more as literal claim, as can be Gautier's declaration that "nothing is beautiful unless it is useless." What links Nabokov with the motto and movement art for art's sake was what Poe called "the heresy of the Didactic"—the rejection of the demand placed upon art that it edify and educate its reader. For Poe as for Nabokov, edification was a noble goal, but it was not the goal of art—because art, strictly speaking, had no goal. Ultimately, Nabokov rejected the phrase *art for art's sake* because of the implication that his singular art could be described by a general term—one that rings of groups and manifestos, of communal efforts and aims—in short, one that abandons art for Art's sake.

Reality, or Artists

> In "real" life we are creatures of chance in an absolute void—unless we be artists ourselves, naturally.
>
> —Vladimir Nabokov, *Ada, or Ardor*

By moving from the abstraction of Art to the concrete work, we have also moved closer to what readers have found mystifyingly cruel in Nabokov's work. To continue on this path we must now turn our attention from art to that which it reflects: reality.

In Nabokov's universe, "life does not exist without a possessive epithet," as "all reality is comparative reality" (*SO*, 118; *LL*, 146). In an interview with Pierre Dommergues, Nabokov remarked: "The word 'reality' is the most dangerous word there is" (Interview with Pierre Dommergues, 95). Humbert Humbert tells us that "reality" is "one of the few words which mean nothing without quotes," and Nabokov concurs with him in *Strong Opinions* where he speaks of "such local ingredients as would allow me to inject a modicum of average 'reality' (one of the few words which mean nothing without quotes) into the brew of individual fancy" (*AL*, 312; *SO*, 94).[7] To understand "reality" as a common fund of shared perceptions is to radically misunderstand the meaning Nabokov ascribes to it.

In the *Apostrophes* interview Nabokov states that the America of *Lolita* (of which so many critics praised the *realism*) was as "imaginary" as the fantastical Antiterra of *Ada, or Ardor*. In another interview he remarks: "The reality of art? It is an artificial, a created reality that is only reality within the novel. I do not believe in such a thing as objective reality" (Interview with Pierre Dommergues, 95).

This is far from a pose limited to interviews. In the third canto of the 999-line poem "Pale Fire" (the poem around which the novel of the same name grows), Shade refers to a certain "vision" which "reeked with truth," and "had the tone, / The quiddity and quaintness of its own / Reality" (*PF*, 60). This position is echoed by *Pale Fire*'s Kinbote who refers to "the basic fact that

---

7. At the end of Humbert's summary of Quilty's play *The Enchanted Hunters*, we learn that "a last-minute kiss was to enforce the play's profound message, namely, that mirage and reality merge in love" (*AL*, 201).

'reality' is neither the subject nor the object of true art which creates its own special reality having nothing to do with the average 'reality' perceived by the communal eye" (*PF*, 130).[8] That "reality" does not denote a common perceptual field or substance, but, instead, purely subjective experience is reflected in that work, as well as those to follow. In *Ada, or Ardor,* the heroine's "metaphysics" uses the term "reality" to denote only the most rare and personal of experiences (cf. *Ada,* 74). This is something she appears to have inherited from her father, Demon Veen, who claims that the ability to perceive "reality" requires "that *third sight* (individual, magically detailed imagination) . . . without which memory (even that of a profound 'thinker' or technician of genius) is, let us face it, a stereotype or a tear-sheet" (*Ada,* 252). For Ada and Demon, as for their creator, "reality" is not passive intake but imaginative engagement with the world around them.

As a result of this special conception of *reality,* Nabokov will say in his own voice of Gogol that at a certain point in the latter's career, "he was in the worst plight a writer can be in: he had lost the gift of imagining facts and believed that facts may exist by themselves" (*NG,* 119). At first sight, this does not seem like much of a plight. Whereas facts are normally conceived of as pertaining to *perception* rather than *imagination,* for Nabokov, the distinction is not operative. This extends to the perception of even the most factual elements—and thus Nabokov will speak of losing "the gift of imagining facts" required of a writer. And just as facts must be imagined, so too must *memories.* Asked if "the inevitable distortion of detail" in the act of remembrance "worries" him, Nabokov replied: "Not at all. The distortion of a remembered image may not only enhance its beauty with an added refraction, but provide informative links with earlier or later patches of the past" (*SO,* 143). Even cherished, faithful, fantastically exact memory is infused with *imagination* as it allows itself to be ruled more by subjective experience than some sort of objective veracity. Not only artistic images, but even facts and memories require imaginative effort to such an extent that "reality," for Nabokov, means nothing without quotation marks.[9]

8. Lest we dismiss this as a false doctrine proffered by a madman, we should note the context in which it is made. It comes in Kinbote's discussion of a Zemblan court painter named Eystein who became famous for his trompe l'oeil skill and who employed "a weird form of trickery" in effecting such compositions: "among his decorations of wood or wool, gold or velvet, he would insert one which was really made of the material elsewhere imitated by paint" (ibid.). Nabokov, like Eystein, while in general employing a trompe l'oeil in the false art and false semblance of a false artist, here includes a "real" decoration, a decoration whose provenance is himself, in the form of one of his own intimately held beliefs.

9. We might note at this point that Nabokov's redefinition of *reality,* to take a psychoanalytical point of reference, is the mirror opposite of the Lacanian "real," which Lacan qualifies as pertaining to the realm of the impossible, the unknowable, and the intolerable. Virginia Blum writes: "So the 'real,' the impossible for Lacan, strung up by Nabokov in inverted commas, the real is the space of contention in the narcissistic economy and one would like to know just why it is that this real is intolerable in both

In his critical writings Nabokov evidences a special fondness for the term "fantasy." This is in part a polemical term used to combat theories of literature focused upon social reform or moral improvement. But it is equally a function of his idea of "reality." "From my point of view," Nabokov writes, "*any outstanding work of art is a fantasy* insofar as it reflects the unique world of a unique individual" (*LL*, 252; my italics). "Fantasy" is thus in no respect opposed to "reality," as Nabokov employs the term, but is instead its artistic reflection. This is clearly evidenced by Nabokov's remark about Proust's *In Search of Lost Time*, that the work "is not a mirror of manners, not an autobiography, not a historical account. It is pure *fantasy* on Proust's part . . . just as Cornell University will be a *fantasy* if I ever happen to write about it some day in retrospect" (*LL*, 210; my italics). Something does not become fantasy by virtue of being fiction; it becomes fantasy by virtue of being imaginatively perceived.[10] What is most confusing about Nabokov's use of the term "fantasy" is the same thing that is confusing about his use of the term "reality." In both cases, he displaces their meaning from the realm of common consensus to that of individual imagination.

But Nabokov does not only speak of "reality," he also speaks of "true reality." Nabokov's position resembles the Romantic vision where individual perception, when infused by the energies of the imagination, is able to reach a "truth"—a "true reality":

> To be sure, there is an average reality, perceived by all of us, but that is not *true reality*: it is only the reality of general ideas, conventional forms of humdrummery, current editorials. . . . Average reality begins to rot and stink as soon as the act of individual creation ceases to animate a subjectively perceived texture (*SO*, 118; my italics).

---

the fictional and the psychoanalytic systems, and what it is about their relationships to the real and to narcissism that make of Lacan and Nabokov such mirror images" (Blum, 203). If Nabokov places "reality" (and it should be noted that Nabokov uses the term *reality* and not the term which Lacan employs, the "*real*"—French, like English, disposes of both terms in essentially analogous fashion) between quotation marks it is not to "string it up" in public punishment for its intolerability, but to safeguard it from being impinged upon from the outside. *Reality* is anything but intolerable for Nabokov—it is the source of life's joy. For another Lacanian reading of Nabokov and narcissism, cf. Couturier's "Narcissism and Demand in *Lolita*."

10. Anecdotal illustration of this position is to be found in an article from the *Crimson* newspaper dating from Nabokov's tenure as a visiting professor at Harvard in 1952 entitled "Recent Capture of White Whale Fails to Mar Melville's Meaning." The article reports the capture of an albino sperm whale off the coast of Peru and speculates on the relation of this fact to Melville's fiction. The article notes: "Vladimir Nabokov, visiting lecturer on Slavic Languages and Literature, and Theodore Morrison, professor of English, both agreed that critics would not revert to a literal interpretation of the novel now that a French vessel has reported the capture of a real albino sperm whale" (*The Crimson*, February 5, 1952).

This act of "animating a subjectively perceived texture"—a ceaseless "animating" of a "texture" (a thin veil for a *writing* of a *text*)—makes of "true reality" a kind of constant aestheticizing, a constant writing, painting, scoring, sculpting of "subjective perception." Nabokov will thus say of the "creative writer" that "he must possess the inborn capacity not only of recombining but of re-creating the given world," as well as, of himself as creative writer: "I tend more and more to regard the objective existence of *all* events as a form of impure imagination—hence my inverted commas around 'reality'" (*SO*, 32; Nabokov's italics). Where Nabokov differs from Romantic theories of the imagination, however, is that there is in his conception no Platonic space or place of ideas which the imagination then *expresses*; its point of origin is himself.

Taking Nabokov's idea of "reality" into careful account allows us to better understand his English novels—from the first to the last. Nabokov's first novel in English is entitled *The Real Life of Sebastian Knight*, and as we move from title to text we can watch the "real" of the title take on all its strangeness. That novel tells the tale of the writer Sebastian Knight, but what is "real" about that life remains highly questionable. Deprived of first-hand access to the writer Knight (who is, ironically, his half-brother), the narrator *imagines* how that life might have been. And as we read still further we are given ambiguous hints to the effect that the brother may merely be a device—a mask behind which Sebastian Knight tells his "real" life—which is to say, an imagined version of it.

The Real Life of Sebastian Knight is, however, not the only one of Nabokov's titles that evokes his idea of *reality*—so too does the last work he lived to complete, *Look at the Harlequins!*. In the scene which gives the book its title, we read:

> "Stop moping!" she would cry: "Look at the harlequins!"
>
> "What harlequins? Where?"
>
> "Oh, everywhere. All around you. Trees are harlequins, words are harlequins. So are situations and sums. Put two things together—jokes, images—and you get a triple harlequin. Come on! Play! Invent the world! *Invent reality!*" (*LATH*, 9; my italics).

Here we learn that the title is synonymous with: "*Invent reality!*" There could hardly be a more fitting close to Nabokov's oeuvre than this.

For Nabokov, the aesthetic criteria of works and of life appear to be *entirely* subjective—or, as we read in *Lectures on Literature*, "everything that is worthwhile is to some extent subjective" (*LL*, 4). This belief fundamentally influenced his compositional practice. As we saw above, it is found at the heart of a number of his most famous fictions—and it also explains much that is unconventional about his autobiography. Therein, Nabokov privileges what seem minor events over major ones, and organizes the work less by chronology than the thematic patterns he traces through his past.[11] Evading a question about the role of the writer, Nabokov says, "as soon as we start defining such terms as 'the writer,' 'the world,' 'the novel,' and so on, we slip into a solipsistical abyss where general ideas dissolve" (*SO*, 136). For Nabokov, however, this "dissolving" of "general ideas" is not to be feared or avoided. Instead of a desire to cling to such conceptions as "'the writer'" or "'the world'" as a means of making sense of one's "reality," one finds in Nabokov that "general ideas" are exactly what must be eschewed to reach "true reality." For Nabokov, instead of engendering an uneasy epistemological vertigo, the proud and independent making of one's own world is a thrilling and joyous act.

In place of the dark or gray tones used to express solipsistic states of affairs in, most famously, the works of Sartre, one finds very little anxiety in Nabokov's writing as concerns shared conceptions, full communication or meaning in history. This is most clearly seen in Nabokov's review of the English translation of Sartre's *Nausea*. As a review, it is utterly unsparing, first pointing out the faultiness of the translation before turning to what he sees as the still greater ineptitude of the original. In the last words of that article, we read something, however, that speaks directly to Nabokov's own view on solipsism: ". . . one has no special quarrel with Roquentin [the novel's protagonist] when he decides that the world exists. But the task to make the world exist as a work of art was beyond Sartre's powers" (*SO*, 230). In the space of a sentence we find here a concise resumé of Nabokov's ideas on "reality" and solipsism. It is not that he would necessarily deny a loss or devaluation of certain common values, nor the need for a radical and resolute decisiveness on the part of the individual confronted by such a state of affairs. For this reason, Nabokov says that one has no special quarrel with Roquentin when he "*decides* that the world exists." But to leave things in such a state of vague indetermination is to leave one's task incomplete. Throughout the brief review, Sartre is taxed with imprecision, and the malaise or nausea of his main character is traced to the vagueness of his creator and the "amorphous" world he creates. Sartre's skill, according to Nabokov, was not enough "to make the world exist as a work of art." In his view, one must more powerfully—which is to say, imaginatively—"animate" the "subjectively perceived texture" to create

11. On this point, Nabokov's first biographer, Andrew Field, observed: "Nabokov's splendid disregard for the mundane obligations of the memoirist is shown by the fact that he does not name his brothers and sisters, and, until the 1966 edition of *Speak, Memory*, he did not even say how many he had" (Field 1967, 34–35).

such a "reality."[12] It is for this reason that Nabokov will refer elsewhere to "the writing of one of those incredible novels where the author, in a fit of lucid madness, has set himself certain unique rules that he observes, certain nightmare obstacles that he surmounts, with the zest of a deity building a live world from the most unlikely ingredients—rocks, and carbon, and blind throbbings" (*SM*, 290). The author's stance here resembles that of a biblical God uttering supernatural fiats as "the materiality of this world may be real enough (as far as reality goes) but does not exist at all as an accepted entirety: it is chaos, and to this chaos the author says 'go!' allowing the world to flicker and fuse" (*LL*, 2).

Nabokov's idea of "reality" thus rejects shared visions of art and the world it mirrors. Integrating this position into Nabokov's aesthetics and ethics has—understandably—presented significant difficulties for Nabokov's critics. Andrews contends that "Nabokov's 'aesthetic,' i.e., his artistic method, *places its first emphasis on external reality*" (Andrews 1999, 53; my italics). Nabokov displayed a remarkable attention to detail and an openness and interest for what went on around him, but in aesthetic matters "external reality" does not seem to have received anything like first emphasis. To claim that it does is to not take Nabokov at his word—and yet, nothing could be more understandable than not taking Nabokov here at his word, given that doing so would seem to imply the exclusion of the reader from the sphere in which his art moves.

The contours of this question can be seen more clearly by turning to a critic who is not only one of Nabokov's finest—but also the one most intimately familiar with the external reality of his life: his biographer, Brian Boyd. In his first major critical study, *Nabokov's Ada: The Place of Consciousness*, Boyd turns to precisely this term, "*reality*":

> what makes reality so elusive is that it is infinitely richer than any single person's knowledge of it, or even the sum of science's specifications. The world is so real

12. Nabokov's brief review was not only an indictment, it was also a retaliation. In 1939 Sartre wrote a negative review of the French translation of *Despair* in the *Nouvelle Revue Française* (in which Nabokov also published) and thought enough of the review to include it in his collection *Situations I* (1947). D. Barton Johnson compellingly argues that Nabokov's introduction to a new translation of *Despair* from 1965, while never naming Sartre, is directly responding to him for two of its ten paragraphs (in which, for example, Nabokov claims that he "shall be interested to see if anyone calls my Hermann 'the father of existentialism' " [*Despair*, 8–9; cf. Johnson 1994, 76]). Johnson adds another piece to the puzzle of animosity between the two writers by noting how close Nabokov's 1926 Russian short story "Terror," evocatively describing the onset of an existentialist loss of connection and value, is to the existentialist novel Sartre would write in the same city (Berlin) eight years later. This idea is well supported by Nabokov's introductory remarks to the 1975 English translation of "Terror," where he notes that the story "preceded Sartre's *La Nausée*, with which it shares certain shades of thought, and none of that novel's fatal defects, by at least a dozen years" (*Tyrants Destroyed*, 112; cf. Johnson 1994, 79). D. Barton Johnson's balanced summary of the relation of the two writers is the finest account of the controversy.

that it always exceeds our knowledge of its reality. . . . Reality is elusive not because it is doubtful whether it exists outside the mind, but because it exists out there so resolutely, so far beyond human modes of perception and explanation in its end-lessly detailed complexity, so real even in its minutest parts. (Boyd 1985, 50)

The difficulty Boyd sets out here to tackle is evident from the outset—and from the circular definition he offers: "the world is so real that it always exceeds our knowledge of its reality." Boyd's intuition seems perfectly clear, and yet his logic seems to falter in his making our restricted knowledge of the world's "re-ality" a *consequence* of the fact that the world is "so real" (implying that if it were somehow less real we would know more about it). And yet even if we read "the world is so real that it always exceeds our knowledge of its reality" as meaning "the world is real and yet we cannot know what lies beyond its limits" we still remain confronted by the problem of the commonality of the thing in ques-tion—and it is this point on which Nabokov and Boyd seem to differ.

For Boyd, Nabokov's "reality" is fairly familiar. It corresponds to what is often meant by the term (a common substance), but is ultimately unknowable because of its constant expansions and the multiplicity of viewpoints ("what makes reality so elusive is that it is infinitely richer than any single person's knowledge of it"). Though he does not note this, Boyd is preceded by Rowe in this regard, who wrote as early as 1971 that Nabokov's writing tends to "free the reader to experience a plastic and consciousness-expanding 'real-ity' " (Rowe 1971, 86). In the section of his study programmatically entitled "Reality," Rowe inscribes Nabokov in a Romantic lineage and comes to the conclusion that, "Nabokovian 'Reality'—*too elusive* and too large for direct expression—is suggested inferentially, intangibly, deceptively" (Rowe, 87; my italics). The stress here, as it is in Boyd, is on the elusiveness of *reality*. But why is this *reality* so "elusive"?

In Boyd's account *reality* is presented as what is often termed the "world": the sum of existing things (as in Wittgenstein's famous phrase, "the world is everything that is the case" [Wittgenstein 1999, 30–31]). While in Boyd's gloss, neither "world" nor "reality" are actually defined as the "world's" "reality" is based on the fact that it is more real than we could ever know it to be, the fact remains that his definition is readily recognizable as in accord with reality as it is most generally defined: enduring substance actually existing and perceived from a multiplicity of standpoints. And yet, reasonable as this position is, it is, as we have seen, the very *inverse* of Nabokov's definition and usage of the term. Both Boyd and Rowe stress how "reality" is "elusive." Reality, however, is only elusive in the optic of communality, not in the optic that Nabokov situates it.

For him, it is described as perfectly graspable in the magic moment of individual, imaginative perception.

Rowe and Boyd, however, have solid grounds for stressing this elusive side of Nabokov's *reality* and both seem to have a specific remark in mind. In an interview from 1962, Nabokov said, "you can get nearer and nearer, so to speak, to reality, but you can never get near enough because reality is an infinite succession of steps, levels of perception, false bottoms, and hence unquenchable, unattainable" (*SO*, 11). For reasons not difficult to envision, Rowe and Boyd refer themselves to this (isolated) remark rather than to the numerous ones where Nabokov stresses that reality is "one of the few words which mean nothing without quotes." The centrality of this remark for Boyd is underlined by his citing it at the outset of a book from 1999, as well as in an interview given a year later (cf. Boyd 1999, 5 and the Nabokov List-Serve for Thomas Bolt's interview with Boyd from *Bomb* magazine in a complete and corrected version of this interview. List-Serve, August 31, 2000). In each case, he refers to this and only this remark amongst the many Nabokov made concerning reality. Both Rowe and Boyd seem to be simply paraphrasing Nabokov and choose to privilege this statement over the many other—more categorical and clear—definitions that Nabokov offered elsewhere. From a philological perspective, this is a questionable choice, but it is not as much an unfounded one. If we look closer, however, we can see that this privileging of an occasional remark over a thoroughgoing and consistent use of the term *reality* elsewhere in Nabokov's works serves a real and important function in Boyd's enterprise—it helps counterbalance the extreme solipsism of Nabokov's idea of *reality*. But before we turn to this question, let us look more closely at the statement that the two critics base their argument upon to see whether it truly does contradict Nabokov's other remarks on the matter.

"...You can get nearer and nearer, so to speak, to reality, but you can never get near enough because reality is an infinite succession of steps, levels of perception, false bottoms, and hence unquenchable, unattainable ..." Nabokov tells us here that reality is another name for a sort of infinity; that its approach is infinite ("an infinite succession of steps"). Does this contradict the numerous statements asserting *reality*'s completely subjective aspect stressed elsewhere? Inasmuch as the approach to reality is seen as an adventure in the world rather than an adventure within the self, it does indeed. In the preceding lines of this passage Nabokov also defines reality as "a kind of gradual accumulation of information" and as "specialization," and claims that a lily is more "real" to a naturalist than to "an ordinary person," and still more "real" to a botanist specializing in lilies—and it is this comparison that leads him to the remark on which Boyd and Rowe base their definitions (cf. *SO*, 10–11).

Nabokov's surprising statement begs the question of in what sense the lily is more "real" for a botanist specializing in lilies than for an "ordinary person." The lily exists just as concretely for the nonspecialist standing before it as the specialist. Following Boyd's definition, the lily would be more real for the botanist than for the ordinary person and still more real for the botanist specializing in lilies, because he links "elusiveness" with *reality*. The more one pursues the object the more it eludes one and the specialist is he who would know this best, having pursued the lily with more energy and intensity than the nonspecialist. And yet, on another level, this cannot be the case as even total ignorance of the name, nature, morphology, and genesis of the lily would not incline the non-specialist to doubt its *reality*, only to wonder what it is.

What then is Nabokov trying to express through this curious—and seemingly nonsensical—analogy, and what does it lead his critics to conclude? Throughout his creative and critical works Nabokov compares and even unites the vision of the artist with that of the scientist studying the minutiae of the natural world. Bringing together scientific and artistic vision is not done to give a clearer outline to objective reality—a point Nabokov shows no interest whatsoever in, but instead of linking the knowledge and attentiveness of the scientist with the passion and purpose of the artist. The lily is more real to the nonspecialist because he or she would more intensely and more subjectively experience it than someone with no special interest in the flower. As "reality" is a purely subjective affair, he or she who experiences something more personally, more passionately and with more emotional and intellectual engagement is experiencing it, in his words, as "more real." In this light we can understand both why it is strange to see Nabokov speak of *reality* as if it could be in greater or lesser supply, as well as in what sense this is not a contradiction of his other statements on the matter. As the passages looked at above make clear, Nabokov understands the word *reality* as meaning the very opposite of what its most accepted, most *general* meaning holds it to be (something well in line with Nabokov's wide-ranging polemic against the *general* and which we will turn to later in this study). Reality can thus be characterized as "an infinite succession of steps, levels of perception, false bottoms, and hence unquenchable, unattainable" because that infinite succession of steps leads not simply into the ever more minute facets of the manifest world, but also and at the same time to the absolutely personalized vision of the individual. The lesson Nabokov endeavors to express through this lily is that, for him, the greater the combined engagement of passion and knowledge, information and inspiration, the greater the *reality*.

What we see reflected in Nabokov's *reality* is a robust absence of interest in shared visions of the world. This is not simply the ivory tower as aesthetic model, but also as a *perceptual* one. This position carries with it, however, a certain danger—and one that finds its place at the center of many of his fictions. In the central formulation of his foreword to Shade's "Pale Fire," the demented annotator Kinbote writes: "Let me state that without my notes Shade's text simply has no human *reality* at all since the human *reality* of such a poem ... has to depend entirely on the *reality* of its author and his surroundings, attachments and so forth, a *reality* that only my notes can provide" (*PF*, 28–29; my italics). Four *reality*'s in the space of a single sentence is a great many. Kinbote claims that the work of art (here, Shade's poem) has no *reality* in and of itself and needs to look to its readers (or in this crazed case, a single reader—himself) for such. For this, as well as for many other reasons, he proves a poor reader, but he illustrates a simple and potent danger contained in Nabokov's aesthetics: solipsism. Nabokov happily exiles himself to the ivory tower of his singular reality and focuses with rare intensity on the passionate pursuit of an inner vision. But what the case of Kinbote—as well as other characters in his fiction—illustrates is the danger of climbing too high or descending too deeply into one's own singular reality. The consequences of such may be innocuous—such as misreading a poem. But they might also prove more sinister.

CHAPTER THREE

THE CRIMINAL ARTIST

Despair

JUST AS LOLITA had a precursor she eclipses, so too does *Lolita*. In "On a Book Entitled *Lolita*," Nabokov notes that the Russian novella "The Enchanter" anticipated his *Lolita*, but that he "was not pleased with the thing and destroyed it sometime after moving to America in 1940" (*AL*, 312). This turned out not to be the case and Nabokov came across a manuscript copy of the story in 1959 and found it not as bad as he had remembered it.[1] *Lolita*, however, does not have just this one precedent; it has a host of them with its pedophile theme surfacing in such prominent places as Nabokov's final Russian novel, *The Gift*.[2] But just as important for the form *Lolita* took as the theme of pedophilia is the theme of the insane artist and his criminal tendencies and these are on spectacular display in a work bearing significant points of resemblance with *Lolita*: *Despair* (1934).

---

1. He did not, however, publish it and it was Nabokov's son Dmitri who translated and published it in 1985.

2. The best summary of these minor and major precursors in Nabokov's work is Dieter Zimmer, "*Zeittafel zur Entstehung des Romans*" (1989) to be found in Zimmer's exemplary German critical edition of Nabokov's works. To that list one further item might be added. Nabokov's father's interests included criminology and in 1902 he authored an article entitled "Carnal Crimes" that, in his son's own description, concerned "little girls *à l'âge le plus tendre*"—"i.e. from eight to twelve years, being sacrificed to lechers" (*SM*, 178). Nabokov notes, however, there that this essay first came to his attention after he had written *Lolita* (ibid.).

In the foreword to *Despair* Nabokov remarks:

I am unable to foresee and to fend inevitable attempts to find in the alembics of *Despair* something of the rhetorical venom that I injected into the narrator's tone in a much later novel. Hermann and Humbert are alike only in the sense that two dragons painted by the same artist at different periods of his life resemble each other. Both are neurotic scoundrels, yet there is a green lane in Paradise where Humbert is permitted to wander at dusk once a year; but Hell shall never parole Hermann. (*Despair*, xiii)[3]

The first question the reader is inclined to ask is why the two books, and the punishment of their protagonists, should be linked? Both are whimsical first-person narrators who tell their own story of crime in blithe, irreverent fashion. Both are murderers. Is this all?

Like *Lolita*, *Despair* is presented as the first-person "memoir" or "confession" (both narrators use both terms to describe their narratives) of a brilliant madman and in it we first find a device later employed to great effect in *Lolita*, as well as in *Pale Fire* and *Ada*. This is the use of an unreliable narrator over whose shoulder peers the glinting eye of the author. This technique involves finding a surprising variety of ways and means for the narrator to disclose or transmit important information to the reader without himself seeming to be aware of its import. Humbert, Kinbote and Van Veen all seem to tell us many (damning) things about themselves without being aware of it, and this was a practice that Nabokov began to explore and refine in *Despair*.

No item in Nabokov's bag of stylistic tricks has received so much attention as this one, and its exegesis has been the basis for both the most insightful and the most outlandish critical findings. The reason for this is easy enough to grasp, as Nabokov's particular mode of employing an unreliable narrator is an open challenge to both the acumen and the imagination of his readers. Booth refers to this gesture as "the secret communion of the author and reader behind the narrator's back" (Booth, 300). Bader notes in the case of *Lolita* that "'point of view' need not be expressed through a separate voice; in Nabokov's case it is more a network of details behind and around Humbert which is not of his conscious making, and of which he may be unaware" (Bader 1972, 58). This "network

---

3. It is a curious fact that though Nabokov rejected the idea of a heaven, purgatory, and hell for men, he accepted it for literary characters. Another example may be found in the person of Flaubert's Emma Bovary who before she makes off with Léon, hears "the last gust of the beadle's parrotlike eloquence" which "foreshadows the hell flames which Emma might still have escaped had she not stepped into that cab" (cf. *LL*, 164).

of details" and the "secret communion" it effects sometimes appear, however, remarkably difficult to grasp.

Humbert says of his cross-country pursuit of mischievous Quilty through numerous hotel registers that he found himself at times in "a border-land mist with verbal phantoms turning, perhaps, into living vacationists" (*AL*, 250–251). Much the same effect is to be found in reading Nabokov's critics—many of whom, not without reason, have literally been pursuing verbal phantoms, as in the works of Rowe, Boyd, D. Barton Johnson, and Alexandrov, who all stress the importance of ghosts and other figures from the "otherworld" in Nabokov's fictions.

Curiously, these critics do not note that Nabokov's technique is as old as Western literature and has a venerable name: *Socratic irony*. In the *Apostrophes* interview, Nabokov remarks, "*moi, je m'en moque de ce Socrate*" ["I could care less about this Socrates."]. And in an interview with Alfred Appel Jr., he denies any "conscious Platonism" (Appel's phrase; SO, 70). In a letter from 1945 to Edmund Wilson Nabokov he was still more explicit: "I detest Plato" (NWL, 159).[4] Whether he detested him or not, he follows in his ironic footsteps. In *Greater Hippias* Socrates lures a traveling Sophist into equating wisdom with money. Socrates and the sophist, Hippias, speak of the wise men of the past and compare them to those of the present. Socrates remarks: "None of those early thinkers thought it right to demand money as payment, or to make displays of their own wisdom before all sorts of people. That's how simple-minded they were; they didn't notice how valuable money is. But each of the modern people you mention [Gorgias and Prodicus, Sophists] has made more money from his wisdom than any other craftsman from any skill." Hippias, caught in the snare, answers, "Socrates, you have no idea just how fine this is. If you knew how much money *I've* made you'd be amazed" (281d–283c; Plato, 1536). This manner of having a character say one thing so that the author may say another is the rhetorical model that Nabokov innovatively explores in his works—beginning with *Despair*.

This is not the only respect in which *Despair* might help us understand *Lolita*. It is an important precursor not only in the unreliable, but also the criminal, narrator. Through both novels flow a drop of Poe's narrative blood, and like the majority of Poe's "grotesque" tales, they are told in the first person and describe perverse, and homicidal, acts recounted with unnerving calm. This filiation is stressed in *Lolita* by the fact that Humbert frequently quotes Poe's works and

---

4. The occasion for this remark appears to be Wilson's articles on Greece for the *New Yorker*. As Wilson's side of the correspondence for this period has been lost it is not possible, however, to know with more precision what, precisely, Nabokov is responding to.

alludes to his person beginning with the book's opening paragraphs and its cloaked citations from Poe's poem "Annabel Leigh" (cf. *AL*, 9ff.).

On the first page of his story *Despair*'s Hermann employs a metaphor that will guide what follows as he claims that "at this point I should have compared the breaker of the law which makes such a fuss over a little spilled blood, with a poet or a stage performer" (*Despair*, 3). Hermann then adopts (without directly referring to) Thomas DeQuincey's playful position from his essay "On Murder Considered as One of the Fine Arts" (1827), and speaks of murder as one of the "creative arts" (*Despair*, 122). He likens the mental going-over of his crime to that of "an author reading his work over a thousand times, probing and testing every syllable"; of his crime, he later explains his lack of remorse with the simple self-evidence that "an artist feels no remorse" (*Despair*, 171, 177). Of the officers investigating his crime he tells his readers that "they behaved just as a literary critic does" (*Despair*, 191). Nabokov is not being especially subtle in setting clearly before the reader how Hermann envisions his trespasses and this red line running through the book is difficult to miss. As with *Lolita*—as with all of Nabokov's works—the author announces in the foreword that the book has "no message to bring in its teeth," and while it indeed may have no special social message, it seems, nevertheless, to offer a carefully encoded message about the relation of art to crime (*Despair*, ix). To underline this point we need only to turn to a later remark of special importance for understanding *Despair* and all that follows it.

In a letter concerning a revised English edition of *Despair*, Nabokov wrote in 1945: "My book is essentially concerned with the subtle dissections [*sic*] of a mind anything but 'average' or 'ordinary': nature had endowed my hero with literary genius, but at the same time there was a criminal taint in his blood; the criminal in him, prevailing over the artist, took over those very methods which nature had meant the artist to use" (*SL*, 57). Hermann is guilty of a special perversion of his natural gifts. Nature "endowed [him] with literary genius" but he allows that gift a dark outlet. The idea here is not merely that two hearts beat in his breast—the criminal and the artist—but that the criminal "took over those very methods which nature had meant the artist to use." That is to say that the gifts are convertible. The imagination, courage, dexterity, and single-minded, even solipsistic, focus required for art ("literary genius") are exercised elsewhere—and with disastrous results.

For Nabokov, "nature" grants "literary genius" to a very select few and intends for them to be used toward artistic ends ("*which nature had meant the artist to use*"). Hermann succumbs to the sin of allowing not just the "gifts" but also the "methods" meant for art to be taken over by the criminal in him—he is, in other words, guilty of applying the "methods" destined for *art* to *life*. In doing so, however, he is not alone.

Khodasevich, or the Line of Intersection

Nabokov's first major critic, his countryman and fellow exile Vladislav Khodasevich, has proven to be among his finest. In a review of *The Defense* from 1930 Khodasevich wrote:

> The artist is doomed to a sojourn in two worlds: the real world and the world of art created by him. A genuine master always finds himself situated on that line belonging to both worlds where the planes of each intersect. The separation from reality, the total immersion in a world of art where there is no flight but only an endless fall is madness. It threatens the honest dilettante but not the master possessing the gift of finding and thereafter never losing the line of intersection. (Bethea, 456)

It would be difficult to imagine a more precise description of the drama and danger that lie at the heart of Nabokov's creation. Though it precedes the publication of *Lolita* by some twenty-five years, no later analysis more accurately describes the motor driving that dark romance. As Khodasevich notes, the special tension in Nabokov's work is that between "the real world" and "the world of art created by him [the artist]," between a way of seeing and feeling which one has in common with others and "total immersion in a world of art."

In an essay written seven years later, Khodasevich noted that the basic theme of Nabokov's work was "life of the artist and the life of a device in the consciousness of the artist" (Khodasevich, 100). This perceptive judgment will be echoed in much later reflections on the theme such as those found in Stegner, Bader (1972), Field (1967), and Rowe (1971). Bader begins her study of Nabokov with an introduction on "The Art Theme" and the thesis—worthy of but without reference to Khodasevich—that "Nabokov's novels are mainly concerned with the artistic imagination and consciousness" (Bader 1972, 4). In this vein, she states that "Nabokov's novels are best seen in the perspective of the game of artifice" and as "different modes of presenting illusion" (Bader 1972, 2). While this is indeed an excellent perspective from which to examine Nabokov's works, it tends at points in her analysis towards abstraction and to the reading of Nabokov's works as allegories of fictionality, metafictionality and the struggle for originality. For this reason she will claim that the real divide between Humbert and Quilty is that Humbert is a true if "inexpert" artist who has "violated" his subject while Quilty is a "commercial artist" and whose "violation" is thereby more "monstrous."[5] Bader's focus on this same "line of

---

5. "Humbert's 'vice' is the inexpert artist's brutal treatment of a tantalizingly undeveloped subject, whose fragile soul Humbert has violated. The grossest violation is Quilty's, the commercial artist's, and

intersection" makes of her work a valuable extension of Khodasevich's early insights, but its persistence in seeing such novels as *Lolita* as allegories of "the literary process" marks the limit of her path-breaking work (Bader 1972, 80).

In a similar vein, Field wrote that *Lolita* is "a tale representing the tragic pain and entrancing beauty of art and the tremendous price it exacts" (Field 1967, 349). Ellen Pifer will take him to task for this idea, and his claim that both the murder in *Despair* and the child-molestation of *Lolita* are "allegor[ies] of the artistic process" (Pifer 1980, 3–4). For Pifer, Field's manner of reading is tantamount to reducing Nabokov's narrative to a string of "mere symbolic events" (Pifer 1980, 3). Field's formulation may be excessive, but his line of speculation—starting in Khodasevich and continuing in Bader—need not be dismissed out of hand. Pifer is doubtless right that he is engaged in an "allegorical mode of interpretation," and yet this is also no easy thing to avoid, and her own later work stresses an overarching idea of "the child's sacred reality" and offers something of an allegory concerning children and creative potential (Pifer 1980, 9).[6]

In an article from 1984 Edmund White located what he saw as an impish, perverse, and even cruel streak running through Nabokov's work in his habit of creating "grotesque versions of himself."[7] Nothing, in fact, has been so baffling to critics of Nabokov as precisely this tendency. One way of approaching this phenomenon is to see it as part of an allegory about art and creation, as we saw above. But might we not see in this tendency something of the order of an experiment? Instead of something broadly allegorical or narrowly personal, might not such a gesture be an exercise and a lesson in the dangers of art? In other words, might we not see Nabokov's habit of creating "grotesque versions of himself"—grotesque versions of the artist—neither as impish or perverse, as did White, nor as an exercise in radical dissociation, as did Nabokov's biographer

---

his crime is so monstrous that it merits the greatest punishment in a novel about artistic creation: he is left deliberately half-created" (Bader 1972, 80).

6. For Pifer, *Lolita* is a story about childhood wherein Nabokov "locat[es] the disease of Humbert's imagination in his betrayal of the child" (Pifer 1995, 317). This, for her, is linked to a larger message about what she calls "the child's sacred reality"—a point from her earlier writings echoed in her most recent essay on *Lolita*, where she notes how "throughout Nabokov's imaginative universe, the child's image shines like a beacon, a beacon that serves, among other things, to highlight this writer's unique position in the development of twentieth-century fiction" (Pifer 2003, 105; cf. Pifer 1995, 319). Lolita represents not only a child, for Pifer, but all that is essential about human "consciousness" and "creativity": "The deprivation Lolita suffers at Humbert's hands, the loss of her childhood, implies in Nabokov's universe a betrayal of human consciousness and its creative potential" (Pifer 1995, 317).

7. Speaking of the Russian short story "Spring in Fialta" (1938), White refers to Ferdinand therein as "one of those many grotesque versions of himself Nabokov planted throughout his fiction" (E. White, 7).

Brian Boyd,[8] but as an intimate part of his thought and art? Might we not see them as monsters and demons carefully carved into the façades of his works to better reveal its mission? To answer these questions we must look more closely at this "line of intersection" traced by Khodasevich.

The Artist's Perspective

Nabokov's first novel offers nothing less than a description of the nature of artistic vision:

> And in those streets, now as wide as shiny black seas, at that late hour when the last beer-hall has closed, and a native of Russia, abandoning sleep, hatless and coatless under an old mackintosh, walks in a clairvoyant trance; at that late hour on those wide streets passed worlds utterly alien to each other: no longer a reveler, a woman, or simply a passer-by, but each one a wholly isolated world, each a totality of marvels and evil. (*Mary*, 27)

To see the individuals of one's world in all their singularity—as each representing "a totality of marvels"—and, in some cases, "evil"—is to see them with an artist's attention. In a front page appeal to aid the unemployed printed in a Russian émigré newspaper on January 2, 1932, Nabokov wrote, "it takes a person idle, cold and with an untenanted heart to turn from another's need or simply not notice it. Fortunately such people are few" (cited by Boyd 1990, 376). In the Russian short story "Perfection" published that same year a character has "a passionate desire to experience everything, to attain and touch everything, to let the dappled voices, the bird calls, filter through his being and to enter for a moment into a passerby's soul as one enters the cool shade of a tree" (*Stories*, 336). For Nabokov, this activity is not only ethical, it is also aesthetic. The most artistic figure in his Russian fiction, *The Gift*'s Fyodor, is described as engaging in the following exercise at a party:

> . . . while the others talked on and he talked on himself, he tried as he did everywhere and always to imagine the inner, transparent motion of this or that other

---

8. Boyd notes in the opening pages of his biography that, "part of my task is to explain why Nabokov could create characters as bizarre as Humbert, Kinbote, or Hermann and allow us to see out from within their minds" (Boyd 1990, 4–5). The thousands of erudite pages that Boyd goes on to write on Nabokov's works and days are thus at least in part to be located under this sign of explaining the nature of Nabokov's bizarre creations. Boyd's sense of task continues undiminished in the second volume of his

person. He would carefully seat himself inside the interlocutor as in an armchair, so that the other's elbows would serve as armrests for him, and his soul would fit snugly into the other's soul. . . . (*Gift*, 35–36)[9]

The activities Nabokov imagined proper to the artist were curiosity, empathy, and pity. What is required is not merely a cold, analytical understanding allowing one to identify the chess-like coordinates of those around one. The artist must also *feel* his or her way into that position. In his *Lectures on Literature*, Nabokov stresses what he calls "the divine throb of pity" necessary for an understanding of Dickens, and in a lecture on Kafka go so far as to define art itself as: "beauty plus pity" (*LL*, 87, 251).[10] Had Nabokov wished for a Latin tag to place upon his literary coat of arms, it seems that he could have found no better one than Terence's *Humani nihil a me alienum puto*.[11]

What then of Nabokov's criminal artists? In a lecture on Chekhov, Nabokov once observed that "criminals are usually people lacking imagination" (*LRL*, 376). Might we apply this remark to Nabokov's most notorious criminal— Humbert Humbert? Nabokov may have chosen to deprive Humbert of many things, but imagination was not one of them. And yet, despite his wide-ranging curiosity, lively imagination and singular perceptiveness, he does not, at least until late in his days and memoir, engage in the empathy and the pity we might expect from someone of his intelligence and imagination. Up until the end of his story, he does not endeavor to regard each individual as "a totality of marvels and evil," does not "enter for a moment into a passerby's soul as one enters the cool shade of a tree." And it is precisely because of this failure to engage in such mobile identification and imagination that he can be depicted as possessing such extraordinary intelligence and sensitivity and yet can act with such brutal insensitivity towards she whom he professes to love above everyone and everything in the world. For Nabokov, what most determines the artist's perspective is his ability to feel his way into another's world, to infuse his sensibility and suffuse his senses with something promising art.

---

biography at the outset of which we read that Nabokov's *Lolita* offered the "imaginative and intellectual challenge of inventing values so thoroughly inverting [Nabokov's] own" (Boyd 1991, 7).

9. Sebastian Knight's brother, at the close of his narrative, speculates that "the hereafter may be the full ability of consciously living in any chosen soul, in any number of souls, all of them unconscious of their interchangeable burden" (*RLSK*, 202).

10. This will lead Rorty to refer to Nabokov's "oversize sense of pity" (Rorty 154–155).

11. "Nothing human is alien to me." The remark is from Terence's play *Heauton Timorumenos* (I.i.2). Nabokov's linguistic nemesis Roman Jakobson (who Nabokov was [wrongly] convinced was a KGB agent) re-tailored the expression to describe himself, declaring on several occasions that "*linguistici nihil a me alienum puto*" (cf. Roman Jakobson, "Closing Statement: Linguistics and Poetics").

The Sense of Art

In his *Lectures on Literature*, Nabokov distinguishes between "the literature of the senses," which he glosses as "true art," and "the literature of ideas, which does not produce true art *unless it stems from the senses*" (*LL*, 237; my italics). For Nabokov, literature born of an abstract idea rather than the senses is destined to wither and die. So fully does Nabokov conceive of the senses as the ground from which art grows that he here offers as a synonym for "true art," "the literature of the senses." In his foreword to *A Hero of Our Time*, he says of commonplace words that "they are tokens of sense, rather than particularizations of sense," and thereby points to the delicate relation between language and the senses (*Nabokov's Congeries*, 254). Merely trafficking in tokens, in signs that point generally and indistinctly toward the felt and sensed world, cannot, for him, lead to the creation of "true art." The writer worthy of the name is able to find language that "particularizes" his or her sensuous world. In *Speak, Memory*, Nabokov notes that "in the works of major Russian poets I can discover only two lepidopterological images of genuinely sensuous quality" (*SM*, 128; those two poets are Bunin and Fet.) "Images" which are "genuinely sensuous" are the only ones truly of value because only they partake of the essence of true art; the rest are without interest.

In *Lectures on Russian Literature*, Nabokov gives a more complete account of this process, claiming that

> Literature must be taken and broken to bits, pulled apart, squashed—then its lovely reek will be smelt in the hollow of the palm, it will be munched and rolled upon the tongue with relish; then, and only then, its rare flavor will be appreciated at its true worth and the broken and crushed parts will again come together in your mind and disclose the beauty of a unity to which you have contributed something of your own blood. (*LRL*, 105)

Nabokov's directions as to how to read are singularly sensuous. The details of a work must not only be isolated and observed in pure analytical fashion, they must be *smelt* and *tasted*; they must be so ecstatically felt that the "unity" produced from sensitive reading is one where "you have contributed something of your own blood." It turns out, however, that to do this, the reader must possess not only a mental readiness, but also a physical sensitivity. Of Kafka's *Metamorphosis*, Nabokov tells us, "we can take the story apart, we can find out how the bits fit, how one part of the pattern responds to the other," but to truly appreciate it, "you have to have in you *some cell, some gene, some germ that will vibrate in answer to sensations that you can neither define, nor dismiss*" (*LL*, 251; my italics).

The intellect can neither master nor control, catalogue nor conserve, "define nor dismiss" that in us which will suddenly, magically, begin to vibrate and come alive—not merely in our minds, but also in our senses. Literary intelligence is all well and good, but, for Nabokov, if it is not coupled with a literary sensitivity—as indefinable as it is irrefutable—it is of no use in truly appreciating a great work of literature.

The other end of aesthetic experience, that of literary inspiration, is unsurprisingly described as being of the same nature. In a late article, Nabokov describes the "inspiration" that has visited him: "The beauty of it is that while completely intelligible (as if it were connected with a known gland or led to an unexpected climax), it has neither source nor object. It expands, glows, and subsides without revealing its secret" (SO, 309). For Nabokov, to truly create art, just as to truly appreciate it, requires the possession of a special and singular sensitivity. But where is this sensitivity to be located?

The Phenomenology of the Spine

> I am trying to analyze the spine-thrill of delight it gives me, this name among all the others.
>
> —Vladimir Nabokov, *Lolita*

In *Lectures on Literature*, Nabokov asks his audience to engage in a special type of reading. On the one hand, he wishes for a passionately interested group of readers. On the other, he is concerned that this enthusiasm could lead, as we saw earlier, to a blind identification with the characters of a work of fiction. He thus asks a reasonable question: "So what is the authentic instrument to be used by the reader?" (LL, 4). He answers:

> It is impersonal imagination and artistic delight. What should be established, I think, is an artistic harmonious balance between the reader's mind and the author's mind. We ought to remain a little aloof and take pleasure in this aloofness while at the same time we keenly enjoy—passionately enjoy, enjoy with tears and shivers, the inner weave of a given masterpiece. To be quite objective in these matters is of course impossible. Everything that is worthwhile is to some extent subjective. (*LL*, 4)

While Nabokov maintains that "everything worthwhile" is "subjective," there is still an "artistic harmonious *balance*" which can be found. Through what instrument are we to reach this balance? What is the "authentic instrument" he refers to? Surprisingly enough, Nabokov has a precise answer to this question: it is the reader's *spine*. "The mind, the brain, the top of the tingling spine," says Nabokov, "is, or should be, the only instrument used upon a book" (ibid.). A few pages later, he describes how this spinal reaction eclipses the colder, more cognitive aspects of reading. "In order to bask in that magic [of a brilliant novel]," Nabokov says, "a wise reader reads the book of genius not with his heart, not so much with his brain, *but with his spine*. It is there that occurs *the telltale tingle* even though we must keep a little aloof, a little detached when reading. Then with a *pleasure which is both sensual and intellectual* we shall watch the artist build his castle of cards and watch the castle of cards become a castle of beautiful steel and glass" (*LL*, 6; my italics). It is through the spine that we may perceive art's innermost architecture.

The account above is anything but an isolated instance. Elsewhere in Nabokov's *Lectures*, in his discussion of Kafka, he states that "no matter how keenly, how admirably, a story, a piece of music, a picture is discussed and analyzed, there will be minds that remain blank *and spines that remain unkindled*" (*LL*, 251; my italics). In his lecture on Dickens, the process is outlined in all its detail: "All we have to do when reading *Bleak House* is to relax and let our spines take over. Although we read with our minds, the seat of artistic delight is between the shoulder blades. The little shiver behind is quite certainly the highest form of emotion that humanity has attained when evolving pure art and science. . . . The brain only continues the spine: the wick really goes through the whole length of the candle. If we are not capable of enjoying that shiver, if we cannot enjoy literature, then let us give up the whole thing" (*LL*, 64). Further on in that lecture, Nabokov takes time out to remind his listeners, "I repeat again and again it is no use reading a book at all if you do not read it with your back" (*LL*, 64). One of Nabokov's Cornell students relates Nabokov's repeated injunction: "let us worship the spine" (Wetzsteon, 245; this maxim is also found in the published transcripts of the lectures—cf. *LL*, 64). Another Cornell student, Nabokov's future annotator and critic Appel, remarked of Nabokov that "he would conclude a lecture with a rhapsodic apostrophe to our writer's style: 'Feel it in your spine . . . the upper spine, the vertebrate tipped at the head with a divine flame!'" (Appel 1971, 84). In *Strong Opinions* Nabokov refers to "the spinal twinge which is the only valid reaction to a new piece of poetry," and even goes so far as to indicate elsewhere in that volume that the reader through proper use of the spine can attain to that which Nabokov everywhere else denies access to—the intention of the writer: "the fact that you read an artist's book not with your heart . . . and not with your brain, but with your brain and spine. 'Ladies and gentleman, the tingle in the spine really tells you what the author felt and wished you to feel'" (*SO*, 134, 41). In an interview from 1967, Nabokov's "advice to a budding literary critic" is simple and straightforward: "Rely on the sudden erection of your small dorsal hairs" (*SO*, 66).

This idea is, however, not limited to Nabokov's pedagogical persona. Shade, often faithful to Nabokov's aesthetic views, is reported by Kinbote (in the note to line 172 of "Pale Fire": "books and people"), to have said when asked about teaching Shakespeare: "First of all, dismiss ideas, and social background, and train the freshman to shiver, to get drunk on the poetry of *Hamlet* or *Lear*, to read with his spine and not with his skull" (*PF*, 155). In the final canto of his poem, Shade relates that the "sudden image" and the "immediate phrase" come with the shiver of "a triple ripple" "over the skin."[12] In Nabokov's English poem "The Poem" (1944), he describes the onset of inspiration as the coming of "the shiver" (*PP*, 157). In his autobiography he writes of the beautiful things he saw in his youth: "I did not know then (as I know perfectly well now) what to do with such things—how to get rid of them, how to transform them into something that can be turned over to the reader in printed characters to have *him* cope with the blessed shivers—and this inability enhanced my oppression" (*SM*, 212; Nabokov's italics, my underlining). The English short story "A Forgotten Poet" contains a reference to "that heavenly draft which suddenly locates the sensorial effect of true poetry right between one's shoulder blades" (*Stories*, 569). To describe the then-forthcoming *Ada*, Nabokov evokes "a much ampler and richer novel, entitled *Ada*, about passionate, hopeless, rapturous sunset love, with swallows darting beyond the stained window and *that radiant shiver . . .*" (*SO*, 91; Nabokov's ellipses, my italics). In *Ada* itself, Van Veen refers to "the French plaisir, which works up a lot of supplementary spinal vibrato" (*Ada*, 19). This description of aesthetic responsiveness is even to be found in Nabokov's private writings. In a letter to Archibald MacLeish in December 1951 he notes that "there is that movement of light in one of your most famous poems that invariably sends a shiver of delight up and down my spine whenever I think of it" (*SL*, 129). In Nabokov's late novel *Transparent Things* we read that the spine is "the true reader's main organ" (*TT*, 75).

Humbert Humbert, that artistic madman, shows, perhaps the greatest spinal sensitivity in Nabokov's works. The mere sight of Lolita's name sends "a spine-thrill of delight" through him (*AL*, 52). Recognizing the magic of the nymphet requires the same spinal sensitivity as Nabokov requires for the work of art:

> A normal man given a group photograph of school girls or Girl Scouts and asked to point out the comeliest one will not necessarily choose the nymphet among them. You have to be an artist and a madman, a creature of infinite melancholy, with a bubble of hot poison in your loins and *a super-voluptuous flame permanently*

---

12. "When inspiration and its icy blaze, / The sudden image, the immediate phrase / Over the skin a triple ripple send / Making all the little hairs stand on end" (*PF*, 67).

aglow in your subtle spine (oh, how you have to cringe and hide!), in order to discern at once, by ineffable signs—the slightly feline outline of a cheekbone, the slenderness of a downy limb, and other indices which despair and shame and tears of tenderness forbid me to tabulate (*AL*, 17; my italics).

At another point early in his chronicle, Humbert notes how "possibilities of sweetness on technicolor beaches had been trickling through my spine"; and later therein to a "spinal music" stemming from the "pleasurable antiphony" created by the concatenation of a pale nymphet encountered in the lobby of the Enchanted Hunters with suntanned Lolita (*AL*, 36, 126). In short, Humbert experiences Lolita's charms as would an artist—in his tingling, singing spine. And this, as we will see, is an essential part of his problem.[13]

Do the Senses Make Sense?

There have been a truly remarkable number of intelligent, sensitive, and erudite readers of *Lolita*, and a great many of them have shared their views and perceptions with the public. And yet, the question of the book's immorality or morality, its ethical message or the absence thereof, remains as uncertain and contested as it was at the time of the book's publication. Is it possible that too little attention has thus been given to the *bad* readers of the book?

The first and best bad reader of *Lolita* was Nabokov himself—in disguise. The purported editor of Humbert's memoir, plodding John Ray Jr. (Ph.D.), reveals himself in his short foreword to be all that the clever reader would wish to avoid. He is wooden, verbose, pretentious and pedestrian. He contends, at cross-purposes to Nabokov's remarks on the subject, that "more important to us than scientific significance and literary worth is the ethical impact the book should

13. I have dwelt at such length on examples of this phenomenon because Nabokov's spine has received surprisingly little attention. One of the few critics to treat the question is Rorty, who refers in passing to what he calls Nabokov's "Housmanian tingles." "Nabokov's talk of tingles," says Rorty, "was certainly influenced by Housman's *Name and Nature of Poetry* (the best-known manifesto in English of what Nelson Goodman calls "the Tingle-Immersion" theory of aesthetic experience)" (Rorty, 147, 149 n. 10). In the talk that Rorty refers to, the Leslie Stephen Lecture (dating from well after Nabokov's Cambridge years), Housman states that "poetry indeed seems to me more physical than intellectual," and in the lecture's crucial passage proclaims:

Experience has taught me, when I am shaving of a morning, to keep watch over my thoughts, because, if a line of poetry strays into my memory, my skin bristles so that the razor ceases to act. *This particular symptom is accompanied by a shiver down the spine*; this is another which consists in the constriction of the throat and a precipitation of water to the eyes; and there is a third which I can only describe by borrowing a phrase from one of Keats' last letters, where he says, speaking of Fanny Brawne, "everything that reminds me of her goes through me like a spear." The seat of this sensation is the pit of the stomach. (Housman, 47; my italics)

have on the serious reader" (*AL*, 5). He continues this thread by claiming that "in this poignant personal study there lurks a general lesson; the wayward child, the egotistic mother, the panting maniac—these are not only vivid characters in a unique story: they warn us of dangerous trends" (ibid.). There was nothing which Nabokov railed against with such energy than reading for "general lessons" and "dangerous trends." John Ray Jr.'s very name is that of Everyman, the mirror (J.R. Jr.) of a Mr. Anyeverybody stuttering anonymous transmission from junior to junior to junior. Should we not heed the numerous signs Nabokov leaves which invite us to read Ray Jr. as a figure for the conformist, generalizing thought he loved to mock? Are we not meant to feel with the droll, jesting, and artfully cadenced Humbert Humbert far more than the lumbering and laboring Ray Jr. and his concern with "bringing up a better generation in a safer world" (*AL*, 6)? At first sight, the answer seems as clear as can be.

Defending the necessity of retaining certain scenes in his editing of Humbert's memoir, Ray Jr. tells us that were one to excise them, "one would have to forego the publication of 'Lolita' altogether, since those very scenes that one might accuse of a sensuous existence of their own, are the most strictly functional ones in the development of a tragic tale" (*AL*, 4–5). Humbert's memoir, so Ray Jr. tells us, presents sensuous scenes not for their own sake, but instead serves a different and definite purpose. They are "the most strictly functional" elements in Humbert's tragic tale. It is in connection with this point that Ray Jr. himself suggests a reason for his selection as the editor of Humbert's transfixing tale: his having won "the Poling Prize" for "a modest work ('Do the Senses Make Sense?') wherein certain morbid states and perversions had been discussed" (*AL*, 3). Might we not imagine that Ray Jr.'s prizewinning work speaks, in its own fashion, of the same danger that Humbert's memoir so vividly, so luridly and so mesmerizingly depicts: the danger that the senses, left to themselves, left to make their own sense, threaten to veer towards "morbidity," towards "perversion"—that is to say, toward the infliction of pain and the forgoing of pity. And yet, what if the senses, as Nabokov claimed, are the ultimate—and only—means

---

This is the only part of Housman's talk that refers to the spine or a physical reaction of shivering and hairs-on-end, making it difficult to read as what Rorty calls it: a "manifesto." The similarity of spinal reaction is worth noting, especially as Nabokov knew and appreciated Housman's poetry. (Though Rorty does not note this fact, Housman rates a mention in Nabokov's first English novel, as well as in his autobiography, his fictional autobiography, his *Lectures on Literature*, and *Pale Fire*—cf. *RLSK*, 66; *LATH*, 22; *LL*, 65–68; PF, 269.) While it is conceivable that Nabokov was influenced by Housman's shaving regime, a much stronger case would need to be made to assert that Nabokov was "certainly influenced" by them. Attributing this idea of physical response to Goodman is also somewhat arbitrary. One might just as well link it to what Northrop Frye called "the proving of art on the pulses" (*Anatomy of Criticism*, 27) or to Emily Dickinson's celebrated remark, "If I feel physically as if the top of my head were taken off, I know this is poetry."

to ensure the beauty and authenticity of the work of art? From what perspective can they then be judged to make sense—or not?

The question of the senses—the sense they make and the perversity they can lead to—is asked on every page in Humbert's memoir. There is, however, a passage near the work's close which presents the question in an especially clear light. Humbert writes:

> Unless it can be proven to me—to me as I am now, today, with my heart and my beard, and my putrefaction—that in the infinite run it does not matter a jot that a North American girl-child named Dolores Haze had been deprived of her childhood by a maniac, unless this can be proven (and if it can, then life is a joke), I see nothing for the treatment of my misery but the melancholy and very local palliative of articulate art: To quote an old poet:
>
> > The moral sense in mortals is the duty
> > We have to pay on mortal sense of beauty. (*AL*, 283)

As the reader may have guessed, Nabokov has invented the old poet for the occasion. But what of his words? There is, first of all, a recognizable Nabokovian concatenation of homophemes (moral, mortals, mortal). More importantly, the key term to Nabokov's aesthetics—*sense*—is on prominent display.

With the question of attribution settled, we might ask what the pithy couplet means. It begins, conceptually, with a "mortal sense of beauty." We might assume that this is the sense of beauty, the feeling of and for beauty, that is *mortal*—that is possessed by those destined to pass and fade; transient beauty for transient beings. The old poet evokes alongside of this beauty a "duty"—an obligation, a debt that comes with mortals' sense of beauty. The tax ("*duty*") that "mortals" must then pay on, and for, their sense of (their experience of) beauty is "the *moral* sense." Thus, in the couplet's tight logic, the tax or "*duty*" that keeps the *sense* of beauty (sensual perception of beauty) from becoming *mortal* (i.e., fatal) for certain *mortals* is the *moral* sense. Phrased otherwise, *mortals'* sense of beauty, if not reined in by the *moral* sense, can be *mortal* (fatal).

If we look to Humbert's favorite writers, we find a parallel for this expression of this ethical responsibility stemming from the perception of beauty. In "The Poetic Principle," Poe remarks: "Just as the Intellect concerns itself with Truth, so Taste informs us of the Beautiful, *while the Moral Sense is regardful of Duty*. Of this latter, while Conscience teaches the obligation, and Reason the expediency, Taste contents herself with displaying the charms, waging war upon Vice solely on the ground of her deformity, her disproportion, her animosity to the fitting, to the appropriate, to the harmonious, in a word to Beauty.

An immortal instinct deep within the spirit of man is thus plainly a sense of the beautiful" (Poe, 76; my italics). In light of this passage we can read the couplet in question as a highly concentrated treatment of the "Duty" of Poe's "Moral Sense." McNeely says this coupling of the concepts is "exactly as Poe does" (McNeely, 190). Six years later, Gerard De Vries writes that "Nabokov compactly paraphrases Poe" in this passage and while both critics are clearly right to read Poe's terms between Nabokov's lines, that what is at issue is a paraphrase is far less certain (De Vries, 145). While Nabokov has Humbert (or his invented "old poet") stage a contest of the faculties where the moral sense must be reluctantly paid as a "duty" on the mortal sense of beauty, in Poe's passage there is no such tension and no such contest. Poe's "Moral Sense" concerns itself indeed with "Duty," but that "Duty" is in no way opposed by the mortal sense of beauty but, instead, "Taste" (which "informs us of the Beautiful") "wages war" on Vice (as does "the Moral Sense"). The only difference is that it does so on separate grounds (the grounds of "deformity, disproportion"). Nabokov is thus not paraphrasing, but *amending* the (traditional) aesthetic position Poe expresses. De Vries extracts the moral from this passage that in Nabokov, "the search for beauty by mortals, the pity and sorrow this search leads to, welds the aesthetic and the moral" (De Vries, 146), but his inability to show how this takes place in Nabokov's works lies in his retaining the traditional vision espoused here by Poe where the perception of beauty automatically leads to moral actions. *Lolita* argues that, on the contrary, this is anything but the case.[14]

As Nabokov made tirelessly clear, for him, art is an affair of the senses. Following his aesthetic prescriptions, the shiver of sensuous excitement is the only reliable barometer of artistic value. In *Strong Opinions*, Nabokov refers to "such combinations of details as yield *the sensual spark* without which a book is dead" (*SO*, 157; my italics). As is much remarked upon (and by no one as much as Nabokov himself), he was fantastically careful in choosing his words. For this reason, we should attend to the *sensual* spark without which, as he says, a book is dead. Given the decidedly nonsexual context, we might have expected the word *sensuous* in its place. That Nabokov perceived a difference between the two terms is witnessed by his remark in "On a Book Entitled *Lolita*," that "no writer in a free country should be expected to bother about the exact demarcation between the sensuous and the sensual" (*AL*, 314). Though he dismisses

14. We might note alongside of Poe another classical aesthetic declaration which might have served as a source for Nabokov's curious phrase (and/or, perhaps, for Poe's own phrase). In his *On the Aesthetic Education of Man*, Friedrich Schiller speaks of the "*sinnlichen Pfand der unsichtbaren Sittlichkeit*" which serves to bridge the gap in the evolution of society from "*der Herrschaft bloßer Kräfte zu der Herrschaft der Gesetze*" (Schiller 1959/1993, 5:576). Though it is impossible to demonstrate with any great degree of accuracy, it is not unlikely that Poe and/or Nabokov found the kernel of their respective phrases in Schiller's "*sinnlichen Pfand der unsichtbaren Sittlichkeit.*"

the need for an artist to concern himself about the distinction, he nevertheless notes that it exists.

What, however, really separates the two adjectives? *Sensuous*, the younger of the two terms, was coined in the seventeenth century by no less a figure than John Milton, who, never frivolous in questions of language, did so in response to the word *sensual*'s growing synonymity with *sexual* (or even, in rarer cases, *lewd*—a semantic shift seen as early as the sixteenth century).[15] The new word, *sensuous*, was thus born under the sign of separating the *sexual* from the *sensual*. Why this was such a pressing concern that a new word needed to be coined was the growing sense that to promote moral behavior one could not simply appeal to reason, as reason would too often encourage simple self-interest. The senses, therefore, needed to be appealed to, and moved—one needed not just to *understand* but to *feel* why one should act morally. One of the most influential treatises on the question, Friedrich Schiller's *On the Aesthetic Education of Man* (1795), could not have taken a more apt epigraph than the one found in Rousseau's novel *Julie ou la Nouvelle Héloise*: "If it is reason that distinguishes man, it is sentiment that guides him."[16] It was precisely this principle that motivated the interminable eloquence of Rousseau's virtuous heroes and heroines. At the outset of his work, Schiller states the problem common to aesthetic and ethical questions: "one is bound to invoke feelings no less often than principles" (Schiller 1959/1993, 5:570). Reason in the form of encapsulated principles can as little guide moral behavior as it can dictate taste in art. For this reason, the senses and the sense they make must play an equally large role in both aesthetic and ethical education. This call to feeling, passing as it does through the ear of the senses, is a delicate thing. While the senses, for Rousseau, for Schiller and, in essence, for most aesthetic speculation since the eighteenth century, offered access to a truth more immediate and intuitive than that which could be reached through reason alone, those same senses, taken not as a *means* to moral betterment, but as an intensely pleasurable *end* in themselves, posed the greatest of dangers. Rousseau's most trenchant, if delirious, critic, the Marquis de Sade, was to evoke, in one hundred different positions, precisely this danger of the senses

15. Cf. the *Oxford English Dictionary*, as well as W. W. Skeat, *Etymological Dictionary of the English Language* (1879–92; Oxford: Oxford University Press, 1993), s.v. "Sensual." Were Milton alive today, and had he similar concerns, he would indeed need to create yet another word, as *sensuous* has become nearly as sexual as *sensual*.

16. One might note in this connection the famous declaration of Alexander Pope in a work that Nabokov shows his intimate familiarity with in *Pale Fire, An Essay On Man*. In the second epistle of that work, Pope stated the relation of passion to reason in the maritime metaphor, "On life's vast ocean diversely we sail, / Reason the card [i.e. compass], but Passion is the gale . . ." Reason can guide—can serve as compass,—but the driving force, as it would later be for Rousseau, is to be found in the passions (Pope, 67–68).

taken not as one among many guides, but as chief and sole counselor. As he fired the senses of his rationalists de Sade instructed them to listen, as did Rousseau, to the counsel of their senses, and that counsel was far from kind.

It is against this at once aesthetic and ethical backdrop that Nabokov composes his couplet. Elsewhere he talks of "the innocent and sensuous eye of the true artist" (*LL*, 116). The question then becomes, for this eye to remain pure and innocent, how one protects its tender *sensuousness* from the willful violence of the *sensual*? That Nabokov chose in his account of what a work requires to be truly "living" the sexier of the pair (*sensual*) proves, ultimately, little. Just as little is proven by the fact that John Ray Jr. chooses the other term, *sensuous*, to stress that those scenes in the work which one might imagine to have a "sensuous existence of their own" are ones which are "strictly functional," and without which the story could not reach its aim. What is of the essence is that if these sensual or sensuous scenes are ones that are a "functional" part of a "tragic" whole, might they not offer some message about the role of the senses in the work of art? In other words, what is the answer to John Ray Jr.'s cryptic question "Do the Senses Make Sense?"

CHAPTER FOUR

SAFELY SOLIPSIZING

Sex: The Ancilla of Art

"LET US SKIP SEX," says Nabokov in an interview in *Strong Opinions*, and in both his fictional and nonfictional writing, he is at some pains to frustrate those searching for sexual symbols, or reading only for the prurient plot (*SO*, 23). "Sex as an institution, sex as a general notion, sex as a problem, sex as a platitude," he states, "all this is something I find too tedious for words" (ibid.). Humbert, with whom Nabokov is of course not always in agreement, similarly informs his reader: "I am not concerned with so-called 'sex' at all. Anybody can imagine those elements of animality" (*AL*, 134). However, works such as *King, Queen, Knave*, *Ada*, *Lolita* and others are far from convincing on this point—and do little to encourage their reader to skip sex.[1]

Elsewhere, Nabokov affirms that art need not blush before the sexual and that "genuine art is neither chaste nor simple" (*A Hero of Our Time*, 258). More

---

1. Closer to the margins of Nabokov's *oeuvre*, one finds, as well, a rare concentration of eroticism in Nabokov's published correspondence with Edmund Wilson—itself a curious mixture of excursuses on poetic meter and droll ribaldry (eventually descending into more and more acrimonious exchanges of ideas on grammar). Among other things, one finds therein practical considerations about the feasibility of engaging in intercourse on the floor of an old-style Berlin taxicab (cf. *NWL*, 147–148). In the salad days of this correspondence one can also read of the strangest of Nabokov's proposed projects: a poem that was to be written at the suggestion of Edmund Wilson narrating Superman's wedding night. *The New Yorker* politely turned it down.

programmatically, he states in the *Apostrophes* interview that "what is referred to as eroticism is nothing other than one of the arabesques of the art of the novel." While "sex as an institution, sex as a general notion, sex as a problem" and "sex as a platitude" may all be "too tedious for words," sex as an artistic device, as "one of the arabesques of the art of the novel," is another matter. If we recognize, as Nabokov enjoins us to, that genuine art is neither chaste nor simple, and choose not to "skip sex," what might we learn from it about the art of fiction?

Safely Solipsizing

> This fatal rage of Masturbation of which the imagination is the artisan, leads to excesses over which the wretched criminal imperceptibly ceases to have any power.
> —Dr. J. D. T. de Bienville, *Nymphomania, or a Dissertation Concerning the Furor Uterinus* (1775).

To return to the coordinates for reading and writing offered by *Despair*, we are now in position to ask an important question: If Humbert, like his predecessor Hermann, goes about the criminal appropriation of the "methods" "meant" for art, what are these methods and how does he appropriate them? The answer is as surprising as it is simple: masturbation.

For reasons easy to imagine, the role of masturbation has received little attention in criticism of *Lolita*, or of Nabokov's work as a whole. And yet, masturbation is the sexual act and activity of the "nympholept," and Humbert refers to it with remarkable regularity in the early chapters of his memoir. We find reference to the "lone gratification" his discrete observations tend towards; he tells us of his ardent striving for the "beggar's bliss" which is all he hopes for in his observing of nymphet beauty (*AL*, 20, 42). Humbert is even something of an impish masturbator as, "little did the good lady [Charlotte] dream that one morning when an upset stomach . . . had prevented me from accompanying her to church, I deceived her with one of Lolita's anklets" (*AL*, 81). Just after Lolita's departure for Camp Q and the kiss which preceded it, Humbert recounts, "I marched into her tumbled room, threw open the door of the closet and plunged into a heap of crumpled things that had touched her. There was particularly one pink texture, sleazy, torn, with a faintly acrid odor in the seam. I wrapped in it Humbert's huge engorged heart. A poignant chaos was welling within me—but I had to drop those things and hurriedly regain my composure as I became aware of the maid's velvety voice calling me softly from the stairs" (*AL*, 67). He even goes so far as to curiously muse upon the possibility that his covert masturbations might somehow affect the futures of those he fantasizes about ("In this wrought-iron world of criss-cross cause and effect, could it be that the hidden throb I stole from them did not affect *their* future?" [*AL*, 21; Nabokov's italics]). Lifting a little roller skater from Nabokov's earlier variation on the theme, *The Enchanter*, Humbert notes how "once a perfect little beauty in a tartan frock, with a clatter put her heavily armed foot near me upon the bench to dip her slim bare arms into me and tighten the strap of her roller skate, *and I dissolved in the sun*, with my book for fig leaf, as her auburn ringlets fell all over her skinned knee, *and the shadow of leaves I shared pulsated and melted on her radiant limb next to my chameleonic cheek*" (*AL*, 20; my italics). This passage may require a second reading to be sure about what is marbling Humbert's cheek, but once seen, it cannot be unseen.

For Nabokov's reader, the interest of masturbation (apart from what James Joyce praised it for—its "amazing availability!"[2]), is the key role it plays in a number of Nabokov's fictions—most centrally in *The Enchanter*, *Lolita*, and *Ada*. Viewed as a theme in Nabokov's work it involves three issues: one of *memory* in the evocation of earlier excitement, one of *actuality* in that the element of actuality is replaced by that of fantasy, and one of *solitude*. Less schematically, what is most at issue in *Lolita* is the role of the *image* as it is isolated from the real reel of life and spliced into the abstracted world of the imagination.

A scene from the first part of *Lolita* narrates something rather simple, and yet has consequences that are ultimately devastating. It is a Sunday morning and Lolita, after a tiff with her mother, has stayed home from church. The living room of the Haze house is depicting in bower-like terms—"the implied sun pulsated in the supplied poplars; we were fantastically and divinely alone"—and the entire scene comes to be more and more bathed in a parodically Edenic light (*AL*, 60). Lolita enters the living room lofting "a beautiful, banal, Eden-red apple" (*AL*, 58). Humbert is at once Adam and Tempter as he snatches it, then offers it to her. They sing and tussle. After a few moments, as Humbert's "corpuscles of Krause" reach a summary state of excitement, we read that "the least pressure would suffice to set all paradise loose" (*AL*, 60). It is given and it is lost.

---

2. Earlier in the story, Humbert nearly obtains his "beggar's bliss" as he gazes on his future lover from behind when he is interrupted by Charlotte. The colors of the passage as well as the phrase a few pages later, "a sudden smooth nether loveliness, as with one knee up under her tartan skirt she sits tying her shoe" (*AL*, 42–44), evoke Leopold Bloom's furtive, crepuscular, seaside masturbation, peeking from afar at the nether loveliness of young Gerty McDowell in *Ulysses* (four copies of which chapter, published separately in Ezra Pound and Margaret Anderson's *Little Review*, were seized and burned by the U.S. Postal Service in 1920—an incident indirectly referred to by John Ray Jr. in his foreword—cf. *AL*, 4). In the facsimile edition of Nabokov's lectures on *Ulysses*, he says of this chapter that "for reasons of time and coeducation I cannot share with you all the plums in this wonderful chapter" (cited by Julian Moynahan in "Nabokov and Joyce," 443).

The playful staging of the lovers' first fall should not blind the reader what it sets slowly in motion. Humbert recounts the scene with high irony, but one can see through that to its ultimate import. He relates:

> What had begun as a delicious distension of my innermost roots became a glowing tingle which *now* had reached that state of absolute security, confidence and reliance not found elsewhere in conscious life. With the deep hot sweetness thus established and well on its way to the ultimate convulsion, I felt I could slow down in order to prolong the glow. Lolita had been safely solipsized. The implied sun pulsated in the supplied poplars; we were fantastically and divinely alone; I watched her, rosy, gold-dusted, beyond the veil of my controlled delight, unaware of it, alien to it. . . . I had ceased to be Humbert the Hound, the sad-eyed degenerate cur grasping the boot that would presently kick him away. I was above the tribulations of ridicule, beyond the possibilities of retribution. In my self-made seraglio, I was a radiant and robust Turk. . . . Suspended on the brink of that voluptuous abyss (a nicety of physiological equipoise comparable to certain techniques in the arts) . . . (*AL*, 60; Nabokov's italics; my underlining)

What Humbert describes here is his ability to achieve a state of "absolute security, confidence and reliance not found elsewhere in conscious life," because he is able to "*solipsize*" Lolita, because he is able to place a "veil of . . . controlled delight" between himself and her which renders her not only "unaware" of his pleasure, but "alien" to it.[3] Humbert's subterfuge allows him to "st[eal] the honey of a spasm without impairing the morals of a minor"—or so it seems (*AL*, 62). As here described, for Humbert it is only in masturbation that an imaginative realm free from the limitations and vicissitudes of one's relations with others, of the constant conflict of desires and the compromised and compromising forms of satisfaction or frustration, can be reached (evoked by the hectic movement from *cur* to *Turk* in the passage's metaphors). External reality of course plays a role in the attainment of this pleasure, but it is a reality made passionate by being made passive to imaginative construction and creation.

3. To augment the aura of solipsism, Humbert is described as wearing in this scene "a purple silk dressing gown" with its suggestions of sovereignty and sensuality. Carl Proffer suggests that the purple robe is an allusion to Gogol's *Dead Souls* (cf. Proffer, 140 n. 47).

I stated that the question of Humbert's masturbation has received little attention. An exception merits noting here. David Packman says of this passage, "Humbert's desire for ejaculation mirrors the reader's desire for plot resolution" (Packman, 52). While such a theory might indeed be developed, it would need be extended beyond not simply every masturbatory act in the novel, nor even every sexual act therein, but every intentional act and to read the passage in such an abstracted light risks missing its import for what is to follow.

In light of this, the reader should not then be surprised when Humbert likens his masturbation here to "certain techniques in the arts" (ibid.).

Still more important for the form his tale will take is the template offered by this masturbatory experience:

> Thus had I delicately constructed my ignoble, ardent, sinful dream; and still Lolita was safe—and I was safe. What I had madly possessed was not she, but my own creation, another, fanciful Lolita—perhaps more real than Lolita; overlapping, encasing her; floating between me and her, and having no will, no consciousness—indeed, no life of her own. And nothing prevented me from repeating a performance that affected her as little *as if she were a photographic image rippling upon a screen* and I a humble hunchback abusing myself in the dark. (*AL*, 62; my italics)

As with the "safely solipsizing" cited above, Humbert stresses the "safety" of his disguised pleasure—the fact that he had done nothing harmful to the twelve-year-old he so desires because he had done nothing to her at all. "What I had madly possessed *was not she*," he claims, "*but my own creation, another, fanciful Lolita*" (ibid.; my italics). Humbert's erotic reverie leads him to make a fundamental division between Lolita in her own right and person, and "another, fanciful Lolita" which is the object of his semi-discreet desire and which he himself "created." The next step is the most artistic and perilous one as he credits his *image* of Lolita with more "reality" than the "real" little girl at his side.

That this was at the heart of Nabokov's intention is clearly reflected by his Russian translation of *Lolita* where he underlines the importance of this operation by rendering the phrase "Lolita had been safely solipsized" as, literally, "Lolita's reality was successfully canceled" (Alexandrov 1991, 170–171). In different fashion, this same point is stressed in the *Apostrophes* interview where he remarks of Humbert that

> It is this sad satyr's *imagination* that makes a magical creature of this young American schoolgirl, as normal and banal in her genre as Humbert the poet is in his own. Outside of the maniacal gaze of Humbert, there is no nymphet. Lolita the nymphet exists only through the obsession that destroys Humbert. An essential aspect of this singular book. (My italics)

Just as in one sense Nabokov invents his nymphet, he cancels—or solipsizes—the reality of the little girl who gives rise to her.

Unsurprisingly, Humbert then likens his image of Lolita to a photographic or filmic image because, after Humbert's masturbatory escapade, that image is depicted as having no more individual agency than such a representation ("no will, no consciousness—indeed, no life of her own").[4] Lolita is solipsized to the point where she ceases, in Humbert's description, to be an *ethical subject* and becomes an *aesthetic object*. Because of the imaginative investment to which she is subject, this other "fanciful Lolita" is described as "perhaps more real than Lolita"—a phrase all the more striking given Nabokov's special usage of the term "reality" as indexical not of the physical reality or durability of some substance or state of affairs, but of the degree of imaginative investment. While Humbert initially describes this imaginative appropriation as a form of shielding Lolita from the beastliness of his desires, it is precisely this method of aestheticizing Lolita that leads to the monstrous acts of the latter half of the book. This scene of venal masturbation leads directly to Humbert's later mistreatment of Lolita by offering him for the first time an image of Lolita separated from her "real" existence, a template for a variously unconscious Lolita, a Lolita considered as an aesthetic object.[5]

Herbert Grabes reads *Lolita* as "tell[ing] the—never really sentimental or tragic—story of a man whose suffering relates from a radically reduced sexual desire which drastically limits his chances of finding sexual satisfaction" (Grabes, 41, 39). While this is at least partially correct, it is at most one half of the equation and Pifer can note with greater pertinence that Humbert's "passion for Lolita originates not in some clinical or chemical disorder but in the depths of his imagination" (Pifer 1995, 311). For Stegner, as for many of *Lolita*'s early critics, the story is indeed one of artistic imagination—but in a purified light. *Lolita*, in Stegner's words, "moves us to a compassionate understanding of the suffering produced by an idealistic obsession with the never-to-be-had" (Stegner, 115).[6] It is important, however, not to rush into the idealistic and to be precise about

---

4. In this connection one should recall Lolita's reason for ultimately leaving Quilty—his insistence that she act in one of his private pornographic films.

5. Humbert's first fantasies, it should be remembered, involve the heavy sedation of the Hazes: "I saw myself administering a powerful sleeping potion to both mother and daughter so as to fondle the latter through the night with perfect impunity. The house was full of Charlotte's snore, while Lolita hardly breathed in her sleep, as still as a painted girl-child" (*AL*, 71). Lolita is not just "as still as a painted girl-child," she is imagined as having no more agency than a painted image. The first night at the Enchanted Hunters Hotel Humbert attempts to sedate his charge, thinking to himself that "by nine . . . she would be dead in his arms" (*AL*, 116). Still later in the telling of that evening Humbert states that "I was still firmly resolved to pursue my policy of sparing her purity by operating only in the stealth of night, only upon a completely anesthetized little nude" (*AL*, 124). The masturbatory template developed earlier is the one that remains. Like a work of art, Humbert imagines her without real life ("dead in his arms"), or with, at best, a distant impersonal life, a "nude" like the ones artists draw, not the naked child a parent might hold.

6. This reading is based on a passage where Humbert remarks "indeed, it may well be that the very attraction immaturity has for me lies not so much in the limpidity of pure young forbidden fairy child beauty as in the security of a situation where infinite perfections fill the gap between the little given and the great promised—the great rosegray never-to-be-had" (*AL*, 264).

what is designated here as unattainable—and why. As readers from Hollander and Trilling onwards have noted, and as Brenda Megerle noted in an essay from 1979, "any compassion the reader feels is experienced because he himself is participating in the very emotions which evoke his 'compassion'" (Megerle, 338). As Megerle's programmatic title, "The Tantalization of *Lolita*," makes clear, a capital element in any reading of the book is "the tantalization which Nabokov finds in the aesthetic experience, and that the erotic emotions the book inspires are the supreme analogue of the artist's desire to 'possess' the aesthetic object"; "Nabokov uses every and any mode that titillates, tantalizes, and lures us on to seek the unattainable" (Megerle, 339, 347). The unattainable as object of Romantic striving is something of which we might be encouraged to, in Stegner's words, have "a compassionate understanding," but Nabokov's text gives clear indications that this should not prevent us from seeing what Humbert does not: that his idealization of Lolita, his "safe solipsism," is anything but safe.

In his "Notes sur la notion d'itinéraire dans *Lolita*" Alain Robbe-Grillet shows a rare sensitivity to this aspect of Nabokov's narrative in referring to "the pre-pubescent doll [*la poupée impubère*] seated next to him in the car" (Robbe-Grillet, 35). This aspect of the novel, rarely taken into account in all its radicality, is graphically highlighted in Edward Albee's transformation of the novel for the stage wherein Humbert appears near the beginning of the play with a life-sized doll in his arms (Albee, 7). This is indeed a heavy-handed way of going about things and Humbert's first speech involves the importance of his love being "the sensation of *MY* being in love. God, what an inadequate term! (*Embraces the doll.*)" (ibid.). What is more, in his dialogue with his creator (who, as we saw, Albee coquettishly calls "A Certain Gentleman"), Albee's Humbert feigns not being aware that what is in his arms is merely a doll ("ACG [A Certain Gentleman]: The doll. Do you plan to explain it? HH (*Hugs it to him.*): What doll?" [Albee, 8]).

While Humbert may claim that his solipsizing was safe, it will most definitely not remain so. The crucial juncture in Humbert's adventure of the image is the morning after their first night together as his solipsized, doll-like, aestheticized and literally anesthetized Lolita comes awake and alive and his pleasures and torments begin with a very real, alive, and lively Lolita. For thousands of miles and hundreds of pages Humbert will keep his gaze riveted not on Dolores Haze seated next to him in their car, but an "another, fanciful Lolita," first "created" for his masturbatory purposes—the true child of his desire. And it is only by fixing his attention on his artfully crafted image that he is able to ignore the real Lolita whom he, all the while, is so hurting. Late in his chronicle he will recall: "There was a day, during our first trip—that first circle of paradise—when *in order to enjoy my phantasms in peace* I firmly decided to ignore what I could not help perceiving, the fact that I was to her not a boy friend, not a glamour man, not a pal, not even a person at all" (*AL*, 283; my italics). Even after their relations where the last thing but imagined, the last thing but "*phantasmatic*," Humbert still thinks in those terms. He can only "enjoy in peace" his vicious circle of paradise if the real little girl he is so desperately mistreating does not too violently interpose herself—and so he decides to "firmly ignore" her in favor of the "phantasm" first formed on this fateful Sunday (*AL*, 284, 283).

Scholium: Moral Masturbation

In the spring of 1948, Nabokov received and read a strange Russian memoir. It was composed in French by a Ukrainian who preferred to remain nameless and was published as an appendix to the French edition of Havelock Ellis' *Studies in Sexual Psychology* (fearing the English public's reaction to its ribald contents, Ellis withheld it from the earlier English edition). In a letter from June 10, 1948, Nabokov wrote Edmund Wilson to acknowledge receipt of, give thanks for, and express amusement at the anonymous Ukrainian's amorous woes. The text left a strong enough impression that it rated an oblique reference in the revised English edition of Nabokov's memoir *Speak, Memory* where, with it in mind, he refers to "various 'sexual confessions' (to be found in Havelock Ellis and elsewhere), which involve tiny tots mating like mad" (*SM*, 203).[7]

The "*Confession sexuelle d'un Russe du Sud*, né vers 1870 . . ." ["Sexual Confession of a Southern Russian, born around 1870"]—translated into English in 1985 as *The Confessions of Victor X*][8]—tells a story of precocious and intense sexual activity. The author's amorous adventures begin in early adolescence, are singularly varied and stringently—even superstitiously—preclude masturbation. The author of the memoir associates masturbation with ruin and malediction to such a point that he describes his intense sexual activity as primarily a means of forestalling it. After this period of initial sexual activity, there follows over a decade of total abstinence (including abstinence from masturbation). This period comes to a close in Italy with a very young prostitute (he does not know her age) with whom he does not have sex, but who masturbates him. (The potentially pedophiliac encounter comes up only at the very end

7. It is presumably with this passage in mind that in his entry on *Speak, Memory* for the *Garland Companion to Vladimir Nabokov* Nivat refers to Nabokov "ridiculing Havelock Ellis's description of an orgiastic prewar Russia" (Nivat, 677).

8. The French edition of Nabokov's correspondence with Wilson, from 1988, incorrectly claims that no English edition of this work exists (*Correspondance: 1940–1971*, 225 n. 1). Cf. *The Confessions of Victor X*, ed. Donald Rayfield (New York: Grove Press, 1985).

of the text, and then only for four pages—cf. Ellis, 435–438.) The experience leads him to at last cede to what he had continued to view as the greatest of vices: masturbation. Shortly thereafter, he contracts a venereal disease which he strongly associates with said masturbation although he is perfectly aware that this is not its (immediate) cause. As a result of the disease he must break off his engagement and finds himself consigned to a life of solitude, bachelorhood, and nearly suicidal sorrow. The memoir ends with what the author had most feared at its outset: a masturbation which makes the sexual act and sexual relations parasitic upon it with real relations serving only to fuel the fire of his solitary exertions. His despair is crystallized in the self-indictment he pronounces at the end of his memoir: "I have become, physically and morally, a masturbator" (Ellis, 445).

In a summary of the Ukrainian's memoir, Simon Karlinsky, the editor of Nabokov's correspondence with Wilson, credits Nabokov's reading of the Ukrainian's text with an influence on *Lolita* (cf. *NWL*, 201–202 n. 1). He makes no mention, however, of masturbation and its associated dangers, stressing instead the pedophiliac note sounded by the young Italian prostitute. The translator and editor of the English translation of the memoir, Donald Rayfield, is equally convinced of the work's influence on *Lolita* and equally silent on the matter of masturbation.[9] A similar claim is made by Ernest Machen in a letter to the *TLS* who argues for the importance of the work (again, only in its portrayal of pedophilia) as a source of inspiration for *Lolita* (Machen, 17). Machen is perhaps right to gently reproach Alfred Appel Jr.'s annotated edition of *Lolita* and Brian Boyd's two-volume biography of Nabokov for not mentioning the work in question, but his claims for influence are excessive, and, more importantly, misplaced. In a preface to *The Enchanter*, Nabokov's son, Dmitri Nabokov, dismisses all these claims of influence.

Independent of whether Karlinsky, Rayfield, Machen, or Dmitri Nabokov is right as to the question of *whether* the anonymous Ukrainian's memoir influenced *Lolita*, is the fact that their cases are posed on false footing. *If* there is a link with *Lolita*, it is not to be found in the person of the potentially underage Italian prostitute the Ukrainian encounters but with what she leads him to do.

Finally, we might note that Ellis' anonymous Ukrainian was not the first confessing memoirist to hold such a belief. The modern father of this confessional genre, Jean-Jacques Rousseau, felt precisely the same way. Rousseau notes how "In my foolish fancies, in my erotic frenzies, in the extravagant acts to which they sometimes led me, I had recourse in my imagination to the assistance

9. Rayfield finds "an almost Tahitian sexuality" in Victor's Ukrainian youth. In a brief prefatory note to the work he invites his reader to read his own conclusions "when he recovers from the confessions" (143).

of the other sex, without ever thinking that it was serviceable for any purpose
than that for which I was burning to make use of it . . ."; and: "For this reason
I have rarely possessed, *but have nonetheless enjoyed myself in my own way—that is
to say, in imagination.* Thus it has happened that my senses, in harmony with my
timid disposition and my romantic spirit, have kept my sentiments pure and my
morals blameless, owing to the very tastes which, combined with a little more
impudence, might have plunged me into the most brutal sensuality" (Rousseau 1959, 12–13; my italics). Elsewhere, in *Emile*, Rousseau remarked that "it
does not require extensive experience to sense how pleasant it is to act with
the hands of others and to need only to stir one's tongue to make the universe
itself move" (Rousseau 1979, 68). In his *Confessions*, he follows his description
of early masturbation with an indication of how that masturbation came to
contaminate his life—and to shape his imagination: how it brought about a manner of thinking and living where the role of solitary imagination played a role
as great as if not greater than that of action. It is then, in a certain indirect but
very real sense, masturbation that leads Rousseau to literary creation—and it is
also masturbation which brings about, in his own account, the irregularities in
his own character.[10]

10. For the most probing analysis of the relation between masturbation and creation in Rousseau, cf.
Jacques Derrida's *De la grammatologie* (esp. pp. 211 ff). One might note that Humbert's text is not without
reference to his fellow Swiss citizen and most famous precursor in his genre. Humbert refers to himself
at one point as "Jean-Jacques Humbert." It seems, as well, that he might have wished to evoke various
elements of Rousseau's confession in the early chapters of his memoir, such as Humbert's "cheerful
motherlessness" (*AL*, 11). One of the central cruxes of the study of Rousseau's person and work has been
what has been referred to as the *morale de l'intention* that Sartre, Marcel Raymond (in *Jean-Jacques Rousseau: La quête de soi et la rêverie*) and others have demonstrated, and which is a *morale* succinctly expressed
in the French saying *qui s'accuse, s'excuse* ("he who accuses himself, pardons himself"). This is indeed
Humbert's game in the first part of the book, but a very deft and involuted version of it.

CHAPTER FIVE

ANESTHESIA

The Definition of Art

TOWARD THE END of his tale, Humbert notes:

> I recall certain moments, let us call them icebergs in paradise, when after having had my fill of her—after fabulous, insane exertions that left me limp and azure-barred—I would gather her in my arms with, at last, a mute moan of human *tenderness* (her skin glistening in the neon light coming from the paved court through the slits in the blinds—her soot-black lashes matted, her grave gray eyes more vacant than ever—for all the world a little patient still in the confusion of a drug after a major operation—and the *tenderness* would deepen to shame and despair, and I would lull and rock my lone light Lolita in my marble arms, and moan in her warm hair, and caress her at random and mutely ask her blessing, and at the peak of his human agonized selfless *tenderness* (with my soul actually hanging around her naked body and ready to repent), all at once, ironically, horribly, lust would swell again—and "oh, no," Lolita would say with a sigh to heaven, and the next moment the *tenderness* and the azure would be shattered. (*AL*, 285; my italics)

Even years later Lolita has not come out of her anesthesia: "*for all the world a little patient still in the confusion of a drug after a major operation.*" But we find here what Humbert opposes to his aestheticizing anesthesia: *tenderness*.

The word recurs four times in the brief passage, and, as we will see, plays a role in Nabokov's world like no other. Nabokov's work is not rich in definitions, and all the less so as concerns art. While at first sight his *oeuvre* seems completely free from such, there is a single exception to be found couched (and crouched) in a paratactical parenthesis from Nabokov's afterword to *Lolita*. Therein, Nabokov informs his readers that

> there are gentle souls who would pronounce *Lolita* meaningless because it does not teach them anything. I am neither a reader nor a writer of didactic fiction, and, despite John Ray's assertion, *Lolita* has no moral in tow. For me a work of fiction exists only insofar as it affords me what I shall bluntly call aesthetic bliss, that is a sense of being somehow, somewhere, connected with other states of being where art (curiosity, tenderness, kindness, ecstasy) is the norm. There are not many such books. All the rest is either topical trash or what some call the Literature of Ideas (*AL*, 314–315).

Tucked away in the parenthesis is the definition of art: "(curiosity, tenderness, kindness, ecstasy)."

Art is first evoked here under the sign of the *curious*. The world of art, to borrow a phrase from a work that Nabokov translated from English to Russian in his youth, "curiouser and curiouser." (Young Alice was so much surprised by the wondrous world she found herself in that "for the moment she quite forgot how to speak good English.") As Nabokov makes clear, not only is all true art born of true curiosity about the standpoints of others, it is curious in the sense that it is singular and strange. As Nabokov says in *The Gift*, in art, "any genuinely new trend is a knight's move, a change of shadows, a shift that displaces the mirror" (*Gift*, 239). In *Lolita* we are reminded that a work of art should come as "a shocking surprise"—a remark echoed in the short story "The Assistant Producer," where we read that "the unexpected is the infra-red in the spectrum of art" (*AL*, 5; *Stories*, 96). (Martin Amis has given an elegant reformulation to this motto: "Great novels are shocking; and then, after the shock dies down, you get aftershocks" [M. Amis, xviii].) *Kindness* is the simplest member of Nabokov's paratactic definition: art reflects kindness toward and kindredness with the world. *Ecstasy* clearly denotes the exhilaration and excitement of artistic creation and achievement. The final term requires a more comprehensive examination.

Tenderness

It has often been noted by both Nabokov and his readers that he has a singularly extensive vocabulary. It has also been noted by both Nabokov and his readers that he chooses his words with extreme care. For this reason, we should give a maximum of attention to a word that recurs in his writings with a regularity and a warmth without equal: *tenderness*. It comes then as no surprise that one finds it in his definition of art, nor is it surprising to find it in Nabokov's evocation of a day when "a reappraiser [of his work] will come and declare that, far from having been a frivolous firebird, [he] was a rigid moralist, kicking sin, cuffing cupidity, ridiculing the vulgar and cruel—and assigning sovereign power to *tenderness*, talent, and pride" (*SO*, 193; my italics). Tenderness is the offering of something or the offering of oneself; a gentle attention and attentiveness. In being characterized by tenderness, art is thus characterized by warmth and generosity. The full extent of tenderness's importance, the way it is employed, and recurs, at key moments in his works—as in the passage from *Lolita* where it is opposed to the anesthesia of Humbert's obsession we saw above—is something which can only be proven through enumeration.[1]

In one of Nabokov's first publications (when he was twenty-two), he differentiates the Russian soul from the English one by finding in the former "this beat, this glow and this dancing madness, this anger and tenderness that lead us to God knows what kinds of heaven and abysses."[2] In a letter to Edmund Wilson from 1956, intimately linking tenderness to art as such, Nabokov states: "I . . . think that at a time when American readers are taught from high school on to seek in books 'general ideas' a critic's duty should be to draw their attention to the specific detail, to the unique image, without which . . . there can be no art, no genius, no Chekhov, no terror, no *tenderness*, and no surprise" (*NWL*, 298; my italics). The word is prominently placed in John Shade's poem in *Pale Fire* as being of the essence of life found again in death: "I'll turn down eternity unless / The melancholy and the *tenderness* / Of mortal life . . . / Are found in Heaven by the newly dead" (*PF*, 53; my italics). In Nabokov's first novel we read: "Bored and ashamed, Ganin felt a nonsensical *tenderness* . . . which caused him to kiss without passion the painted rubber of her proffered lips, although this *tenderness* did not succeed in silencing . . ." (*Mary*, 11; my italics). At another point we read of "a marvelous romance that developed with genuine, *tender* care" (*Mary*, 56; my italics). One special night meeting of Ganin and his Mary is described as "especially *tender*"; they exchange "*tender* letters"; he kisses her "*tender* neck" (*Mary*, 68, 69, 74; my italics). Of all that he is mistaken about, Hermann

---

1. Michael Wood refers to "Humbert's liking for tenderness as a word," without offering examples as well as, elsewhere, to the relation of tenderness to suffering in "Signs and Symbols" (cf. Wood, 142, 71). Alexandrov claims that "the ethical resonances of the words *tenderness* and *kindness* evoke the implications of Nabokov's 'otherworldly' theme" (Alexandrov 1991, 160).

2. From an essay entitled "*Kembridzh*" (Cambridge) cited by Galya Diment in her entry in the *Garland Companion*, "Uncollected Critical Writings," 733; my italics.

is perhaps most mistaken in thinking that "the essential, though hidden, feature of my soul is *tenderness*" (*Despair*, 198; my italics). Nabokov's description of his treasured lepidoptera offers many such examples as where, in the Russian story "Christmas" (translated by Vladimir and Dmitri Nabokov), the Attacus moth that emerges magically at the end of the story and which is intimately bound up with the soul of the departed as the father mourns the loss of his son, we read of the unfurling of the wings: "And then those thick black wings, with a glazy eyespot on each and a purplish bloom dusting their hooked foretips, took a full breath under the impulse of *tender*, ravishing, almost human happiness" (*Stories*, 136; my italics). Nabokov repeatedly refers in the Russian poem "Mother" (from 1922) to butterflies as "my *tender* ones" (*Nabokov's Butterflies*, 107; my italics). In *Strong Opinions*, Nabokov calls certain proofreaders of his work, "limpid creatures of limitless tact and *tenderness*" (*SO*, 95; my italics). He employs the word in his description of his treasured St. Petersburg: ". . . St. Petersburg mornings where the fierce and *tender*, damp and dazzling arctic spring bundled away broken ice down the sea-bright Neva" (*SM*, 111; my italics). In *Glory*, Martin, searching for his thought, states that "there are besides—how shall I say?—glory, love, *tenderness* for the soil, a thousand rather mysterious feelings" (*Glory*, 156; my italics). In that same work, in a passage particularly rich in autobiographical detail (one describing Martin's first years at Cambridge), we read that "it was as if Martin had found the right key to all the vague, *tender*, and fierce feelings that besieged him" (*Glory*, 63; my italics). In *The Gift*, Fyodor says of his first love that "all her shortcomings were concealed in such a tide of fascination, *tenderness* and grace, such enchantment flowed from her most fleeting, irresponsible word, that I was prepared to look at her and listen to her eternally," and on the same page, in his tiny treatise on the forms his youthful poetic efforts took, he cites the line, "Of loveliness intangible and *tender*" (*Gift*, 150; my italics). One also reads in *The Gift* of the "heights of *tenderness*, passion and pity as are reached by few loves" (*Gift*, 178; my italics). In *The Real Life of Sebastian Knight*, the narrator says of his parent's marriage that it was "a quiet and *tender* union" and of time that Clare and Sebastian spent together says that "it is hard to believe that the warmth, the *tenderness*, the beauty of it has not been gathered, and is not treasured somewhere, somehow" (*RLSK*, 9, 85; my italics). In *King, Queen, Knave*, Fyodor's first meetings with Martha are "natural and *tender*" (*KQK*, 138; my italics). In "Signs and Symbols," we find in the monologue of the boy's mother: "She thought of the endless waves of pain that for some reason or other she and her husband had to endure; of the invisible giants hurting her boy in some unimaginable fashion; of the incalculable amount of *tenderness* contained in the world; of the fate of this *tenderness*, which is either crushed, or wasted, or transformed into madness; of neglected children humming to themselves in unswept corners" (*Stories*, 597; my italics). Asked in "The Last Interview" about a possible return to the United States, Nabokov replies: "I'm sluggish, but I'm sure I'll go back with *tenderness*" (Interview with Robert Robinson, 123; my italics). In the foreword to *Bend Sinister*, we read that "the puddle thus kindled and rekindled in Krug's mind [is] . . . a rent in his world leading to another world of *tenderness*, brightness and beauty" (*BS*, xv; my italics). In *Look at the Harlequins!* Vadim refers to "my sweet, docile, *tender* Iris"; later, "a wave of new warmth, new intimacy, new *tenderness*, swelled and swept away all the delusions of distance"; there is also "the torturous *tenderness* I had always felt for Annette"; an occasion where the narrator "uttered some wild words—of regret, of despair, of *tenderness*"; and even an instant where *tenderness* becomes the very "*stuff*" of love: "Save for a few insignificant lapses—a few hot drops of overflowing *tenderness*, a gasp masked by a cough and that sort of stuff—my relations with her remained essentially innocent" (*LATH*, 53, 61, 136, 159, 173; my italics).

But the work which most extensively expresses tenderness is *Lolita*. In an interview from 1963, Nabokov says of Lolita, "there is a queer, *tender* charm about that mythical nymphet" (*SO*, 21; my italics). Humbert has a particular fondness for the term. In addition to the tenderness-filled passage with which we begun, he sheds "tears of *tenderness*"; makes a "dreadful grimace of clenched-teeth *tenderness*"; and bemoans that "two months of *tenderness* would be squandered forever" (*AL*, 17, 22, 66; my italics). The nymphet herself is full of tenderness: "What drives me insane is the twofold nature of this nymphet—of every nymphet, perhaps; this mixture in my Lolita of *tender* dreamy childishness and a kind of eerie vulgarity . . . and then again, all this gets mixed up with the exquisite stainless *tenderness* seeping through the musk and the mud" (*AL*, 44; my italics). Humbert refers to Lolita's "*tender*, mysterious, impure, indifferent, twilight eyes," and to the "smooth, *tender* bloom" of her face (*AL*, 120, 204; my italics). Speaking of the arrangements for his wedding with Charlotte, Humbert states that "I knew I would not dare be too *tender* with cornered Lolita," and on the next page "confesses to a certain titillation of his vanity, to some faint *tenderness*" in his status as Charlotte's lover (*AL*, 74, 75; my italics). During rehearsals for "The Enchanted Hunters," Humbert states, "I was so struck by the radiant *tenderness* of her smile that for an instant I believed all our troubles gone" (*AL*, 202; my italics). A good priest works on Humbert's conscience "with the finest *tenderness* and understanding" (*AL*, 282; my italics). When Lolita at last reveals her lover's name, she does so "not *untenderly*" (*AL*, 272; my italics). Humbert's poem for Quilty (and which also serves as a death sentence) evokes "when I was helpless moulting moist and *tender*" (*AL*, 300; my italics). At the moment John Ray Jr. terms Humbert's "moral apotheosis" we read: "No matter, even if those eyes of hers would fade to myopic fish, and her nipples swell and crack, and her lovely young velvety delicate delta be tainted and torn—even then I would go mad with *tenderness* at the mere sight of your dear wan face, at the mere sound of your raucous young voice, my Lolita" (*AL*, 278; my italics). Finally, in an interview from 1961, Nabokov notes of *Lolita*, "it is a tender book. A *carte de Tendre* of the United States" (Interview with Anne Guérin, 27). It is perhaps then not "mask" which is the key word (in answer to Humbert's much commented-on query) but instead "tenderness."[3]

With this voluminous perspective, let us return to the passage with which we began. Here, *tenderness* is opposed to the brute sensuality which overmasters Humbert at the end of the passage. To be tender is to give affection and care to those in need of it. It is, gently, patiently and even passionately seeing not just from one's own standpoint, but from the standpoint of someone else. But in this passage, as Humbert bemoans, this tenderness does not win out over the demands of the senses. In a pivotal scene from the novella which gave rise to *Lolita*, as the main character's bliss reaches its peak, he is described as "senselessly discharging molten wax" (*Enchanter*, 74). This most sensual, sense-focused of sensations, the taut inner radiance of orgasm, is tagged with a "senselessness" which consigns it to the most incoherent of realms. There is no getting around this senselessness, and yet it inevitably provokes the question asked in that same work: "What if the way to true bliss is indeed through a still delicate membrane?" (*Enchanter*, 4). And is this not precisely the danger which is played out in Nabokov's novel of the senses, *Ada, or Ardor*, where sex is at turns presented as that which would allow for the transcendence of the agonizing distance between two young lovers of genius—as well as that which would prevent such a transcendence? In *Lolita*, the marvels of the excited senses lead to no transcendence, but rather to the ever greater occlusion of *tenderness*. To continue to offer himself the sensual feasts he does, Humbert, as someone eminently capable of imagining the inner life and suffering of another, must blind himself to Lolita's concerns. Her inner life does not concern him during their cross-country romps because in some sense his affair is with a second Lolita, "*more real*," as he says, than the other, and which has the advantage for him of "*having no will, no consciousness—indeed, no life*" of its own (*AL*, 62; my italics).

3. The pride of place reserved for this word seems in some measure familial as one finds in Dmitri Nabokov's "On Revisiting Father's Room" a reference to the publication of a volume of his father's verse, "perhaps the most innovative, most *tender*, and most haunting of all his work" (130; my italics). Véra Nabokov stresses in a letter to her son from 1975, "Things that are precious, honesty, *tenderness*, broadmindedness, life in art, and true, unselfish, touching attachment, are the greater values by far" (cited by Schiff, 46–47; my italics). Elsewhere, she notes of her husband's change of language that he had substituted a "*mariage de raison*" for his more passionate affair with the Russian language, which "as it sometimes happens with a *mariage de raison*—became in turn a *tender* love affair" (ibid. 98; my italics).

Intacta

Late in his narrative, Humbert informs his readers that "it is not the artistic aptitudes that are secondary sexual characters as some shams and shamans have said; it is the other way around: sex is but the ancilla of art" (*AL*, 259). The catchiness of the remark should not blind us to its implications. In elegant and involuted fashion, Humbert tells us here that art is not sublimated sex or drive (*pace* Freud), *but the inverse*.[4] Does this make sense? Humbert implies that the artistic instinct in man may find expression not only in artistic activity itself, but also in *sex*. Sex is thus but one particular manifestation of the larger phenomenon of *artistic drive*. While what Humbert is here doing might be dismissed as mere mockery of the Freudian conception of the relation between drive and art, there is something fundamental expressed in his remark. What remains more darkly and deeply implied therein is that not just sex, but all life should be seen as lying under the province of *artistic drive*.

Humbert's remark here is a gauge of his *aestheticization* of Lolita—and life. This is a gesture which one finds, in varied forms, throughout Nabokov's works. In *The Defense* the artistic chess player Luzhin falls victim to his conception of reality as art (the art of chess), suffers greatly, and ultimately takes his own life in a moment of maximal confusion. Vadim makes an error which is the inverse of Humbert's in *Look at the Harlequins!* where he confounds his real-life daughter with his literary creation (*LATH*, 195). To return to Humbert's case, the most dramatic and most striking passage in this respect is one which directly precedes Lolita's final flight. During Humbert's cross-examination of Lolita, they pass in front of a storefront:

> It was indeed a pretty sight. A dapper young fellow was vacuum-cleaning a carpet of sorts upon which stood two figures that looked as if some blast had just worked havoc with them. One figure was stark naked, wigless and armless. Its comparatively small stature and smirking pose suggested that when clothed it had represented, and would represent when clothed again, a girl-child of Lolita's size. But in its present state it was sexless. Next to it, stood a much taller veiled bride, quite perfect and *intacta* except for the lack of one arm. On the floor, at the feet of these damsels, where the man crawled about laboriously with his cleaner, there lay

---

4. Humbert's claim is thus like Wallace Stevens' where the later declares that "the aesthetic order includes all other orders but is not limited to them" (Stevens, 905). A more coherent position, if only from an artistic point of view, is that made by Rilke a generation earlier where he claimed in his *Letters to a Young Poet* that sexual and artistic creation flow from the same source and are essentially the same phenomenon.

a cluster of three slender arms, and a blond wig. Two of the arms happened to be twisted and seemed to suggest a clasping gesture of horror and supplication.

"Look, Lo," I said quietly. "Look well. Is not that a rather good symbol of something or other?" (*AL*, 226)

Lolita makes no reply and it is left to the reader to answer the question Humbert poses. The dismembered mannequin is the last figure of the "safely solipsized" Lolita, and the one which shows the cracking of the mold. More precisely, it is a "rather good symbol" of Humbert's burgeoning awareness that his Lolita is neither a disembodied image, nor a lifeless model, neither a "painted girl-child" nor an "anesthetized little nude." She is also not a mannequin, of course, but the grotesque figure is indeed a "rather good symbol" of the no longer "intact" (that is, no longer undamaged and no longer virginal) Lolita. Humbert's vision is parodic and excessive, but as we saw earlier, in Nabokov's peculiar universe this in no way prevents it from being richly communicative. More than any other, this sardonic symbol signifies what Nabokov, speaking of the relation between Humbert and Lolita in the *Apostrophes* interview, referred to as "the void between them."

CHAPTER SIX

Humbert's Green Lane

Ill at Ease

HUMBERT HUMBERT OWES HIS FAME to the discomfort he has caused his readers. At the outset of his memoir, and for quite a few pages thereafter, Humbert dismisses and discredits the cares and concerns of others with what many readers—such as Trilling, Booth, Appel, Pifer and many others—have described as unnerving facility. But how exactly does he do this? In the name of what values, through what reasoning, and playing upon what weaknesses or vanities does he so successfully place his readers so ill at ease?

The first and best answer to the question of how Humbert manages to unsettle his reader is that he is eloquent. He possesses fantastic verbal range, depth, and dexterity. Just as importantly, he is surprising. Eloquence is no blank slate simply awaiting persuasive words to fill it; it is not an inert substance waiting to be used for adornment. It is a reactive. It can only be made to function by coming into contact with the specific desires and fears, ambitions and anxieties of those exposed to it. What then are the elements involved in this reaction? What chords does Humbert strike, what fears or desires does he evoke, and what ambitions does he flatter?

The first minor chord is pity. Humbert begins by telling us of love and loss at a tender age. In the triple tradition of the confession, the case study, and the court case, he makes use of a sad past to explain and excuse a deplorable present. With freakish and acidic irony he tells us of the early loss of his mother: "(picnic, lightning)" (*AL*, 10).[1] This first loss is followed by another: that of Humbert's love, Annabel Lee. Here too, his description is a bewildering and bravura mixture of plangent lyricism and merciless self-parody. The latter is as central to Humbert's persuasiveness as the former. Nabokov not only approvingly cited Flaubert's dictum that, "irony does not impair pathos—on the contrary, irony enhances the pathetic side"—he knew how to follow it (cf. *LL*, 149). In *Lolita* this element of artificiality is flawlessly assimilated into the story itself, exacerbated and extenuated to the point that parody and poignancy are indissociable from one another.[2] This self-parody serves Humbert's purposes particularly effectively by immunizing, so to speak, his description. If you find his story unbelievable, his complaints mawkish, his reasoning faulty, he is protected from this criticism by the sword of irony and shield of parody. If you find his story credible, his complaints compelling, his reasoning sound, then the parody becomes something else: the sign of his suffering. Everyone is familiar with the phenomenon of a pain so great it can only be spoken of in a mocking tone used to protect the teller. Humbert calls upon this phenomenon. His urbane self-parody is kept up in the opening sections of his memoir with such delicate intensity that, by keeping his own guard up, he tempts his readers to lower theirs a notch.

To the suggestion of childhood trauma and arrested development he adds the question of cultural relativism. Humbert industriously evokes distant times and places where sexual relations between people vastly separated in age was not only not condemned, but was encouraged. "Hugh Broughton, a writer of controversy in the reign of James the First," he informs us, "has proved that Rahab was a harlot at ten years of age"—two years younger than Lolita when they become lovers (*AL*, 19). And we should not forget that "lecherous old men of eighty copulate with girls of eight, and nobody minds" (ibid.). As Eric Rothstein has noted, "Nabokov's own way of keeping us unsure as to values is to flood the written text with them," and the relativity of cultural norms is an essential current therein (Rothstein, 30).

Alongside of this delicate game, Humbert plays another one with his reader: a game of letters. Readers are notoriously vain—above all about reading. We all

---

1. Martin Amis shows himself a student of such parentheses in his introduction to *Lolita*: "Then, once the book begins, Humbert's childhood love Annabel dies, at thirteen (typhus), and his first wife Valeria dies (also in childbirth), and his second wife Charlotte dies ('a bad accident'—though of course this death is structural), and Charlotte's friend Jean Farlow dies at thirty-three (cancer), and Lolita's young seducer Charlie Holmes dies (Korea), and her old seducer Quilty dies (murder: another structural exit). And then Humbert dies (coronary thrombosis)"(Amis, vii). For a systematic treatment of Nabokov's artful use of parentheses, cf. Duncan White's "'(I have camouflaged everything, my love)'." White's central thesis is that, "stylish cruelty is the hallmark of the Humbertian parenthesis" (D. White, 50).

2. On the question of parody in *Lolita* cf. especially Appel 1967, Frosch, and Edmund White.

know the experience of finding value and interest in a phrase because it contains an allusion we think only a select group will recognize. We also all know the experience of realizing that the phrase in question had nothing to speak for it except for its hidden heredity. In unpredictable fashion, Humbert invokes the literary sensitivities and education of his reader. From the very first lines of his memoir, he begins to weave lines—and names—from the only poem that Edgar Allan Poe ever wrote for his first cousin and child-bride (Virginia Clemm was thirteen and Poe twenty-five when they married in 1836), and which he wrote only after her death: "Annabel Leigh." The poem has a childlike, hypnotic repetitiveness (the distinctive rhythm which led Emerson to unflatteringly dub Poe "the jingle man") that well suits Humbert's hypnotic purposes (we might recall that he initially chose the pseudonym "Mesmer Mesmer" before deciding that the "double rumble" in "Humbert Humbert" better expressed "the nastiness."[3] More allusions follow. In more cryptic fashion, Humbert invokes the adult sorrows and longings of Rousseau, Baudelaire, and Proust. (In noting the frequency of French referents we should recall that French is Humbert's native language—the presence of Poe being fully compatible with this preference given that only later in Humbert's fictional lifespan does Poe's English influence begin to eclipse his French one.) In pedophiliac proclivity Poe is followed by Dante and Petrarch: "After all," Humbert reasons, "Dante fell madly in love with his Beatrice when she was nine, a sparkling girleen, painted and lovely, and bejeweled, in a crimson frock, and this was in 1274, in Florence, at a private feast in the merry month of May. And when Petrarch fell madly in love with his Laureen, she was a fair-haired nymphet of twelve running in the wind, in the pollen and dust, a flower in flight, in the beautiful plain as descried from the hills of Vaucluse" (*AL*, 19).[4] Humbert does not of course mention that Dante himself was only eight years old when he met the, in reality, eight-year-old Beatrice (or Bice) Portinari, or the fact that the Laura of Petrarch's love was roughly six years younger than the poet—but then again, why would he?

Humbert's artistic comparisons do not, however, stop on the level of biographical parallels and literary allusions. He tells us that to perceive a nymphet, to recognize one in a crowd, you must be an "artist and a madman" (*AL*, 17). One of the principal things that artists and madmen share in Nabokov's world

---

3. "There are in my notes 'Otto Otto' and 'Mesmer Mesmer' and 'Lambert Lambert,' but for some reason I think my choice expresses the nastiness best" (*AL*, 308).

4. More indirect references to another unhappy literary lover, Lewis Carroll, might be found in the work, but they are slight, if they could be said to exist at all (e.g. *AL*, 26, 39, and other references to Carroll's dubious hobby: photographing young girls). In a remark made to *Lolita*'s annotator Alfred Appel Jr., Nabokov stated, "I always call him Lewis Carroll Carroll because he was the first Humbert Humbert" (*AL*, 381 n. 131/1).

is their indifference to what others think of their inspired (or deranged) states. Nabokov loans a great many of his characters experiences and opinions which were also his own, and this giving of very personal gifts is not limited to likeable fellows such as *Glory*'s Martin and *The Gift*'s Fyodor, but extends to characters Nabokov himself singles out as "scoundrels" and "wretches," such as *Ada*'s Van, *Pale Fire*'s Kinbote, and, of course, *Lolita*'s Humbert. Humbert receives just such a gift from his creator—a mighty and a dangerous one: the gift of artistic vision. Nabokov not only graces Humbert with the perceptual and linguistic powers necessary for art, he lends him the credo that a true artist creates in sublime isolation and owes account only to his own genius. And it is here that things begin to go awry.

We saw earlier that Nabokov evoked a similarity between *Despair* and *Lolita*. That similarity consisted in *Despair*'s Hermann being given gifts of "literary genius . . . which nature had meant the artist to use"—and which he turned to other ends (murder). Humbert is also given gifts of literary genius—and on a far grander scale. *Despair* is not *Crime and Punishment*, and no reader of the book has yet gone on record as having felt anything like a real or compelling identification or complicity with Hermann, as Trilling and a host of others have with Humbert. As Nabokov makes clear from the outset, we are to have contempt for Hermann—he does not excite admiration, he does not persuade—and for this reason he is not dangerous. Humbert, however, is another story.

Humbert's eloquence also depends upon a further element that unifies the ones mentioned above—something that was not at Hermann's disposal: *love*. For all his blindness and madness and hurt, Humbert loves. And for the Humbert of the first part of the novel, the lover and the artist see the world in the same all-enlivening, all-consuming way. The reader might recall here that Humbert follows Nabokov's remarks on reality to the letter. This is the heart of his eloquence and the essence of his alibi: his justifications for his love, and for his pursuit of that love despite the rules of society and reason outlawing it, are in every way analogous to Nabokov's justifications for art. In his descriptions, Humbert calls upon the inner vision, the sudden image, and the irrefutable call of the senses that are all hallmarks of Nabokov's vision of art. His subtlest reasoning is then in the careful parallel he establishes between the proud creation of great art and the heedless pursuit of love. By subtly describing, and avidly pursuing, Lolita as one would the inspiration lying at the outset of a work of art, Humbert tempts the reader to look at her as precisely that—and it is this most slippery step that allows for sensitive and schooled readers to be seduced, subdued, or entrapped. We are led astray because we are offered the wrong optic through which to see Lolita—*the optic of art*—and we are often too eager to be worthy of it to suggest that it should not here apply.

A Moral Apotheosis

As we saw earlier, in the preface to his revision and retranslation of *Despair*, Nabokov says of the resemblance between *Despair*'s Hermann and *Lolita*'s Humbert, that, "both are neurotic scoundrels, yet there is a green lane in Paradise where Humbert is permitted to wander at dusk once a year" (*Despair*, xiii). Why does Humbert merit this brief reprieve? What does he do that allows him an annual walk in Paradise?

Humbert does not remain wondering before this storefront with its symbolically disfigured mannequin we saw at the end of an earlier chapter, and it is for this reason that one might speak of a turn in his thinking and feeling. The deceptively perceptive John Ray Jr. tells us that what we are to read is "a tragic tale tending unswervingly to nothing less than a moral apotheosis" (*AL*, 5). The epithet is doubtless inflationary, but it should not prevent us from seeking its referent. Humbert is hardly promoted to divine status, and does not offer a strong case for canonization. But he does appear to do something laudable and deserves his reader's full attention.

In a note to *The Annotated Lolita*, Appel, without offering his reasoning, locates this "moral apotheosis" in the closing pages of the book and Humbert's hearing a chorus of children's voices from afar and his realization "that the hopelessly poignant thing was not Lolita's absence from my side, but the absence of her voice from that concord" (*AL*, 308). Though he does not note Appel's precedent, Alexandrov locates this "moral apotheosis" in precisely this same scene (cf. Alexandrov 1991, 171). Dawson also refers to this scene as the "seeming 'moral apotheosis'" that John Ray Jr. announces (Dawson, 128–129). Boyd locates Humbert's "great epiphany" in the same place as Appel (Boyd 1991, 249). In an article published four years later attacking the group of critics he terms "revisionists,"[5] Boyd refers in passing to Humbert's "moral apotheosis" as taking

5. Boyd uses the term "revisionists" to refer to critics endeavoring to recast the chronology of the book's last scenes and who contend that the final section of the book—with Humbert's reunion with Lolita and murder of Quilty—is all a hallucination. Humbert states on the last page of the book, "When I started, fifty-six days ago, to write *Lolita* . . ." (*AL*, 310). According to Ray's foreword, Humbert died on November 16, 1952. Fifty-six days earlier we find ourselves on September 22, the day he received Lolita's letter. These critics are Elizabeth Bruss in 1976, Christina Tekiner (1979), Toker (1989), Dolinin (1995), Connolly (1995), and, most recently, George Ferger (2004). The argument—marshaled for different readings of the novel by the critics listed here—is that the entire last section of the novel beginning with Humbert's receiving of Lolita's letter is imaginary and that Nabokov meant for his reader to consider it as such. In a carefully argued essay, Boyd demonstrates that the dating inconsistency was in every likelihood a slip of Nabokov's pen (cf. Boyd 1995). Andrews uses this same curious term to denote those critics who turned away from the idea of an "aestheticist" Nabokov (cf. Andrews, 38).

place in "the scene above Elphinstone"—the same scene where Humbert hears the children's chorus (Boyd 1995, 85).

While the passage is tender and touching, it is only part of the change Humbert undergoes, and, for the moment, it alters nothing in his behavior. When the reader replaces this scene, recounted at the very end of the book, in its actual chronology, we see that this supposed moral turn does not prevent him from continuing to search for his lost love with the same desperate intensity as before. This "moral apotheosis" is best sought for in *Lolita*'s tenderest chapter, where we read:

> Somewhere beyond Bill's shack an afterwork radio had begun singing of folly and fate, and there she was with her ruined looks and her adult, rope-veined narrow hands and her goose-flesh white arms, and her shallow ears, and her unkempt armpits, there she was (my Lolita!), hopelessly worn at seventeen . . . and I looked and looked at her and knew as clearly as I know I am to die, that I loved her more than anything I had ever seen or imagined on earth, or hoped for anywhere else. She was only the faint violet whiff and dead leaf echo of the nymphet I had rolled myself upon with such cries in the past; an echo on the brink of a russet ravine, with a far wood under a white sky, and brown leaves choking the brook, and one last cricket in the crisp weeds . . . [Nabokov's ellipses] but thank God it was not that I worshiped. What I used to pamper among the tangled vines of my heart, *mon grand péché radieux*, had dwindled to its essence: sterile and selfish vice, all *that* I canceled and cursed. You may jeer at me, and threaten to clear the court, but until I am gagged and half-throttled, I will shout my poor truth. I insist the world know how much I loved my Lolita, *this* Lolita, pale and polluted and big with another's child, but still gray-eyed, still sooty-lashed, still auburn and almond, still Carmencita, still mine. . . . No matter, even if those eyes of hers would fade to myopic fish, and her nipples swell and crack, and her lovely young velvety delicate delta be tainted and torn—even then I would go mad with tenderness at the mere sight of your dear wan face, at the mere sound of your raucous young voice, my Lolita (*AL*, 278; Nabokov's italics).

Nabokov was to remark of this scene years later that in reading it, "the good reader should feel the forerunner of a tear," and given what Nabokov puts into the passage, this might seem like a reasonable request (Interview with Anne Guérin, 27). In another interview, Nabokov confessed to himself having felt more than a forerunner, and to having written the passage through his own tears (Interview with *Les Nouvelles Littéraires*).

Nabokov's tears are his own affair—just as are ours. But what the passage describes is essential for any understanding of the moral turn Humbert appears to make toward the end of his story. Here he has recognized the sensuous adulation of his past as "sterile and selfish vice," and he has seen beneath and beyond a dark layer of lust a radiant one of love. He realizes that he loved her, and loves her, and will always love her—however she might change and whatever she might become. He loves her not for senses she might have fired, but simply for herself—as anyone should be loved. In a line as simple as it is tender, Wallace Stevens once wrote, "and there you were, warm as flesh, / Brunette, yet not too brunette." As we all know but can easily forget, to love someone is to love them for exactly as brunette as they are, to love them for the way that they are, and to love them as they change in a way that can only be their own. "I don't think Lolita is a religious book," Nabokov once stated, "but I do think it is a moral one. And I do think that Humbert Humbert in his last stage is a moral man because he realizes that he loves Lolita like any woman should be loved" (quoted by Rampton, 202 n. 34). Humbert's change in tone and his turn in thinking is one towards *love*, and the tender empathy that characterizes it. To do such, to love, merits, even in the darkest of stories, attention, care, and a special, if slight, dispensation. Francis Bacon wrote of "that which the Grecians call *Apotheosis*," and which he described as "the supreme honour which a man could attribute unto man" (Bacon, 23). If we recall that there is no greater grace and no higher honor that we might be offered than love, might Humbert not deserve his extraordinary epithet, and his crepuscular stroll, after all?

The green lane that Nabokov grants Humbert a yearly stroll in has received little attention from the book's critics—and the little it has received has been of a rather indignant sort. Julian Connolly states that "Nabokov imagines that his hero will be 'permitted to wander at dusk' in a 'green lane in Paradise' once a year" (Connolly 1997, 35). This displacement of terms fundamentally changes their tenor, as if Nabokov only "imagines" that this will come to pass, and that he may well be wrong. As the entire process takes place in his imagination, this is an unnecessary stress to place (it is not that Nabokov "imagines" that his "permission" might come from some other corner). It is Nabokov himself who is doing the permitting: he rules his aesthetic universe and what he "imagines" is not a possibility or a hope. De Vries will show an equal unease in accounting for the passage, stating that, "as Nabokov is so kind as to permit him to leave Hell 'once a year' (February 29th seems fair enough) 'to wander at dusk' in 'a green lane in Paradise,' I am sure that the angels surrounding Dolly will keep her out of his way" (De Vries, 152). De Vries too will recast Nabokov's special dispensation, attributing it to mere "kindness" on Nabokov's part, as if he had some polite obligations towards his creation. De Vries' situating of Humbert's "yearly" walk on February 29th seems to display nothing so much as how inexplicable the remark appears to him.

The Garden

Nabokov wrote to his friend and colleague Morris Bishop in 1956 that "*Lolita* is a tragedy."[6] The story is a tragedy for the same reason that Humbert is granted a brief stroll in paradise—because Humbert realizes the fault in his character and the crime of his conduct, but does so, alas, too late to halt the progress of the poison. The tragedy is the loss of Lolita—and she is lost from virtually the beginning of Humbert's memoir. She can be said to be absent from the book which bears her secret name (only to Humbert is she "Lolita"—she is "Lo" to her mother, "Dolly" at school, "Dolores on the dotted line," and so forth) because of the ultimately less than safe solipsism to which Humbert subjects her. She is everywhere referred to, everywhere described, everywhere poetically loved, but of her *thoughts* and *feelings*, Humbert offers us scarce a glimpse.[7] Humbert is able to take advantage of her, to "deprive her of her childhood," as he says, because of his refusal to think from her standpoint—to think beyond the lyricism of his love and the practical precautions of maintaining a tractable little concubine (*AL*, 283). Near the end of the novel, hearing a chance remark that Lolita makes to Eva Rosen, Humbert remarks:

> . . . and it struck me, as my automaton knees went up and down, that I simply did not know a thing about my darling's mind and that quite possibly, behind the

6. Letter from March 6, 1956. Morris Bishop Collection, Cornell University. Cf. also Bishop's widow Alison Bishop's remark, "Nabokov described *Lolita* to us [to her and her husband] as a tragedy" (in Gibian and Parker, 217). Though he does not quote this letter (and may well not have known of its existence), Martin Amis reaches a similar, but different conclusion: "Quilty's death is not tragic. Nor is Humbert's fate. Nor is *Lolita*. But Lolita is tragic, in her compacted span. If tragedy explores thwarted energy and possibility, then Lolita is tragic—is flatly tragic" (Amis, ix).

7. De Vries alludes to this absence by noting that Humbert is present in all sixty-nine chapters of the novel (as the text is his first-person confession one wonders how it could be otherwise), while Lolita is present in only thirty-seven of those chapters (De Vries, 148–149). This however is to confuse quality with mere quantity. What is of interest in the book, what is revealing and what might sketch something like a difficult to read message therein, is the means and nature of this occlusion of Lolita from the story that bears her name. First-person confessions of love and crime may well be dependent upon the absence of the loved object, but the task which *Lolita* assigns its readers is the understanding of its nature.

juvenile clichés, there was in her a garden and a twilight, and a palace gate—dim and adorable regions which happened to be lucidly and absolutely forbidden to me. (*AL*, 284)[8]

A few pages later, enumerating his indignities, Humbert continues: "Now, squirming and pleading with my own memory, I recall that on this and similar occasions [the occasion in question is Lolita's mourning her mother's death], it was always my habit and method to ignore Lolita's states of mind while comforting my own base self" (echoing his earlier confession that he had "firmly decided to ignore what I could not help perceiving" [*AL*, 283]), and finally adds, "I must admit that a man of my power of imagination cannot plead ignorance of universal emotions" (*AL*, 287). Despite the gift of artistic perception with which nature graced him, he does not enter into the souls of others as one enters into the cool shade of a tree. He never ventures out from under the tree of his own desire, and his interactions with Lolita resemble nothing so much as his pulling her into that darkness.

The Pattern of Remorse

Though not containing vengeful acts of the sort that Pia Pera includes in her *Lo's Diary*, where Lolita sodomizes a drugged and sleeping Humbert Humbert with a pen (Reader: symbol!), the account Nabokov transmits through Humbert does not lack an element of vengeance.[9] This is not simply effected by Nabokov gesturing to his readers over Humbert's shoulder, but is also presented through the vengeance Humbert wreaks upon himself (we might refrain from modifying Pera's mise-en-scène accordingly). Humbert tells the story of his refusal or inability to think from the standpoint of someone else, and in doing so, follows a self-imposed constraint that he does not break until the book's closing chapters. "Fortunately," Humbert states, "my story has reached a point where I can cease insulting poor Charlotte for the sake of retrospective verisimilitude" (*AL*, 71). We should take in the full import of the phrase: that there is a logic of "retrospective verisimilitude" at work throughout Humbert's entire memoir and which results in his endeavoring to

---

8. It is unlikely, but possible, that Nabokov had in mind Nietzsche's remark in his *Gay Science*: "We all have our hidden gardens and bowers [*Wir haben Alle verborgene Gärten und Pflanzungen in uns*]" (Nietzsche, 3:381). Nabokov was doubtless aware that the etymology of *paradise* is "garden" or "park."

9. Cf. Pia Pera *Diario di Lo*. Venezia: Marsilio, 1995. 332–333; Pia Pera *Lo's Diary*. Trans. Ann Goldstein. New York: Foxrock, 1999, 266).

convince his reader of what he himself was convinced of at the time the events in question took place. Because of the self-imposed constraint of retrospective verisimilitude, because he is, in his words, "a conscientious recorder," he will not intersperse his text with commentary contemporaneous to the moment of writing—at which point, as the novel's closing sections show, he experiences the bitterest regret and the most intense self-loathing for what he has done. These are the rules of the game, and he cannot allow for more than a faintly intelligible "pattern of remorse daintily running along the steel of his conspiratorial dagger," for his story to fulfill its end (*AL*, 74, 75).

In her study of Nabokov, Toker chooses not to take into account this systematic logic of "retrospective verisimilitude" that is such an essential element of Humbert's narrative. She writes: "'I cannot paint / What then I was,' says Wordsworth in 'Tintern Abbey' when he tries, and fails, to revive the raptures known by his former self. The fact that throughout more than half the book Humbert does not fail to paint 'what then he was' means that despite his protestations he has not yet succeeded in canceling his obsession. . . . If Humbert were, indeed, cured of his obsession, the tenderness of his remorseful memories of Dolly . . . would color the whole of his retrospective narrative and interfere with his presentations of pedophilia as incomparable bliss" (Toker 1989, 208). Such a view leaves completely out of account the above remark, as well as the possibility that Humbert might be trying to teach his reader something and that the complicity he courts for his cruel acts at the outset of the work might serve some real purpose in his account (other than trying to get an imaginary jury to sympathize with him—a project he ultimately decides to discard). Toker's position leads her to void Humbert's "moral apotheosis" of any reality—*literally*. She does this by basing her argument on a line of reasoning that relegates the events of the last section of the book to Humbert's fantasy: "The problem of reconciling Humbert's persistent perversity with the event that purports to have removed it must have been a major challenge for Nabokov. He found his solution in a crafty handling of dates that in effect untells Humbert's tale" (Toker 1989, 209).

To return to Humbert's principle of "retrospective verisimilitude," in his reconstructed diary recounting Humbert's first days in the Haze house, we find the following entry: "*Monday. Delectatio morosa.* I spend my doleful days in dumps and dolors" (*AL*, 43). The annotated edition of *Lolita* glosses this abstruse beginning of the week as follows: "Latin; morose pleasure, a monastic term" (*AL*, 357 n. 43/2). This is not false, but it is also not what Nabokov is referring to. The term is indeed Latin and it is indeed a monastic term, but more can be said of it. It is a technical term in Christian theology and denotes a problem that goes to the heart of the Christian conception of sin. *Delectatio morosa* is pleasure taken in sinful thinking or imagining which comes to the sinner unbidden, which is *involuntary*.[10]

Up to the very end of Part I of his memoir (when he first sleeps with Lolita), Humbert has endeavored to limit his sin to an "internal" and involuntary one, to engage in nothing worse than *delectatio morosa*. He has, as he so often stresses, tried to "preserve the morals of a minor." Nabokov once remarked of his creation that "you can defend what [Humbert] feels for Lolita, but you cannot defend his perversity" (Interview with Anne Guérin). In these terms then, it is only when Humbert acts, when his fantasies take on flesh, that they become cause for a denunciation. Though one might well question the propriety of sharing them with others,[11] fantasies per se are not to be condemned. Cause for denunciation comes with *acts*. Such a denunciation, however, should be accompanied by a desire to understand how a man not insensitive or unimaginative or generally unable to control himself effects this passage from pardonable fantasy to unpardonable act. It is for this reason that the intermediate stage of Humbert's passage to the act should be of such interest to the attentive reader and that I have dwelt on it at such length in the preceding. The mental operation that allows the in other respects sensitive and intelligent Humbert to proceed to such cruel and indifferent acts is crystallized in the Sunday masturbation scene where it is with an "image" of Lolita that Humbert interacts, a Lolita which was "my own creation, another, fanciful Lolita—perhaps more real than Lolita; overlapping, encasing her; floating between me and her, and having no will, no consciousness—indeed, no life of her own" (*AL*, 62). This is then how Lolita becomes a case of arrested development, not only on her own account, as schoolmistress Pratt remarks, but on Humbert's as well. Even when their contact is no longer phantasmatic, it remains so in an important sense in that though it is with Lolita's body that he makes love, it is with the moving image he has created of her that he *engages*—and that image is credited, as was the masturbatory one with which he began, with having, like all images, "no will, no consciousness, no life of its own." And it is for this reason that it can be the passive subject of anything Humbert likes.

As we just noted, up until the very end of Part I of *Lolita*, Humbert has endeavored to "preserve the morals of a minor." In his *narration*, however, he

---

10. It is thus classified alongside of *gaudium*, dwelling with complacency on sins already committed, and *desiderium*, the desire for what is sinful, as "internal sins" in orthodox Catholic theology.

11. *Lolita*'s eccentric first publisher, Maurice Girodias, saw in the work an endeavor to alter parent-adult relations in modern society—a project that he heartily approved of. (Nabokov was surprised to learn from his European agent that Girodias thought that the book "might lead to a change in social attitudes towards the kind of love described in *Lolita*" [letter from 1955 cited by Boyd 1991, 266].)

has not done much to preserve the morals of his reader. He has passionately dedicated his remarkable rhetorical resources towards seducing or subduing the reader into an acceptance of, or complicity with, his dark fantasies and darker acts. Bertrand Russell once noted that there is nothing so useful to democracy as immunization against eloquence.[12] Might we not see *Lolita* in a similar light? Does not Humbert's memoir ultimately tell his reader: "What I have done is monstrous, let no amount of eloquence ever convince you that such acts are anything but: look at them for what they are, look at them for the pain they cause."[13] Stated somewhat differently, Nabokov's book tells us that the artist cannot live in the world as he lives in the world of words—and that this is a lesson worthy of expressing in the world of words.

Scholium I: Surprised by Sin?

When he first read Milton's *Paradise Lost*, William Blake was so shaken by the experience that he concluded that Satan's eloquence could have come from but one source: Satan. In his view, the great poet had been surprised by the sin of his creation and, both unwillingly and unknowingly, *seduced* by it. He had "been of the Devil's party without knowing it." Milton, who wished to do nothing less than "justify the ways of God to men" (Milton, 213), found himself in Satan's camp—and so clever was the seducer that he never knew it.

One of the first intuitions of Western aesthetic speculation was a simple one: that imitation carries a subtle danger with it, that the worse may be mistaken for the better reason, that charisma will override probity, passion override reason. It is this idea that led Plato to recommend that, after receiving ample honors, poets be asked to leave his ideal republic for another one. As aesthetic speculation progressed, so too did the dangers of imitation. In the most significant modern milestone, Hegel's *Lectures on Aesthetics*, we find a related problem. He suggests that Mary Magdalen, "the beautiful sinner," was perhaps responsible for a great deal of sin even as late as his own day because the contrition in

---

12. "To acquire immunity to eloquence is of the utmost importance to the citizens of a democracy" (*Atlantic Monthly*, October 1938).

13. It should be stressed that the question here is not whether it would be possible, under certain truly extraordinary circumstances and given the relativity of personal development and cultural norms, for a person of Humbert's age and one of Lolita's to have a sexual relationship which would be noncoercive, mutually fulfilling, tender, rich, and psychologically damaging for neither party. Such a scenario is indeed difficult to imagine, but we live in an exceptional world, and both physical and emotional development follows exceptional paths. The issue is with the story as Humbert relates it, and in that story his relation with Lolita is anything but noncoercive, mutually fulfilling, tender, rich, and psychologically damaging for neither party.

which so many inspired artists depicted her was so moving that it tempted others to contrition—and it did not escape the subtle dialectician that one cannot repent a sin not committed (Hegel 13:78). In impersonating Humbert Humbert, might Nabokov himself have been surprised, subdued, or seduced by the sin he depicts? Or, as Humbert expresses the most biting and moving contrition for his dark acts, might this less beautiful sinner not have also romanticized sin and glamorized contrition?

In his *Areopagitica*, Milton declared that as concerned himself, he could not "praise a fugitive and cloistered virtue," and there is every evidence that he put this principle into practice in the composition of Satan's monologues. In that blazing eloquence where the worse easily appears the better reason,[14] virtue is to come to grips with the image of vice which is most likely to seduce it—and virtue must vanquish it. Anything less would have been unworthy of his high enterprise. As to the eloquence and perfidy with which Nabokov invests Humbert, is there not every reason to see it in the same sulfurous light?

Scholium II: The One Lolita

"You think it is Lolita," said Severo with a smile.

—Heinz von Lichberg, "Lolita" (1916)

From the first hour of *Lolita*'s publication fifty years ago, critics strove to explain its genesis. So too did Nabokov. "As far as I can recall," he wrote a year later, "the initial shiver of inspiration was somehow prompted by a newspaper story about an ape in the Jardin des Plantes who, after months of coaxing by a scientist, produced the first drawing ever charcoaled by an animal: this sketch showed the bars of the poor creature's cage" (*AL*, 311). This might seem simple enough—except for the fact that both article and animal were his own mischievous invention (cf. this study's conclusion).

Nabokov had little use for influence, and lots of use for deception. When asked if other writers—whether they were cherished ones such as Joyce, or despised ones such as Thomas Mann—influenced his work, he voiced strong negative opinions. In 1969, he solemnly informed an interviewer that he was not one to provide much "sport" for "influence hunters" (*SO*, 151–152). Nabokov, right about much, was not right about this. A number of hunts have since taken place, but by far the most intense and interesting has been the one lately

14. Milton says of his darkest creation that "his tongue / Dropt Manna, and could make the worse appear / The better reason" (Milton, 234).

led by German journalist Michael Maar that culminated in *The Two Lolitas*. The second Lolita of the book's title is not a metaphor; it is not a reference to themes of doubling or psychoanalytical projections. This "Lolita" is a short story published in 1916 by a Hessian aristocrat, Heinz von Eschwege, under the pseudonym Heinz von Lichberg, telling the tale of a middle-aged man's doomed love for a young Spanish woman named "Lolita."

Plagiarism is a harsh word. When Martial coined it to denounce a certain Fidentius he claimed was stealing his work, he borrowed the term from the vocabulary of kidnapping. Maar offers three explanations for his philological find and none of these is plagiarism—at least not in so simple or scandalous a form. The first explanation is that the coincidence of name (Lolita) and theme (an older man's love for a fatally younger woman) is precisely that—one of the more or less unlikely coincidences that color art and life. The second explanation is somewhat more complicated and Maar gives it a corresponding name: "cryptomnesia." Nabokov came into contact with Lichberg's "Lolita" at some point, and then forgot it. Years later, his memory stirred by a similar interest, the story came back to him in encrypted form and he "remained quite unconscious of this resurgence of memory in what seemed to him to be entirely his own creation" (Maar, 57). In support of cryptomnesia, Maar cites instances of such from the diaries of Thomas Mann. The third explanation is closest to plagiarism and also the one Maar personally opts for. Nabokov deliberately lifted elements from Lichberg's story and then artfully concealed this fact—what Thomas Mann, again brought to the bar, proudly called "higher cribbing" (Maar, 58).

There have been many claims that Nabokov took his story from real life, either from the realm of his own desires or, to chose a single example, from those of his chess partner and colleague at Stanford University, Harry Lanz. Lanz, nympholept and scholar (he married his wife in London when she was a mere fourteen and shocked Stanford faculty when he arrived in town with her, then seventeen, and their year-old child.). Best known for his *In Quest of Morals* (1941), he came to know Nabokov during the latter's brief summer stay in Stanford and allegedly revealed to Nabokov the wild array of his pedophile adventures. Nabokov suggested to Field that Lanz "may have been in the back of my mind" when writing *Lolita* (cf. Haven, 74). The case history of the then-anonymous Ukrainian in Havelock Ellis as well as the case of Sally Horner have also been summoned as potential points of inspiration. But as intensely as inspiration for the novel has been sought in life, the search in literature has been just as eager—and Maar's find is the most recent and indeed most remarkable instance therein.

To suggest that Nabokov willingly concealed something important from his readers is the anything but absurd. He often did do so, and was proud of it. But to claim that he consciously concealed Lichberg and his "Lolita" in his own requires demonstrating several things that *The Two Lolitas* fails to do. First among these is offer compelling evidence that, in the absence of any historical proof (there is nothing whatsoever to indicate that Nabokov knew Lichberg-Eschwege or his work beyond the fact that they lived for a time in the same city and that Nabokov possessed midlevel German reading skills at the time), the coincidence of name and theme is more than coincidence. Maar is an able writer and an intelligent critic but the evidence he offers is tenuous. He does enterprising things such as juxtapose early photos of Nabokov and Lichberg at the top of a page under which it is noted that Lichberg "preserved an air of the solitary poet about him"—and that this was "not so utterly distant from the young Vladimir himself" (Maar, 47) and there is much padding of this sort in the slim volume that does little to advance Maar's argument. He branches out in his claims in subsequent chapters to find equally tenuous parallels between Lichberg's writing and a number of minor works by Nabokov's such as his 1938 play *The Waltz Invention*.

Whether it be for the major work *Lolita* or the minor one *The Waltz Invention*, Maar fails to supply something else essential to his undertaking: a plausible motive for Nabokov choosing to refuse a debt that could have been so easily paid. Maar claims no special literary value for Lichberg's "Lolita" (he is, on the contrary, openly disparaging). The debt is then to be found in the coincidence of name and age. Lichberg was not the first to name a work "Lolita." Couturier has pointed to the remarkable frequency of the name in titles of French works, from Isidore Gès's *En villégiature: Lolita* from 1894, through René Riche's *La chanson de Lolita* (1920), René Gast's *Lolita, roman algérien* (1927), and the entry for the name in Valéry Larbaud's *Des prénoms féminins* (also 1927), to a pulp book entitled *Cette saloperie de Lolita* (1953) (Couturier 2005, 21–22 n. 3—cf. Maar, 27n. 28). That leaves age. Nabokov's Lolita is a mere twelve when she first becomes Humbert's lover. Lichberg's Lolita is indeed young, but how young is difficult to tell. Lichberg describes her as *"blutjung"*—an ambiguous idiom like "of a tender age" and translated as "terribly young" in the book's appendix (Maar, 13, 87). In that same paragraph Lichberg does indeed refer to Lolita as a "child," but as the phrase is an allusion to a famous line by Goethe (a fact not noted by Maar) used by Lichberg to foreshadow her death,[15] it cannot be taken as a reliable indicator that the girl is prepubescent (Maar, 87–88).

As Maar began to publish his findings—first in a series of articles published by the *Frankfurter Allgemeine Zeitung* in March and April 2004, then in an English

---

15. The allusion is to the final line, *"In seinen Armen das Kind war tot* [In his arms the child was dead]," of Goethe's famous poem *"Der Erlkönig"* (1782).

resumé in the *TLS*[16]—rebukes poured in from such figures as Nabokov's son and literary executor, Dmitri, and from the foremost German critic of Nabokov, Dieter Zimmer. The vehemence of these responses was surprising. It is understandable and laudable to protect the memory of the loved and departed in an age where false information can spread with such rapidity and ease. But the idea that if the door of influence were opened a crack the monster of anxiety would come crashing in is a false one. As for Maar, and the real author of his find (he was alerted to the existence of the story by a certain Rainer Schelling [Maar, 11]), they should be thanked for their services. That such an interesting scoop should be stretched out over the course of five major articles is of the nature of journalistic work. Maar is an interesting writer and his work is well translated, but the argument of even such a trim book as his is too spare. Nabokov once wrote that "some law of logic should fix the number of coincidences, in a given domain, after which they cease to be coincidences, and form, instead, the living organism of a new truth" (*Ada*, 361). While presenting an interesting item of philological curiosa, *The Two Lolitas* falls short of the point at which such coincidence begins to shimmer, shift, and give way to the living organism of a new truth.

16. Maar, "Curse of the First Lolita." In this article Maar's claims are more mild and equivocal than in the argument's book form. The *TLS* article is in large part a literal translation of Maar's first *Frankfurter Allgemeine Zeitung* article, "*Was wußte Nabokov?*"

PART TWO

STYLE AND MATTER

I LOVE INDECENT LITERATURE!

—VLADIMIR NABOKOV

Letter to Edmund Wilson, April 17, 1950.

CHAPTER SEVEN

A RIDDLE WITH AN ELEGANT SOLUTION

Oui, encore une fois, à quoi est-il bon, je le demande en vérité, un livre qui n'est
ni instructif, ni amusant, ni chimique, ni philosophique, ni agricultural, ni élégiaque,
un livre qui ne donne aucune recette ni pour les moutons ni pour les puces, qui ne
parle ni des chemins de fer, ni de la Bourse, ni des replis intimes du coeur humain,
ni des habits moyen âge, ni de Dieu, ni du diable, mais qui parle d'un fou . . .
—Gustave Flaubert, *Mémoires d'un fou*

IF THE ARGUMENT MADE in part one of this study is correct and
what Nabokov meant to offer his readers was a lesson in cruelty and tenderness, a
question remains: Why did he not simply say so—why he instead vehemently
and repeatedly stated that there was no such lesson—and in fact no lesson of
any sort—to be taken from his work? If Nabokov chose to offer an artistic
lesson in tenderness, and yet was in no way prepared to openly concede this,
one possible reason is that he had an interest in dissimulation. And an interest
in dissimulation, as we will see shortly, he did have—several, in fact. But before
examining this interest in deception and dissimulation, let us look at what
Nabokov was deceptive about.

As we saw earlier, in the afterword to *Lolita*, Nabokov states that the book
was not written for any other purpose than to write it and that, "there are gentle
souls who would pronounce *Lolita* meaningless because it does not teach them
anything. I am neither a reader nor a writer of didactic fiction, and, despite John

Ray's assertion, *Lolita* has no moral in tow. For me a work of fiction exists only insofar as it affords me what I shall bluntly call aesthetic bliss" (*AL*, 314–315). What else does he then say of it? Asked in an interview: "Would you like to talk about *Lolita*?" Nabokov replied, "Well, no" (*SO*, 6). Prodded to go a little farther, he replied to the question, "Why did you write *Lolita*?" that, "it was an interesting thing to do. Why did I write any of my books, after all? For the sake of the pleasure, for the sake of the difficulty. I have no social purpose, no moral message; I've no general ideas to exploit, I just like composing riddles with elegant solutions" (*SO*, 16). In an interview from 1962, he remarked that "*Lolita* is a special favorite of mine," noting that "it was my most difficult book—the book that treated of a theme which was so distant, so remote, from my own emotional life that it gave me a special pleasure to use my combinatorial talent to make it real" (op. cit.). It is not *Lolita*'s emotional or ethical poignancy, not any message about art or life, but the pure pleasure of its extraordinarily difficult composition that makes it, for Nabokov, such a "special favorite." This is a note struck in still other interviews, as where Nabokov says that *Lolita* "was like the composition of a beautiful puzzle—its composition and its solution at the same time, since one is the mirror view of the other" (*SO*, 20). In a related vein, he remarks that "of all my books *Lolita* has left me with the most pleasurable afterglow—perhaps because it is the purest of all, the most abstract and carefully contrived" (*SO*, 47). The pleasure, glow, and purity of the work are what Nabokov directs his readers' attention to—and these are things that he sees stem from how "abstract and carefully contrived" it is. If we are to believe the bluff and blithe remarks of these interviews, *Lolita* was then, in the absence of exploitable general ideas, simply a riddle with an elegant solution. But what is that solution—and what is the riddle that it solves?

From the moment of its publication in 1955, Nabokov consistently eschewed the two most readily conceivable reasons for the writing of such a book as *Lolita*: that he identified with his seemingly monstrous narrator, and that he wished, through such "a shining example of moral leprosy" (to borrow John Ray Jr.'s phrase [*AL*, 5]), to prove a moral point or transmit a social message. Defending himself against the first accusation—that his creature shares the tastes of its creator—he noted that, "people tend to underestimate the power of my imagination and my capacity of evolving [sic] serial selves in my writings," which in point of fact was quite true (*SO*, 24).[1] This is the gentle version.

---

1. In his critical biography of Nikolai Gogol, Nabokov remarks: "It is strange, the morbid inclination we have to derive satisfaction from the fact (generally false and always irrelevant) that a work of art is traceable to a 'true story.' Is it because we begin to respect ourselves more when we learn that the

Nabokov more often expressed himself more vehemently, noting his many years of conjugal bliss, his staid habits, and so forth. In a definitive remark, Nabokov noted in the final interview he gave: "If I do have any obsessions I'm careful not to reveal them in fictional form" (Interview with Robert Robinson, 125).

Elsewhere in his afterword to *Lolita*, Nabokov remarked that "one of my very few intimate friends, after reading Lolita, was sincerely worried that I (I!) should be living 'among such depressing people'—when the only discomfort I really experienced was to live in my workshop among discarded limbs and unfinished torsos" (*AL*, 316).[2] He noted in another interview that "Humbert Humbert is a vain and cruel wretch who manages to appear 'touching,'" just as he referred to his talented narrator elsewhere as "the despicable Mr. Humbert [*l'immonde Monsieur Humbert*]" (*SO*, 94; *Apostrophes*). This distancing himself from this creation leads Nabokov to protest that "it is not my sense of the immorality of the Humbert-Lolita relation that is strong; it is Humbert's sense. *He* cares, I do not. *I* do not give a damn for public morals" (*SO*, 93; Nabokov's italics). Thus, though it might be possible that within the world of the novel Humbert may be endeavoring to express a moral message or something of the sort, under no circumstances should that message to be confused with a message sent by Nabokov in sincerity and earnestness to his readers. He does not care about "public morals."

Though ironic (and even impish), these remarks are perfectly consistent with ones that are less so and that Nabokov had been making since his youth. His strong distaste for the idea of writing with a "moral in tow" can be found as early as his Russian essays of the 1920s where he denounces literature marred by "the loathsome tint of social intent" (the remark is from an essay from 1927; Diment, 735). His position in debates about "engaged" literature during his years of European exile was clear. He was against the idea that the artist needed to engage himself or his art in something other than art and this led to attacks on his work by Russian expatriate critics who deplored what they described as his lack of political and social conscience. Later discussions of the deadly

---

writer, just like ourselves, was not clever enough to make up a story himself?" (*NG*, 40). There is every likelihood that Nabokov would have found himself in agreement with Umberto Eco's answer to the question, "with which of your characters do you identify?": "My God, with whom should I ever identify? With the adverbs, of course." (Eco 2000, 531). One should bear in mind in this connection the discretion, and even self-protectiveness, necessary for modern American mediatic figures to retain some degree of privacy—Nabokov's student Pynchon and his much-admired Salinger being prime examples of the lengths to which some must go to procure the needed measure of writerly peace.

2. This metaphor in all likelihood an allusion to the passage in the book where Humbert and Lolita observe the dissembled mannequins in a shop window (cf. *AL*, 226).

direction of works of art by Soviet and Nazi propaganda officials did, as one would expect, little to temper his views on the question.

While Nabokov's position was a product of the troubled times he lived in, he did not see the question as specific to it. Social moralizing and political preaching were for him dangerous and perennial traps—ones so dangerous that he saw both Gogol and Tolstoy, writers he adored, fall into them. Nevertheless, certain special factors contributed to the extremity of his remarks concerning *Lolita*. Nabokov had learned enough about Anglophone literary culture to know that the story of a coercive sexual affair between a very young American girl and a very suspicious European man was one that would need special handling if it were to make it to press without censorship (a fact made all the more clear to him through the experiences Wilson's *Memoirs of Hecate County* had with the censors less than a decade earlier[3]). And all the more so when the narrative was written in the first person—and with freakish charm. Matters were doubtless compounded as the work first appeared in Paris, a city reputed for its literary liberality, and in a publisher's catalogue alongside works with such striking titles as *The Whip Angels*, *The Enormous Bed*, and *I'm For Hire!* After years of visiting professorships and financial precarity, Nabokov had at the time he finished *Lolita* at last landed a semi-permanent professorial position at Cornell University, and if his post did not carry with it a princely salary, it was nevertheless one he was not eager to jeopardize. Cornell was not exceptionally conservative in 1955, but nor was it exceptionally liberal, and the social and political climate which reigned elsewhere in America in those years reigned there as well. Given this state of personal and public affairs, Nabokov first thought that attaching his name to the work was impossible and that the only way for him to publish it would be under the veil of anonymity. Gradually persuaded that this would only raise the likelihood that the work would be censored (anonymity serving, as a rule, to heighten the censor's attention), he agreed, with much trepidation, to publish the work under his own name. From this point onward, he went to no small pains to stress that the work was not a social commentary, not a sublimated confession, and not a work—like *I'm For Hire!*—of erotic import. *Lolita*, as he said again and again, was a riddle, a puzzle, an exercise, and an amusement—and nothing more.

Nabokov's famous afterword to *Lolita* in which he sets the tone for his remarks on the novel that he will follow for years, was first a foreword. It was

---

3. The New York Society for the Suppression of Vice called for the prosecution of Doubleday and Company (for publishing obscene material as defined by the New York Penal Code). The court found Wilson's book "obscene" and thereby not subject to protection by the First Amendment in *People v. Doubleday* (1947).

written not for publication with the novel (and consequently does not appear in the first edition), but to accompany the first excerpts of *Lolita* to be published in the United States.[4] It was part of a carefully prepared mediatic effort on the part of Nabokov, his friends, and his publishers to remove *Lolita* as far as possible from the realm of the social, and in so doing defuse the burgeoning scandal surrounding the book in the hope that it might be published without legal interdiction in the U.K. and America. Nabokov had the unsought and unhoped-for imprimatur of Graham Greene and a select, and growing, group of others, but *l'affaire Lolita*, as it came to be called, was far from over.[5]

When one turns to Nabokov's remarks made further from this mediatic spotlight, one obtains, however, a different image of his novel. Seen in their totality, Nabokov's descriptions of the intentions lying behind and woven into his most famous work varied in the extreme—a fact that was slow to receive attention from his critics. Put on trial, Flaubert was eager to avoid penalty and prohibition of his book and said—repeatedly—something tactically intelligent and literally true: that *Madame Bovary* was art for art's sake. But this belief in art for art's sake—in the special sovereignty and independence of the work of art—by no means excluded the conviction that his book was "moral, extremely moral" (Flaubert, 2:665). Nabokov's equally beloved Proust was to respond similarly in relation to his own work of art for art's sake, writing to Daniel Halévy to remind the latter of the "profoundly moral" character of his novel (letter from December 1921; Proust 1970–1993, 21:181). In much the same fashion Nabokov, in a letter to Edmund Wilson written a year before the work was first published, says: "I consider this novel to be my best thing in English, and though the theme and situation are decidedly sensuous, its art is pure" (*NWL*, 285). In a letter to Wilson from the following year, he remarks that "it depresses me to think that this pure and austere work may be treated by some flippant critic as a pornographic stunt" (*NWL*, 296). In another letter to Wilson, from

---

4. In the 1957 issue of the *Anchor Review* before being appended the following year to the first American edition (by Putnam).

5. As a highly respected literary authority and renowned writer, Greene did *Lolita* a huge favor by including it in his list of the best books of the year (as we saw earlier). John Gordon did it an even bigger one by being so vocally disgusted by the choice. It is perhaps not without interest, however, to note here a matter which has been neglected in accounts of the work and its publication. This was that Greene had ambiguous antecedents as regards such a subject and which might have been seen by enemies of his literary cause as motivating his choice. In the 1930's Greene wrote two memorable reviews of Shirley Temple movies. The first, relatively tame, notes a "mature" "coquetry," in Temple's performance in *Captain January* (1936). In the second, a review of *Wee Willie Winkie* (1937), Greene noted Temple's "agile studio eyes," "dimpled depravity," and "neat and well-developed rump twisted in the tap-dance." Temple's parents and Twentieth Century Fox filed a libel suit charging that Greene had "procured" Temple "for immoral purposes" in his article and Greene and the magazine were required to pay £3,500 in damages. Cf. duCille, 15.

the year following *Lolita*'s (first, French) publication, Nabokov is even more to the point as he enjoins Wilson—in terms essentially identical to those of Flaubert and Proust before him—to "please mark that it [*Lolita*] is a highly moral affair" (*NWL*, 298). (It appears that Wilson, like Morris Bishop, had for at least a time only read part I of the work, which gives it, as the reader can easily surmise, a much more sinister feel—as if *Crime and Punishment* ended just after Raskolnikov's murder—that is, without the "punishment.")[6]

Once *Lolita* had been safely and successfully published in both England and America, had been translated into dozens of languages, and had not only established a solid reputation for itself but made its author once again a rich man, Nabokov began to speak differently about it not only in private, but also in public. This images of the writer as the author of riddles, designer of puzzles, as the cold creator of lifeless forms that we saw earlier came to be counterbalanced by one of Nabokov himself crying while composing Humbert and Lolita's last scene together (cf. *Les Nouvelles Littéraires* interview). In a little attended-to remark made in another French interview, Nabokov said of *Lolita*, "there is a moral to the work—and a very moral one: do not hurt children. This is precisely what Humbert does" ["*il y a une morale très morale: ne pas faire du mal aux enfants. Or, Humbert fait ce mal*"] (Interview with Anne Guérin).[7] (Nabokov was to say that composers of dictionaries who defined "nymphet," as "'a very young but sexually attractive girl,' without any additional comment should have their knuckles rapped" [*SO*, 131]).[8] In an English interview quoted earlier, Nabokov is equally categorical: "I don't think *Lolita* is a religious book, but I do think it is a moral one" (Rampton, 202 n. 34). For Nabokov—as was the case for many of his literary idols—that a work of art be conceived of as a thing apart, not serving any near or narrow goals or aims, as art for art's sake, in no way excludes his conceiving of it as "moral." *Lolita* is a moral book—and

6. Wilson notes in a later letter that though he liked the novella from which the novel grew (*The Enchanter*), he did not like the book. The thrust of his somewhat vague critique is ultimately realist as he writes that "it isn't merely that the characters and situation are repulsive in themselves, but that, presented on this scale, they seem quite unreal" (*NWL*, 288). The published correspondence between the two writers offers ample room for conjecture as to extraliterary reasons for Wilson's ambivalence. Though he did not like it, Wilson did make some efforts to promote the work—e.g. his letter to Jason Epstein from 1955 where he writes: "Here's a manuscript by my friend Volodya Nabokov. It's repulsive, but you should read it" (cited Boyd 1991, 264). As Jason Epstein remarks in his recent memoir *Book Business*, he did read it, did not find it repulsive, but nor did he find it a work of genius (like Wilson, he preferred Nabokov's earlier works).

7. Though she does not cite this remark, Pifer (1980, 2003) reads *Lolita* very much in this light.

8. Terry Holt relates the following anecdote: "On the Halloween after *Lolita*'s American release, Nabokov demonstrated his own feelings on the matter of nympholepsy. A little girl, about Lolita's age, appeared at the Nabokovs' door that night. her costume was minimalist: a label, 'Lolita,' pinned to her neat dress. Nabokov spluttered at her, 'You tell your mother that this is an obscenity'" ("Shades of Nabokov," 3).

its moral is that one must see the world as it is and not simply through the embellishing eyes of a gifted imagination; that there is nothing to excuse abuse and coercion—above and especially in the case of those most in need of love, care and respect—children—and that there is a tragic and moral poignancy in such a realization.

To understand the sense in which Nabokov claimed that *Lolita* was a "moral" book, as well as why his remarks about that book were so divergent, we need to look more closely at how he felt about the world and its particular facts and facets, and it is to this matter that we should now turn so as to approach the elegant solution to the riddle Nabokov poses his reader.

CHAPTER EIGHT

THE PARTICULARITY OF LITERATURE

> The only real number is one, the rest are mere repetition.
> —Vladimir Nabokov, *The Real Life of Sebastian Knight*

WHILE WORKING AT Harvard University's Museum of Comparative Zoology in the 1940s, Nabokov, instead of relying on a generic description of band formation on butterflies' wings, developed a new classificatory technique involving the counting of stripes, and in some cases scales, on the wings of the butterflies in question (cf. Field 1977, 270). At work on a later lepidopterological project, he spent six hours a day months at a time posted in front of a microscope examining, treating, and removing the complex genitalia of thousands of members of the "blue" family of butterflies. At the height of his fame, in 1968 and 1969, Nabokov took time out to correspond with a certain V. O. Virkau about a "fragrant bog orchid," its various names in German and English as well as whether or not it was to be found in sphagnum bogs in the northern Russia. In short, Nabokov showed a passion for detail. While this is what one would expect from a natural scientist, his stress on exact and detailed observation and description was found with equal intensity in his other area of specialty: literature.

In the introductory remarks to his *Lectures on Literature* entitled "Good Readers and Good Writers," Nabokov stresses that "in reading, one should notice and fondle details" (*LL*, 1). In line with this pedagogical dictum, one of Nabokov's students at Cornell related the following experience: "'Caress the details,' Nabokov would utter, rolling the r, his voice the rough caress of a cat's tongue, 'the divine details!'" (Wetzsteon, 245). Indeed everything about Nabokov's pedagogical approach reflected this caressing stress on the details of the work of art. In the 1958 course description for a lecture course at Cornell, he informs prospective students that the works in the class will be "studied from the point of view of structure and style with great attention given to technical details and factual, specific features" (quoted in SL, 238). They could hardly, however, anticipate the fantastic attention he would ask them to give to such technical details and factual features. The course's final examination has survived and on it students were asked to describe Emma Bovary's sunshade and shoes, to enumerate the contents of Anna Karenina's handbag, to map the Liffey's movement through Dublin and Gregor's movements though the Samsa flat. In directing his classes' attention to a passing image of "silvery pools in a dark sea" from Dickens' *Bleak House*, Nabokov remarked, "Some readers may suppose that such things as these evocations are trifles not worth stopping at; but literature consists of such trifles. Literature consists, in fact, not of general ideas but of particular revelations, not of schools of thought but of individuals of genius" (*LL*, 116). One should notice and fondle details because in them resides the essence of the work. For Nabokov, great art contained no "trifles" in the disparaging sense of the term—or, if it did, the trifles were not fleeting images and factual precisions, but general themes and ideas that floated vaguely above and around such silvery pools and dark seas as Dickens described.

In a letter to Wilson from 1946, Nabokov harshly criticizes André Malraux's *La condition humaine* on the grounds that he found it unlikely that mosquitoes in the "imaginal stage" were to be found in early spring in Shanghai—an observation which seems to have decisively contributed to his judgment of Malraux as, though a nice person, a "third-rate writer" (*NWL*, 175–176; Nabokov goes on to note that, "Malraux's work belongs to the *Compagnie Internationale des Grands Clichés*" *NWL*, 176). In another letter to Wilson, Nabokov criticizes Henry James' "The Aspern Papers" on the basis that the narrator, describing a cigar seen by night from a darkened window, refers to its having a "red tip." Nabokov objects that the light of a cigar by night is "blunt," and dismissively suggests that the locution would be more apt to describe a dog's penis—an observation which shapes his less than favorable general impression of James' work in that letter (cf. *NWL*, 53).[1]

1. Nabokov could be even harsher on the matter, stating elsewhere in his letters to Wilson that James was "impotent" and "a complete fake" (*NWL*, 213, 278). He would, however, later note in an interview something far more favorable than anything he confided to Wilson: "my feelings toward James are rather complicated. I really dislike him intensely but now and then the figure in the phrase, the turn of the epithet, the screw of an absurd adverb, cause me a kind of electric tingle, as if some current of his was also passing through my own blood" (*SO*, 64). On the relation between Nabokov and James, see Robert Gregory's "Porpoise-iveness without Porpoise: Why Nabokov Called James a Fish."

Attention and fidelity to detail were also a criterion employed for writers Nabokov unconditionally admired. His lectures on literature go to great length to notice and fondle the brilliant details of his favorite works, and he regularly compliments the skill and sharpness of perception of Kafka and Dickens, Flaubert and Proust, Austen and Stevenson, Tolstoy and Chekhov, as well as other treasured authors. His book on Gogol pays more attention to such details than to the general ideas other critics focused upon and his elephantine edition of Eugene Onegin is a tour de force in caressing the details of his favorite poet. Though Nabokov only rarely discussed contemporaries, when he did this principle applied to them as well. In the grateful remarks he wrote in response to the issue of TriQuarterly dedicated to him, his praise (which is not slight) of Anthony Burgess's contribution takes the form of noting: "I particularly appreciate his Maltese grocer's cat that likes to sit upon the scales and is found to weigh 2 rotlos" ("Anniversary Notes," 12).[2] The contemporary of whom Nabokov spoke in perhaps the most glowing terms is Alain Robbe-Grillet. In a letter from 1959 the Nabokovs refer to Robbe-Grillet as "the greatest French writer of the day (V. opinion backed by Vera's humble one)."[3] In Bernard Cwagenbaum's documentary Vladimir Nabokov est un joueur d'échecs, Nabokov refers to Robbe-Grillet's Le voyeur as "one of the finest novels" of our time. Nabokov was of course not the only writer and reader of his time to hold Robbe-Grillet in high esteem, but it is likely that his particularly intense admiration had something to do with the hallmark of Robbe-Grillet's singular style: fantastically minute and precise description. Here and elsewhere, and with both ancients and moderns, there is every reason to believe that Nabokov would have heartily agreed with Hume's assessment in his Enquiry Concerning Human Understanding that "accuracy is, in every case, advantageous to beauty" (Hume, 10).

What the above makes clear is that, for Nabokov, the province of art is the province of the particular detail. "In high art and pure science," Nabokov said, "detail is everything"—and he meant it (SO, 168).[4] Gentle souls such as The Gift's Fyodor or The Defense's Luzhin (who is thrilled by "Sherlock composing a monograph on the ash of all known sorts of cigars" [Defense, 34]) are blessed with precisely such attentiveness to detail—just as are the darker and more complicated cases of Humbert and the notorious Veens in Ada, or Ardor. There

---

2. Burgess, of course, admired Nabokov—but, as a later remark shows, within limits. When asked to compare Nabokov to Joyce, he replied, "he's unworthy to unlace Joyce's shoe" (Paris Review interview, 144).

3. Letter written from Genoa December 7, 1959 to Morris Bishop, Morris Bishop Collection, Cornell University. As the letter, like the better part of Nabokov's correspondence, is typed, it is difficult to precisely ascertain authorship, but this letter, like the better part of Nabokov's correspondence from this period, was almost certainly written by his wife—something noticeable in stylistic traits.

4. In a French interview from 1968, Nabokov he offered an equally lapidary formulation: "le détail, tout est là" ["all is in the detail"] (interview with Pierre Dommergues, 97).

is indeed no article of aesthetic faith which sheds clearer light on Nabokov's conception of the task of the artist than this. "One of the functions of all my novels," remarked Nabokov, "is to prove that the novel in general does not exist" (*SO*, 115). This is not the death of art, the author, or literature, and what Nabokov is speaking of here should not be mistaken for a historical diagnosis. The novel does not exist "in general" not because of the *novel*, but because of the *general*, because "the part is more alive than the whole" (*LRL*, 373). The corollary of his conviction that "the detail is everything" is that generalities— from *the Good* to *the novel*—are, in essence, nothing. And for this reason Nabokov stresses that "the book I make is a subjective and specific affair" (*SO*, 115).[5]

Interviewed by a Wellesley student in 1941 about his strong opinions, Nabokov offered an even more overarching claim for specificity: "there is no such thing as art . . . there are artists, but they are individuals with different forms of expression."[6] Nabokov is n5ot eager to enter into a hermeneutic circle in which art, artist, and artwork revolve; he dismisses the generality and clings passionately to the particular case. Where art exists, it does not do so as a generality, but in spite of generalities: "the *isms* go; the *ist* dies; art remains" (*LL*, 147). Perhaps no better name for this caressing of the particular detail might be found than the scholastic one that Nabokov on occasion employs: *quiddity*. In *The Gift*, Nabokov refers to the "genuine quiddity" which lay at the center of Fyodor's interests, and in his notes to *Eugene Onegin* he refers to "the quiddity of individual artistic achievement (which, after all, alone matters and alone survives)" (*Gift*, 9; *EO* 3:32).

Generality

> The larger the issue, the less it interests me.
>
> —Vladimir Nabokov, *Strong Opinions*

In the remarks he made in the margins of his copy of Joshua Reynolds' *Discourses*, William Blake exclaimed: "To Generalize is to be an Idiot. To Particularize

---

5. As concerns how protective of the specificity of this subjective affair was, cf. Nabokov's letter to Jason Epstien from 1956 regarding the cover art for Nabokov's then forthcoming *Pnin*: "I am sending you some photographs of Pnin—like Russians, with and without hair, for a visual appreciation of the items I am going to discuss. . . . 3. The nose is very important. It should be the Russian potato nose, fat and broad, with prominent nostril curves. See Zhukovski for nostrils, Obrastov for a replica of Pnin's fat glossy organ . . . 4. The terribly important space between nose and upper lip. This must be simian, large, long, with a central hollow and lateral furrows . . ." (*SL*, 190).

6. *Wellesley College News*, May 7, 1942. Eight years later, E. H. Gombrich will begin what would become the best selling art-historical work ever, *The Story of Art*, nearly verbatim: "There really is no such thing as Art. There are only artists" (Gombrich, 1).

is the Alone Distinction of Merit" (Blake, 641). As concerns the discourses he himself read, Nabokov drew the same conclusion. The consequence of his stress on particularity is a vehement opposition to Generalizing in all its forms. From his first work to his last, Nabokov will tirelessly champion "the supremacy of the detail over the generalization" (*LRL*, 373).

In an essay written in 1931, Nabokov announced, "I've nothing of a systematizer in me" ("L'écrivain et l'époque," 139). There was indeed nothing which Nabokov was so obstinately skeptical of as systematizing visions and projects. Distancing Chekhov, whom he adored, from Dostoevsky, whom he loathed, Nabokov remarks that whatever Chekhov's occasional faults, "*au moins, [il] ne secrète pas d'idées generales*" ["at least, [he] does not secrete general ideas"]— whereas, for Dostoevsky, this unsightly process could be found on every other page (Interview with Anne Guérin, 26).

Nabokov is, if possible, even more categorical in an unpublished lecture note dating from his first semester at Cornell (in 1948) that outlines the concerns of the coming course: "I am not concerned with generalities, with ideas and schools of thought, with groups of mediocrities under a fancy flag. I am concerned with the specific text, the thing itself" (cited by Boyd 1991, 133). It is this same stress on the particular detail and this same aversion to generality that leads to the confusing position he takes on the idea of "commonsense" in his "The Art of Literature and Commonsense." Therein, commonsense is not part of literature—it is its opposite. Nabokov's attack is understandable only when one sees commonsense as a synonym for unthinking acceptance of received ideas and general claims. It is a denunciation of the tendency to privilege generality over and against the particular detail (as commonsense indeed dictates). For Nabokov, literature follows different lines as "the main delight of the creative mind is the sway accorded to a seemingly incongruous detail over a seemingly dominant generalization" (*LL*, 374).

Though Nabokov is both adamant and militant on the matter of generality, he is also careful not to push his position into incoherence. In philological questions, faithful and loving attention to the particular was a principle and a method, but not dogmatism. In "Good Readers and Good Writers," we read that "If one begins with a ready-made generalization, one begins at the wrong end and travels away from the book before one has started to understand it" (*LL*, 1). Here, his argument is commonsensical and points out that in reading we should begin with what is on the page. If we begin with what we bring to it rather than what we find here, we are moving not in the direction of the work and its innermost attention, but away from it. With this in mind, Nabokov says that "There is nothing wrong about the moonshine of generalization when it comes *after* the sunny trifles of the book have been lovingly collected"

(*LL*, 1; Nabokov's italics). What must be grasped is priority—the details of the work of art, the specific thing in all its specificity, comes first—and that only thereafter can one indulge in generalities—an activity, nevertheless, that is not one he recommends, his choice of the term "moonshine" clearly designating that generalizing is an activity that is dreamy, drunken, and inexpertly mixed. As a necessary result, when a generality is granted admission into his aesthetic world, it always remains firmly anchored in the detail of individual perception:

> This world I said was good—and "goodness" is something that is irrationally concrete. From the commonsensical point of view the "goodness," say, of some food is just as abstract as its "badness," both being qualities that cannot be perceived by the sane judgment as tangible and complete objects. But when we perform that necessary mental twist which is like learning to swim or to make a ball break, we realize that "goodness" is something round and creamy, and beautifully flushed, something in a clean apron with warm bare arms that have nursed and comforted us ... (*LL*, 375)

Symbols, Allegory, and Myth

> As an artist and a scholar, I prefer the specific detail to the generalization, images to ideas, obscure facts to clear symbols, and the discovered wild fruit to the synthetic jam.
> —Vladimir Nabokov, *Strong Opinions*

The villainous Demon Veen remarks:

> I don't give a hoot for the esoteric meaning, for the myth behind the moth, for the masterpiece-baiter who makes Bosch express some bosh of his time, I'm allergic to allegory and am quite sure he was just enjoying himself crossbreeding casual fancies just for the fun of the contour and color, and what we have to study ... is the joy of the eye, the feel and the taste of the woman-sized strawberry that you embrace *with* him, or the exquisite surprise of an unusual orifice—but you are not following me ... (*Ada*, 437)

As Demon veers towards the venereal it becomes difficult to follow him. His point remains, however, clear. What drives the Veens' fine perception of art, just as what drives Nabokov's, is an an- or anti-allegorical impulse. Speaking of his teaching days at Cornell, Nabokov once noted, "Every time one of them [his students] used the word 'symbol,' I gave them a bad grade" (interview with Pierre Dommergues, 97). Similarly, he later reminisced: "I once gave a student a C-minus, or perhaps a D-plus just for applying to [Joyce's *Ulysses*] the titles borrowed from Homer" (*SO*, 55).[7] In both cases, the enemy is the same: generality.

Given Nabokov's grading scale, it should come as no surprise that ways of reading or writing which systematically undermine the sovereignty of the detail are anathema. "I detest symbols and allegories," we read in "On a Book Entitled Lolita" (*AL*, 314). In the list of items offered as advice to an imaginary "budding literary critic" Nabokov writes: "Ask yourself if the symbol you have detected is not your own footprint. Ignore allegories" (*SO*, 66). This position should not be seen as simply part of the bluff and bluster of Nabokov's American literary persona, as thirty years earlier he had offered the same advice to his mother. In a letter from 1935 concerning his *Invitation to a Beheading*, he warns her that she "shouldn't look for any symbol or allegory" therein (cited by Boyd 1990, 419). Responding later to a work analyzing, precisely, symbols in his own writing (the work was Rowe's), Nabokov said that "the notion of symbol has always been abhorrent to me. . . . The symbolism racket in schools attracts computerized minds but destroys plain intelligence as well as poetical sense. It bleaches the soul. It numbs all capacity to enjoy the fun and enchantment of art" (*SO*, 304–305). Searching for symbols is an activity that bleaches away the color of life, stifles the poetic, and renders the work unintelligent and unintelligible. And so it, like allegory, should be ignored.

As we can see from the above, Nabokov's polemical opposition to symbolism and allegory stemmed directly and consistently from his vision of the importance of the particularity, the importance of the detail viewed and felt in and for itself. One of the implications of this stress on the particular is that much interpretation of Nabokov's works has found itself cornered, as some of his more energetic and aggressive readers—such as Susan Sontag—have noted. Focusing on and fondling divine details might suffice to pass an exam, but not, however, to write a work of criticism. Nabokov welcomes the process of analysis—detailing the specific parts—but rejects syntheses proposing what are always for him hollow wholes. The critic wishing to pay tribute to his strong opinions and also follow his critical guidelines thus finds little room for hermeneutic maneuver. This has hardly prevented, as it hardly should, critics from interpreting his works—but it has also shaped those interpretations. To a real extent Nabokov was "against

7. The first edition of Joyce's *Ulysses* employs chapter titles taken from scenes of the *Odyssey* ("Telemachus," "The Lotus-Eaters," "Ithaca," etc.). Joyce removed the chapter titles from the second and all subsequent editions of the work—which Nabokov held for a fine idea. In Borges' 1935 text "The Approach to Al-Mu'Tasim," the narrator holds these Homeric titles in similar esteem ("The repeated, but insignificant, contacts of Joyce's *Ulysses* with the Homeric *Odyssey* continue to enjoy—I shall never know why—the harebrained admiration of the critics" (Borges 1962, 42).

interpretation" if by interpretation we understand synthesizing judgments, and Couturier is right to remark that, for Nabokov, "interpretation, like translation, is itself always a betrayal," just as Brian McHale is right to claim that "more forcefully even than Susan Sontag, Nabokov declared himself to be 'against interpretation'" (Couturier 1993, 382; McHale, 279). And so, instead of speaking generally about Nabokov's polemical opposition to generality, let us turn now to a particular case—the most remarkable in his oeuvre.

Freud, or The Particular Problem

> I said I always preferred the literal meaning of a description to the symbol behind it. She nodded thoughtfully but did not seem convinced.
> —Vladimir Nabokov, *Look at the Harlequins!*

One of Nabokov's students once related how one day in class, as Nabokov was vehemently denouncing Freud, the heating pipes in his Cornell University classroom began to clank and clang. Nabokov stopped and exclaimed: "The Viennese quack is railing at me from his grave!" (Boyd 1991, 308). And cause he had to rail. Not only in classes, but in books, articles, interviews and conversation, Nabokov made tireless fun of psychoanalysis and its father. Playing with the projections of a Freudian reader in *Lolita*, Humbert relates: "sometimes I attempt to kill in my dreams. But do you know what happens? For instance I hold a gun. For instance I aim at a bland, quietly interested enemy. Oh, I press the trigger all right, but one bullet after another feebly drops on the floor from the sheepish muzzle. In those dreams, my only thought is to conceal the fiasco from my foe, who is slowly growing annoyed" (*AL*, 47). Just to be sure, Humbert reminds his reader later in the novel, "we must remember that a pistol is the Freudian symbol of the Ur-father's central forelimb" (*AL*, 216).[8]

In one of the more felicitous formulas made from atop his favorite hobby-horse, Nabokov denounced what he called "the oneiromancy and mythogeny of psychoanalysis" ("Conclusive Evidence," 133). This denunciation could hardly be more pervasive. The opening paragraphs of both of the first two chapters of Nabokov's autobiography make disparaging reference to Freud, condemning, "the vulgar, shabby, fundamentally medieval world" of his thought (*SM*, 10). In the screenplay for *Lolita*, "the Freudian prison of thought" and "the Freudian

---

8. In this, and many other things, *Lolita* tends toward the grotesque. To choose a glaring instance, Humbert relates a plan for a proposed mural in the Enchanted Hunters Hotel (where Humbert and Lolita first become lovers) that would depict "a choking snake sheathing whole the flayed trunk of a shoat" (*AL*, 134).

nursery-school of thought" are both vehemently evoked, and dismissed.[9] *Ada, or Ardor* abounds in references to the "expensive confession fests" of psychoanalysis; *Strong Opinions* laments the incursions of "the Austrian crank with a shabby umbrella" (*Ada*, 364; *SO*, 116). In the latter work Nabokov goes so far as to claim that psychoanalysis has dangerous ethical consequences in its penchant for the disculpation of crimes (ibid.).[10] In regard to Freud's venture into the realm of political analysis, his co-authored study of the political life of Woodrow Wilson's drives, Nabokov wrote to the magazine *Encounter* which published sections of the work in 1967: "I welcome Freud's Woodrow Wilson not only because of its comic appeal, which is great, but because that surely must be the last rusty nail in the Viennese Quack's coffin."[11] The only positively phrased thing Nabokov is on record saying about Freud is his remark in a televised French interview that, "I admire Freud greatly as a comic writer" (*Apostrophes* interview). Nabokov's disparaging remarks are indeed legion and, as Shute writes in the entry "Nabokov and Freud" in *The Garland Companion to Vladimir Nabokov*, "Nabokov's antipathy to psychoanalysis scarcely requires documentation" (Shute, 413).[12] We might thus dispense with any further instances, and turn to the question of why Nabokov felt such antipathy in the first place—as well as the question of what, if anything, Nabokov's antipathy has to teach us about his vision of art.

So as to contextualize Nabokov's remarks we should recall that creative writers of Nabokov's generation, and of the one directly preceding it, were hardly unanimous in their appreciation of Freud. The Surrealists found Freud's

9. *Lolita: A Screenplay*, 728. Kubrick removed all such references from his shooting script. Nabokov's screenplay if shot as written would have lasted, by Kubrick's estimate, some seven hours. For an informative treatment of the preparation and shooting of the film, cf. Richard Corliss' *Lolita* (London: British Film Institute, 1995).

10. Such accusations are perfectly unfounded in the sense that Freud never sought to pardon or explain away *real* crimes, and, in fact, tended to avoid discussing actual criminals or any possible relation between psychoanalysis and criminology. The remark however is not without an oblique pertinence given that the rise of criminology coincides with, and is to an extent influenced by, the rise of psychoanalysis. As Freud developed a theory in which violent fantasies are seen as the normal consequence of the conflict between individual desire and collective prohibition, the step from the disculpation of violent *fantasies* to the disculpation of violent *acts* was, for many, not great.

11. Cited by Paul Roazen in "Oedipus at Versailles," 12. Recent evidence (an unpublished manuscript, letters, early drafts, and fragments all in Freud's hand) proves what many close to Freud had long disputed—that Freud played an important role in the redaction of a project with William C. Bullitt begun in the late 1920s and first published as *Thomas Woodrow Wilson* in 1967. Bullitt was Freud's patient for a time in the 1920s in Vienna (which he denied) and the maverick diplomat impressed Freud enough for the latter to consent to co-authorship (which was well on its way at least as early as 1930).

12. Though Shute does not note this in her article, the importance and scale of Nabokov's antipathy to Freud is discussed in the first book-length study of Nabokov, that of Page Stegner, who remarks: "In one sense *Lolita* might be considered an extensive parody of Freudian myths and Freudian explanations for psychological aberration" (Stegner, 103). In an essay from 1976 Claude Mouchard very rightly noted

insights into the wild realms of dream and drive tremendously exciting (though Freud was politely befuddled by them), and D. H. Lawrence and a variety of other authors of the age found undreamt-of truths revealed to them in Freud's writings. In other quarters, however, there was quite a bit of disliking, distrusting and even raging against psychoanalysis. There were categorical cases and conditional ones. Paul Valéry, to take a celebrated example, was not a fan—nor was Joyce, who said of psychoanalysis that it was "neither more nor less than blackmail" (Humbert continues the joke by referring to psychoanalysts as "dream-extortionists" [*AL*, 34]). A darker drama is to be found in the ambivalent relation of Virginia Woolf to psychoanalysis. After gently mocking Freud's ideas throughout much of the 1920s, she changed her mind in the 1930s. In 1939, Freud invited Woolf and her husband Leonard to afternoon tea in his Hampstead home (the Woolfs were friends of Freud's English translator, as well as his publishers). Upon her arrival, Freud presented Virginia with a flower— a Narcissus—a gesture that given Woolf was to take her own life by drowning two years later, is more than a little uncanny.[13]

In Nabokov's case we find, however, something quite different from what we find in any of the writers mentioned above. Geoffrey Green qualifies Nabokov's disdain in the only monograph treating the subject, *Freud and Nabokov*, as "the grandest and most extravagant contempt for psychoanalysis known in modern literature"—and with good reason (Green 1988, 1). From his first works to his last, in Russian, in English, and in French, Nabokov shows himself ever ready to combat what he calls "madly frolicking Freudianism" ["*le freudisme folâtre*"] ("Pouchkine," 81). From the 1920s to the 1970s, the emphasis remains the same: psychoanalysis is associated with the medieval and the superstitious,

---

that "The challenge to the 'Freudians' in Nabokov's works, and especially in his prefaces, is almost an obligatory rite of passage" (Mouchard, 131). Along such lines, Jeffrey Berman is perhaps right to claim that "Nabokov has created a new art form, psychiatry baiting," though less correct in asserting that this invective is "mirthless" (Berman, 211, 213). Of Berman's work, Virginia Blum writes (without citation or page reference) that "Berman suggests that Nabokov's repugnance to Freud and Freudianism arose as a result of Freud's Germanic background, which Nabokov unconsciously equated with fascism" (Blum, 238 n. 4). Berman does write of this German association (cf. Berman, 218) and both at the beginning and the end of his essay does suggest that more can or will be understood of Nabokov's dislike of psychoanalysis through knowing more of Nabokov's biography (from someone professionally engaged in the study of psychoanalysis this is hardly surprising), but he nowhere suggests that Nabokov's dislike for Freud "arose" from such associations, nor that such an unconscious association would or could explain it.

13. In a 1920 article entitled "Freudian Fiction" (*TLS*, March 25, 1920), Woolf's gently contemptuous attitude towards psychoanalysis can be found in her remark: "A patient who has never heard a canary sing without falling down in a fit can now walk through an avenue of cages without a twinge of emotion since he has faced the fact that his mother kissed him in the cradle. The triumphs of science are beautifully positive." This light-hearted statement acquires a certain weight when one notes that during a psychotic episode in her teenage years Woolf claimed to have heard birds singing to her in Greek.

with stupidity and credulity; he associates it, as we saw, with prison, pre-school, the premature and the pre-modern. Nabokov's message seems that Freud's ideas should be mocked and thwarted, as he endeavors to do in the forewarnings to Freudian readers he includes in the prefaces to so many of his works. But what, precisely, about Freud's ideas is seen to be so harmful? And why can't he simply leave it in peace?

One of Nabokov's sharpest criticisms is that Freudian thought is essentially *determinist*, thereby linking it with the movements he most intensely loathed. In a lecture given at Stanford University in 1941, while trashing Eugene O'Neill's *Mourning Becomes Electra*, he claims that in that play, "Fate [leads] the author . . . by one hand, and the late professor Freud by the other" ("The Tragedy of Tragedy," 336). What Nabokov found objectionable here was what he saw as the collusion of Freud and fate in creating a deterministic world. More polemically, Nabokov denounces what he calls a "police state of sexual myth" in Freud's thought (*SM*, 300). As is explicit here and implicit elsewhere, Nabokov even associates psychoanalysis's prying eye with totalitarianism. In a French interview, Nabokov notes how "psychoanalysis has something Bolshevik about it—an inner policing . . . symbols kill the individual dream, the thing itself" ("*le psychanalyse a quelque chose de bolchévick: la police intérieure. . . . les symboles tuent la chose, le rêve individuel*") (Interview with Anne Guèrin, 27). What psychoanalysis shares with Bolshevism is the totalitarian tendency to neglect the rich singular instance in favor of a dangerously hollow generality.[14]

Nabokov thus saw Freud as representing not only many things he did not like, but also that which he most intensely disliked: the generalizing of the particulars and particularities. This general idea about the tendency to generalize raises the question of Nabokov's familiarity with Freud's ideas and work. Did

14. In an essay from 1929 entitled "*Die Stellung Freuds in der modernen Geistesgeschichte*," Nabokov's despised Thomas Mann argued that far from representing an obscurantist thinking which might prepare the soil for the sowing of totalitarianism, psychoanalysis opposes itself to irrationalism and combats the unthinking veneration of the obscure, the mythic, the unconscious, and the dark night of dream and drive. For Mann, Freud's work may use the mythical, but it does so to deprive fascism of its use. Nabokov clearly saw things differently—and, incidentally, took every opportunity to insult Mann, including him in lists of renowned writers whom he deemed "mediocrities" (alongside of such luminaries as Gide, Faulkner, Dostoevsky, and Rilke). In 1945, an indignant Nabokov wrote to Wilson, "How *could* you name that quack Mann in one breath with P[roust] and J[oyce]? (*NWL*, 148). In "On a Book Entitled *Lolita*," Nabokov refers to "topical trash or what some call the Literature of Ideas" and lists as examples of such Balzac, Gorky, and Mann (*AL*, 315). In an interview for the German weekly *Die Zeit* in 1959 where he once again makes disparaging remarks about Mann, his exasperated interviewer asked if there were any German authors he *did* like (the answer was yes: Kafka; *Die Zeit*, April 17, 1959, p. 6, translation by Dieter Zimmer). It is difficult to know what role extraliterary factors such as Mann's bourgeois persona, his homoeroticism, or his pro-Bolshevism might have played in Nabokov's dislike, but it is likely that Mann's view of Freud did not improve Nabokov's image of him.

he simply have a general idea of psychoanalysis, or did he have, instead, a precise and detail-rich understanding? This is something that Nabokov deliberately makes difficult to ascertain with any great certitude. When asked about his familiarity with psychoanalysis, he replied, "Bookish familiarity only. The ordeal is much too silly and disgusting to be contemplated even as a joke" (SO, 23). But even this degree of "bookish familiarity" is difficult to ascertain. Nabokov's first biographer, Andrew Field, notes that Nabokov was familiar with Freud through English translations (Field 1977, 262–263). Field does not offer any textual support of this claim, but it is almost certainly based on a letter preserved in the Nabokov Archive at the New York Public Library from Véra Nabokov to him wherein she responds on her husband's behalf to Field's query: "he [Nabokov] actually read *many* of Freud's works (in English translation)" (letter from Montreux January 31, 1966, Nabokov Archive, Berg Collection, New York Public Library; Véra Nabokov's emphasis). Expanding upon his remark that he found Freud richly comic, Nabokov specified, "he must be read, however, in the original."[15] In an unpublished and undated note card (but which was written, in all likelihood, during the 1960s), found in Nabokov's papers and bearing the title "Freud," we read: "*Ever since I read him in the Twenties* he seemed wrong, absurd, and vulgar to me" (Nabokov Archive, Berg Collection, New York Public Library, undated folder, "Notes on Various Subjects"; my italics). On this basis we can ascertain that he read Freud relatively early and that he read him in translation—with forays into the original for comic relief. No further certainties can be had, but there is room for a conjecture.

Whatever other writings of Freud's Nabokov might have read, there are signs that he was familiar with Freud's case study of the "Wolf-Man" ("*Aus der Geschichte einer infantilen Neurose*") dating from 1918 and available in English translation by the "Twenties" when Nabokov, at the earliest, first read Freud. There are a number of reasons to suggest that the text was known to Nabokov. The first is that along with the case studies of Schreber, Anna O., and the "Rat-Man," it is among the most famous ever published, and Nabokov was much interested in case studies—especially, but not exclusively, while composing *Lolita*. What is more, the case history of the "Wolf-Man" contains the first, and by far the most outlandish, references to an "*Urszene*," a "primal scene,"

---

15. Though Nabokov repeatedly claimed varying degrees of ignorance of the German language, it was never as great as he pretended. Not only did Nabokov live in Berlin for some eighteen years, but before moving there he knew German well enough to translate certain short pieces by Heine and Goethe into Russian. In an interview from the 1971 with *Bayerischer Rundfunk*, Nabokov gave the reason for his reticence to (fully) learn the language: "Upon moving to Berlin I was beset by a panicky fear of somehow flawing my precious layer of Russian by learning to speak German fluently" (cited by John Updike in *LL*, xx).

in Freud's writing, and one of the few additional clues Nabokov's remarks on psychoanalysis offer as to his familiarity with Freud is his ridiculing of the idea of a primal scene (cf., for instance, *AL*, 34). An additional factor is that this is a case that Nabokov would have special reason to find interesting. Despite Freud's cloaking of the identity of his patient, it is clear from a reading of the case study that the "Wolf-Man" was, like Nabokov, a White Russian rendered destitute by the Revolution and living in precarious European exile. While somewhat older than Nabokov, he seems, from Freud's account to have been at least somewhat of Nabokov's set (wealthy, cosmopolitan, cultivated, multilingual, living part of the year in the country and part of the year in the city)—all of which makes it plausible that Nabokov might have caught wind of the story in one or another émigré circle if he hadn't already become familiar with Freud's text upon, or shortly following, its appearance.[16] Finally, amongst the remarkable array of neurotic symptoms from which the Wolf-Man suffered was a "*Schmetterlingsphobie*" ("butterfly phobia")—something that could hardly have failed to excite the interest of someone whose feelings on the subject were so very much the opposite (cf. Freud 1968–78, 12:147).

While it is eminently plausible that Nabokov developed his particular dislike from reading Freud's case history of "The Wolf-Man," the question remains— whether it was this text or another that formed the foundation of Nabokov's familiarity—*why* Nabokov felt such energetic hostility towards Freud? There was much that he found wrong-headed in popular authors but some element or elements in Freud's thought or influence led him to dedicate special intensity and effort to denouncing him. Nabokov might well have considered psychoanalysis a comically or sadly misguided undertaking without feeling the need to initiate measures to counteract its influence. Was his outspoken antipathy simply the result of his sense that psychoanalysis represented a danger for the general public (which, we might recall, he did not usually concern himself overmuch with)? Or did psychoanalysis perhaps present a particular danger for himself, and his art?

Like many an artist, Nabokov associated childhood with creation. His hostility to psychoanalysis would have been fueled by Freud's upsetting of the vision of Edenic youth that Nabokov so ardently cherished. That the idea of the bright, happy, and innocent child of previous centuries be replaced by a toddler torn by conflicts of the most violent sort is unlikely to have sat well with him, even if that idea was not truly Freud's invention. In any case, it should then come as no surprise that one finds in Nabokov's works no ambivalent children

16. The identity of Freud's Wolf-Man later became known to the general public, and Freud's former patient (who remained resolutely uncured) went on to write a memoir of his analysis: cf. *The Wolf-Man by the Wolf-Man*, and Karin Obholzer's *The Wolf-Man: Conversations with Freud's Patient—Sixty Years Later*.

like little James who no later than the second page of Woolf's *To the Lighthouse* wishes for "an axe . . . or a poker, any weapon that would have gashed a hole in his father's breast and killed him, there and then" (Woolf, 4).[17]

It seems safe to assume that one of the reasons artists have been less than eager to embrace psychoanalysis, and have been motivated, as in Nabokov's case, to combat it, is that it doesn't depict the artist in a very favorable light. Psychoanalysis's view of art removes the site of creativity from the conscious, controlling mind to the creator's unconscious drives and depths. For an artist, like Nabokov, so concerned with controlling the work under his hand, this could not have been a pleasing idea. To exchange an imaginative world where the artist reigns in unquestioned sovereignty for one where that imaginative realm is secretly controlled by an unconscious and exceedingly immature regent was unlikely to have appealed to him. This places him alongside a number of artists with such an antipathy but it does not explain the exceptional vehemence of his response.

As we have seen, Nabokov intensely disliked art, and interpretations of it, which he saw as mythologizing. Inasmuch as psychoanalysis makes recourse to such mythological types and archetypes, Nabokov would have found himself oft estranged by "the oneiromancy and mythogeny of psychoanalysis." To a certain extent, this is a simple question of the disparity of the two thinkers' interests. For Freud, mythology was a key for the unlocking of the mysteries of the psyche because he saw myths as encrypted signs and frozen forms of human drives, desires, and developments. Myths were the encoded history of our common psychological past. As Freud held to a reasonably prevalent evolutionary model of culture (wherein so-called primitive cultures employing "mythological" systems of thought were considered to be very like our own, but at an earlier stage of historical development), mythology was a treasured tool for understanding the mysteries of human development—both singular and collective. This is all well and good for anthropological and psychological purposes, but what of art? For Nabokov, approaches to the understanding of the human mind and its creations that relied upon the analysis of myths constantly risked committing the worst sin in his aesthetic canon: the failure to pay close

17. Another motivation might be the simple fact that psychoanalysis depended for its very functioning on the trespassing upon of Nabokov's treasured principles of discretion and decorum. In the description of young Martin in Nabokov's novel *Glory* (1932), which a comparison with *Speak, Memory* shows to contain a number of autobiographical details and experiences (as Nabokov himself was later to acknowledge), we read: "From early childhood his [Martin's] mother had taught him that to discuss in public a profound emotional experience—which, in the open air, immediately evanesces and fades, and, oddly, becomes similar to an analogous experience of one's interlocutor—was not only vulgar, but a sin against sentiment" (*Glory*, 12). Psychoanalytic treatment is of course not a "public" discussion, but for Nabokov it seems to have been nearly tantamount to it.

attention to the particularity of the work of art. Such approaches, like, for him, allegory and symbolism, granted conceptual license to interpret everything in terms of something else—and this he found intolerable and at cross-purposes with good reading and good writing.

And yet, while all these motivations for Nabokov's hostility are to the point, and, in all likelihood, contributed to his resistance and resentment, there seems to be a more fundamental reason for this hostility. Whatever Nabokov's familiarity with Freud's work ultimately was, what one easily gleans from his remarks on the question is that what most infuriates him is the idea of a system of psychic substitutions. Thomas Frosch astutely observes that "ultimately, we have to understand Nabokov's anti-Freudianism in the context of a hatred for allegory and symbolism in general" (Frosch, 43). Nabokov represents Freud's vision of the world as not only sexually perverted and socially deranged, but also as denying the particular detail its rights. When examined within the context of Nabokov's remarks on art his remarks on Freud appear perfectly consistent. Readers have understandably tended to slip on the glaze of his remarks, chosen sides with or against Nabokov, and, within a few pages, have generally forgotten the whole business.[18] Such taking sides has not, however, led to clarity on the question and has tended to occlude the fact that what Nabokov so strenuously objects to is the violence done to the particularity of perceptual life and the particularity of his own literary works by the generalizing system which, for him, is psychoanalysis. Like Michel Foucault, Nabokov would reproach less psychoanalysis's failure to be or become a science (pace Karl Popper's critique of the unverifiability of psychoanalysis's hypotheses), than its very pretension to be a science, its aspiration to function in the realm of the human sciences as would a natural science—as a totalizing, unifying discourse.[19]

Now that its terms and sources somewhat more clear we can ask whether Nabokov's implicit virulent criticism is justified or not. As concerns the

18. This tendency is best seen in Green's *Freud and Nabokov*, which ends: "These were two great men, two great achievements, two great writers" (Green, 116). It might be noted that all of the influential first-generation critics of Nabokov "side" with him. Stegner does so (cf. Stegner, 36), as will, a few years later, Field in denouncing psychoanalysis's "slavish" following of doctrine (cf. Field 1967, 264). Appel will continue in this same line, but most extreme in this respect is Boyd, who goes to some lengths to insult Freud, as well as Jacques Lacan (cf. Boyd 1990, 91, 260; Boyd 1991, 435; and, where psychoanalysis seems to be intimately identified with "postmodernists," Boyd 1999, 3). Green is certainly justified in noting: "What needs to be faced is the extent to which Nabokov's readers are reluctant to depart from the mode of reading he prescribed for them and to what degree this may be a perceived filial obligation" (Green 1988, 4).

19. Though their approach could hardly be more different from Nabokov's, Gilles Deleuze and Félix Guattari's critique of psychoanalysis in their two-volume *Capitalism and Schizophrenia* objects to precisely this same element of Freud's thought. Just as does Nabokov, Deleuze and Guattari reproach psychoanalysis

question of the importance accorded to individual images, details, sensations, or perceptions, Freud's case is a difficult—and strange—one. In his writing—above all in his case histories—there is fantastic attention paid to the most minute and seemingly derisory detail of his patients' lives. And yet, this attention to the individual detail is coupled with a tireless drive to interpret those details within psychic schemas that would be common to groups ranging in size from metropolitan Vienna to all of humanity. As Nabokov's charge is made in the name of art, the question can be asked with more precision on its grounds. To this end, let us take the most artistic example Freud offered: his analysis of the unhappy peace Leonardo da Vinci struck with his desires. Freud was to refer to this work in a letter to Lou Andreas-Salomé ten years after its publication as "the only beautiful thing I have ever written," and beautiful or not it is likely a case that Nabokov would have had at least passing familiarity with (cf. Freud and Andreas-Salomé, 90). In this imaginary case history, Freud centers his analysis around a memory which Leonardo relates from earliest childhood in which a bird—according to Freud, a vulture—lands upon the edge of the young Leonardo's cradle and parts his lips with its tail feathers. In German, as in Italian, the word for tail (*Schwanz* in German, *coda* in Italian) is often used to refer to the male sexual organ. Freud finds it highly improbable that the memory in question is in fact a memory and declares it instead (on scant but plausible evidence) a "fantasy"—and then reveals to his readers another "fantasy" lurking behind it: "fellatio." In an effort to contravene the skepticism he anticipates from his reader, Freud writes that "like any psychic creation, like a dream, a vision, or a hallucination, such a fantasy must have a meaning" (Freud 11:86; translation modified). This remark perfectly reflects Freud's vision of the particular detail. On the one hand, we find an intense and intelligent suspicion that *everything* in the world merits inspection and reflection.[20] On the other, as every dream or act must have a meaning other than itself, the details culled from inspection and reflection are translated into the terms of general schemas which cannot do justice to those particulars Nabokov treasured.

Three years after Freud published his study of Leonardo, Freud's fellow analyst Oskar Pfister published a work with the mesmerizing title "Cryptolalia, Cryptographia, and the Unconscious Visual Puzzle in Normal Individuals"

---

for funneling a multiplicity of symptoms into a limited number of set syndromes (Oedipus, incest, etc.). Cf., on this question, *Capitalism and Schizophrenia*, vol. 1: *Anti-Oedipus* and the chapter "One or More Wolves" in vol. 2: *A Thousand Plateaus*).

20. Of a detail, Freud states elsewhere: "It is only a trifle [eine Kleinigkeit] out of which anyone other than a psychoanalyst would make nothing. . . . The psychoanalyst, however, thinks differently: for him nothing is too trifling [klein] to be an expression of concealed psychic operations [Äußerung verborgener seelischer Vorgänge]" (Freud 1968–78, 8:190).

wherein he claimed to have discovered in Leonardo's painting *Virgin and Child with St. Anne and a Lamb* the hidden form of a vulture in the folds of Mary's dress, which vulture, following Pfister, became visible when one turned the painting on its side. Freud wrote in the margin of his edition of Pfister's study: "a remarkable discovery has been made. . . . in the picture that represents the artist's mother, the vulture, the symbol of motherhood, is perfectly visible."[21] For most, however, this form has been anything but "perfectly visible." What is more important: there is every reason for it *not* to be.

This is because Freud, in his most ambitious attempt at understanding the mind of an artist in light of his revolutionary theories, fell prey to an error of detail. He bases the better part of his analysis on the bird in question being a vulture (*Geier*). "The key to all of Leonardo's accomplishments and misfortunes," says Freud, "lies hidden in the infantile fantasy about the vulture" (Freud, 11:136). The bird in question is, however, not a *vulture* but a *kite* (*nibbio* in Leonardo's Italian). Though Freud quotes the original in his text (and was relatively fluent in Italian), he unaccountably bases his translation on a German translation of a Russian novel that integrates Leonardo's Italian text into its plot. This error greatly weakens Freud's argument as kites are significantly smaller, look much different, and, more importantly, are *not* the bird the Egyptians used in their hieroglyph for "mother," *not* the bird believed in European folklore of the Middle Ages to be exclusively of female sex, *not* the bird believed to be inseminated by the wind, and thus *not* the bird cited by the Church Fathers in association with the Virgin Birth. Though Freud's error was pointed out as early as 1923, neither Freud nor those close to him ever publicly acknowledged it (cf. Maclagan).

It is, however, not the only one of its kind. In a respectful essay full of praise for Freud's acumen in psychological matters, Meyer Schapiro noted that the reader of this strange childhood memory can explain, or begin to explain, much in it by simpler and more coherent means. The passage with the cradle-visiting kite in question is to be found on the reverse of a page in Leonardo's notebooks concerned with the study of the flight of birds. Numerous birds are mentioned and drawn therein, but more than any other is the one that Leonardo felt best allowed one to observe the mechanics of flight—the kite (cf. Schapiro, 150–152). This might explain why Leonardo's imagination would have been occupied with the kite—but why he might have suddenly remembered—or, as Freud claims, fantasized, about a crib-side visitation remains a mystery. To answer this question, Schapiro turns to the convention in classical biography

21. Cf. Oskar Pfister, "*Kryptolalie, Kryptographie und Unbewusster Vexierbild bei Normalen*"; cf. also Freud 1968–78, 8:187–188.

of animals visiting gifted men in their cribs, and such visitations were to be found in texts which related the lives of those whom Leonardo saw as his great forebears in the arts and sciences. Cicero relates the legend of bees settling on Plato's lips and thereby anticipating the future sweetness of his speech. Pausanias relates this same swarming and settling of bees upon the infant lips of Pindar. In other legends, ants filled the mouth of the greedy baby Midas with grains of wheat as he slept, and a nightingale was said to have alighted on the mouth of the infant lyric-poet-to-be, Stesichorus.[22]

What is more, still other elements of Freud's account allow for simpler and more coherent explanation. Eric Maclagan, an English student of the Renaissance who was the first to point out Freud's translational error, also noted the looseness of another important link in his argumentative chain. Freud notes how Leonardo, in cold, and even parsimonious fashion, recorded in his diary the expenses for his mother's funeral and uses this detail to buttress his vision of Leonardo's sexuality. And yet, as Maclagan points out, the burial in question was in all probability not for Leonardo's mother, but for his servant (Maclagan, 54–57). Another pivotal point in Freud's biographical reconstruction, the idea that Leonardo was adopted by his illegitimate father only three years after his father's marriage, is contradicted in a French study of Leonardo's life which Freud himself owned and made notations in (Spector, 58; cf. Gay, 273).

To turn from personal to public history, Freud set great weight upon Leonardo's choice and manner of depicting St. Anne, Mary and the Christ Child. The reasons for this choice of subject are, however, perhaps not as mysterious as Freud suggests. Schapiro notes that in 1494 (that is, shortly before Leonardo began work on the first sketches for the painting), St. Anne's cult received new attention through a much-discussed work by a German abbot (entitled *Tractatus de Laudibus Sanctissimae Annae*), and that in that same year Pope Alexander VI issued an indulgence for those who recited a prayer to Anne and Mary while bowing before an image of Anne, Mary, and the Christ Child. Such prayers were to be rewarded with relief from ten thousand years of punishment in purgatory for mortal sins, and twenty thousand years for venial sins (cf. Schapiro, 160). That Leonardo would have undertaken a painting of Anne, Mary, and the Christ Child at this time need not then be explained by psychic turmoil and the experience of having had two mothers as the demands of the market offer a perfectly coherent explanation.[23]

22. All instances cited by Schapiro (cf. Schapiro, 153).

23. As concerns, the body positioning, Schapiro cites precedents in a Dürer completed before 1500 and a Cranach from 1509 where Anne and Mary sit on the same bench and Anne's face seems younger than Mary's. This latter fact need not so surprise Freud, observes Schapiro, as it was a convention of the time to represent age and degree of authority by varying size and level of the figures rather than by signs

What should interest us here is less the number of Freud's errors than their cause. More than anything else, this seems to lie in Freud having reached his conclusions about Leonardo's character *before* coming across the childhood memory upon which he based his analysis. In a letter to Jung from October 1909 (several months before Freud began research for the essay in question), Freud wrote: "the mystery of Leonardo da Vinci's character has suddenly become clear to me. This would then be the first step into the biographical. The biographical material is, however, so slight that I despair of being able to make my convictions clear to others" (Freud and Jung, 255). As he had already arrived at his theory, the details later amassed remained ever secondary—and he correspondingly went to no great effort in analyzing them for and as they were.

In other domains, Freud's ready memory, precise observational skills, his erudition, and his taste for exploring and unlocking difficult riddles and rebuses would not have failed to interest Nabokov. But as concerns the arts, as concerns seeing life in and for its precious details, Freud was, for him, nothing less than a danger. And yet, there is a final irony in Nabokov's attacks on Freud as prophet and promulgator of the general. In vilifying Freud, Nabokov followed only the most general lines of attack. He never criticized Freud for such things as misunderstanding or misapplying the insights of those who came before him, and his strictures are, in truth, never particular. And so if Freud were indeed to choose someday to rail at Nabokov from beyond the grave, he might find no better grounds for doing so than that his antagonist too fell prey to the ever-present and ever-powerful seductions of the general.

Fellow Generalists: Marx and Darwin

In *The Gift*, (fictional) Fyodor researches and writes, for the purpose of "firing practice," a biography of the (real) materialist Chernyshevsky. To help us understand the latter, he cites a passage from Marx's *Holy Family*. To make Marx's observations "less boring," he puts them into blank verse (*Gift*, 244–245).

Nabokov held Marx in much the same esteem he held Freud—and not simply because he found him boring. As with Freud and Freudians, Nabokov disliked Marx and Marxists because of what he saw therein as a dangerous tendency

---

of age (Schapiro, 163). Schapiro, cruel in his philological kindness, finally notes that Leonardo's smile, that, for Freud, of his mysterious mother, is not unsimilar to many a smile from Verrocchio, with whom Leonardo studied and lived from an early age and who was a friend of Leonardo's father (Schapiro, 165).

towards generalization—one where "Wealth and Work emit Wagnerian thunder in their predetermined parts" (*BS*, 73). That this privileging of the general over the particular led, for Nabokov, to an insensitivity to works of art is stressed by a passage from his lecture on Flaubert where in trying to clarify the meaning of the word *bourgeois* he offers a neat summary of its parallel parts: "Marx would have called Flaubert a bourgeois in the politico-economic sense and Flaubert would have called Marx a bourgeois in the spiritual sense; and both would have been right, since Flaubert was a well-to-do gentleman in physical life and Marx was a philistine in his attitude towards the arts" (*LL*, 127). While this is rather unfair—Marx was, in point of fact, fairly sensitive in his attitude towards the arts, and was singularly wary about making hasty connections between the structure of economic life and the superstructure of art (the reason he was unable to write the study of Balzac's works he had planned)—it clearly enough expresses Nabokov's view of the artistic effects of Marx and Marxism.

While references in Nabokov's writings to Marx and his followers are fewer than those to Freud and his, the tone and the critique are essentially the same.[24] In a letter to Wilson from 1940, Nabokov proclaims, "without its obscurities and abracadabra, without its pernicious reticences, shamanic incantations and magnetic trash, Marxism is not Marxism" (*NWL*, 31). Marxism is thus inseparable from its conservatism ("pernicious reticences"), its primitive, or even mystic, ideology ("shamanic incantations"), and its clanking materialism ("magnetic trash"). In *Speak, Memory* Nabokov notes: "there is in every child the essentially human urge to reshape the earth, to act upon a friable environment (unless he is a born Marxist or a corpse and meekly waits for the environment to fashion *him*)" (*SM*, 302; Nabokov's italics). Marxists are thus, in Nabokov's view, the meekest and most accepting of creatures: they are passive shapes, not active shapers.

Fyodor's materialist Chernyshevsky is motivated by "a love of generalities . . . and a contemptuous hatred of particularities" (*Gift*, 240).[25] His ineptitude and insensitivity are seen to flow directly—and ironically—from his doctrine:

> Chernyshevski explained: "We see a tree; another man looks at the same object. We see by the reflection in his eyes that his image of the tree looks exactly the same

---

24. As to the question of familiarity, Nabokov was intimately familiar with Marx through research preparatory to chapter 4 of his novel *The Gift*. It should be noted, however, that in discussing the Soviet Union, Nabokov often conflates Marx with Lenin, and the latter, for reasons not very difficult to imagine, is treated with every bit the contempt with which Marx and Freud are treated. For one example, cf. an unfavorable comparison from *Strong Opinions*: "Lenin's life differs from, say James Joyce's as much as a handful of gravel does from a blue diamond, although both men were exiles in Switzerland and both wrote a vast number of words" (*SO*, 118–119).

25. Years later, *Pale Fire*'s vulgar and homicidal Gradus, a notch down the moral scale, is said to have "worshiped general ideas . . . with pedantic aplomb. The generality was godly, the specific diabolical"

as our tree. Thus we all see objects as they really exist." All this wild rubbish has its own private hilarious twist: the materialists' constant appeals to trees is especially amusing because they are all so badly acquainted with nature, particularly with trees. That tangible object which according to Chernyshevski "acts more strongly than the abstract concept of it" . . . is simply beyond their ken. . . . Chernyshevksi did not know the difference between a plow and the wooden *soha*; he confused beer with Madeira; he was unable to name a single wild flower except the wild rose; and it is characteristic that this deficiency of botanical knowledge was immediately made up by a "generalization" when he maintained with the conviction of an ignoramus that "they [the flowers of the Siberian taiga] are all just the same as those which bloom all over Russia!" There lurks a secret retribution in the fact that he who had constructed his philosophy on a basis of knowing the world was now placed, naked and alone, amidst the bewitched, strangely luxuriant, and still incompletely described nature of northeast Siberia: an elemental, mythological punishment which had not been taken into account by his human judges (*Gift*, 243–244).

God punishes for not looking closely at his creation. In *Bend Sinister*, the book's revolutionaries-cum-fascists "relied entirely upon generalizations and [were] quite incapable of noting, say, the wallpaper in a chance room or talking intelligently to a child" (*BS*, 79). The product of Marxism and materialism is, for Nabokov, a conservatism and a passivity where the particular details of the world are lost in the sea of intoxicating generalities.[26]

To this elite company of reviled generalizers should be added Charles Darwin. In 1941, Nabokov worked on, and eventually discarded, a paper he announced as an attack on Darwin's ideas on the evolution of protective camouflaging markings. The drafts for the paper did not survive, but as Nabokov himself noted, a passage from it did, woven into the narrative fabric of *Speak, Memory* (in the chapter devoted, appropriately, to butterflies). Contrary to expectations,

---

(*PF*, 152). In this same work, the not-always-unreliable annotator Charles Kinbote offers his readers a chromatico-political representation of the general and specific in Nabokov's ravaged homeland: "Ideas in modern Russia are machine-cut blocks coming in solid colors; the nuance is outlawed" (*PF*, 243).

26. Cutting against the grain of Nabokov's rejection of an "overconcern with class or race" in literary matter are several recent readings of *Lolita* (*SO*, 101). Mizruchi has related Humbert's travels and travails to the collective historical trauma of the Holocaust and added to it a critique of consumer culture and the objectification of American class relations (with explicit reference to Horkheimer and Adorno) in her "*Lolita* in History" (2003). Steven Belletto's analysis of the role of race—primarily "through imagistic associations and verbal pairings" in *Lolita*—takes up the other half of Nabokov's interdiction (cf. Belletto, 16). Belletto's conclusion as concerns a reading of *Lolita* is that "Nabokov evokes images of miscegenated blood and racial difference to further distance his authorial presence from Humbert's poisoned perspective" (Belletto, 1).

it contains nothing one might be tempted to call a scientific explanation for Nabokov's assertion that the elaborate designs and self-protective mimicry of many butterflies go beyond the bounds of the utilitarian. What one finds is a simple championing of the "nonutilitarian delights" Nabokov claims to perceive in "Nature" (*SM*, 125). What is given therein to be understood is that the Creator in creating this world not only employed the Newtonian necessities of a mechanistically functioning world, but also gave expression to a demiurgic *aesthetic* sense: nature for art's sake. I will return to this question, and to Nabokov's reading of Darwin, later (in relation to the question of *deception*). For the moment, let it suffice to note Nabokov's remarks on Darwin in the context they occur in: Nabokov objects to Darwin's general, in his eyes, excessively utilitarian view of nature.

Freud, Marx, and Darwin are all branded by Nabokov as being universalizing, generalizing, systematizing thinkers—founders of systems whose structures of interpretation strip the particular detail of its individual color and particular fire. All three authors are presented as thinkers who interest themselves in the particular only inasmuch as that particular represents a generality: the unconscious, the superstructure, natural selection. In the cases of all three figures, Nabokov's defense of the detail will oppose itself to all systems of thought, no matter their explicatory power, which would tend to negate or minimize particular details, which would tend to see in the detail the rule, not the exception. It is for this reason that no member of the reviled triumvirate of generalizers is reproached on his own ground, no alternative models are presented, no sustained critiques are offered, and no intimate familiarity with the discourse from which the works spring is demonstrated: for example, Nabokov does not reproach Marx for misusing or misunderstanding the insights of Ricardo and Smith, Freud for misinterpreting the import of Fechner and Charcot, or Darwin the theories of Lamarck or the flights of his birds. In a very real sense, Freud and Marx (and, to a lesser extent, Darwin) are only examined, and are only condemned, for the *generality* of their discourses. They are *generally* condemned for their tendency to judge generally, for the fact that their systems could never hope to do justice to the fine particularity of perceptual life, and can thus only ever offer the blinding lie of a worldview.

Scholium: Freud's Followers

The tendency toward generalization that Nabokov noted is a phenomenon more familiar from works of psychoanalytical literary criticism than from Freud's own writings. For this reason Nabokov will ride his anti-Freud hobbyhorse with more energy starting around the time (in the 1960s) when critical studies, and, amongst them, psychoanalytical studies, of his work begin to appear. In the first monograph on Nabokov, Stegner writes that "it is really the popular version of the psychopathologist's interpretation of the conscious and subconscious world, made into a religious cult by confused and unhappy pseudo-intellectuals, that Nabokov deplores" (Stegner, 36). That many patients who seek out psychoanalytical therapy are indeed "unhappy" is obviously the case (it is indeed the point), and to group both practitioners and patients as such is not only unfounded, but irrelevant. Nevertheless, and however excessive the terms employed, Stegner is right to see that "it is really the popular version" of psychoanalysis that Nabokov most "deplores." This is on clear display in the objections he published to a chapter in Rowe's *Nabokov's Deceptive World* (1971) that treats of sexual symbols. "The fatal flaw in Mr. Rowe's treatment of recurrent words, such as 'garden' or 'water,'" Nabokov tells us, "is his regarding them as abstractions, and not realizing that the sound of a bath being filled, say, in the world of *Laughter in the Dark*, is as different from the limes rustling in the rain of *Speak, Memory* as the Garden of Delights in *Ada* is from the lawns in *Lolita*" (SO, 36). The seeker of symbols, for Nabokov, will conflate the dissimilar and miss the distinctiveness of the detail—and psychoanalysis gives special direction to this quest for symbols and is thus to be combated.

A much different view of the situation—and of Nabokov's antipathy—is to be found in Rorty, who informs us that "Freud was the one person Nabokov resented in the same obsessive and intense way that Heidegger resented Nietzsche. In both cases, it was resentment of the precursor who may already have written all one's best lines" (Rorty, 153–154). Rorty's statement is not borne out by the facts. Heidegger not only shared Nietzsche's language and vocation, he saw himself as the follower and the fulfiller of Nietzsche's epochal project. This would indeed not prevent Heidegger from nurturing an "obsession," expressing "resentment," or from thinking that Nietzsche had written all his best lines, but things stand differently with the other half of Rorty's comparison.

As we saw above, Nabokov and Freud have little in common. The greatest convergence of interest between the two writers is the importance both accorded to impressions from earliest childhood (which Rorty does not mention). The treatment and significance accorded to those impressions is, however, without anything one would be tempted to call similarity. They do not share language, vocation, interests, or aims. The relation of Nabokov to Freud is, in fact, far less of the order of a "precursor who may already have written all one's best lines," than that of another, perhaps equally important, kind of precursor: one who would have so totally misunderstood those lines.[27]

Rorty's claim is exaggerated—or, at least, insufficiently developed. But in the prominent place it ascribes to Freud it pales in comparison to Harold Bloom's treatment of the same topic. Bloom tells us that Nabokov's "loathing of Freud reduces[28], I think, to a fear of meaning, to a need to defend against over-determined sense" (Bloom, *Nabokov's Lolita*, 2). Bloom is certainly right that Nabokov's loathing is motivated by "a need to defend against over-determined sense," the only question is whether this stems from what Bloom calls a "fear of meaning" or what Nabokov insists is a defense of meaning. On the next page Bloom proclaims Freud "the greatest of modern knowers," and announces that "rejecting Freud is not a possible option in our time, that the whole of part two of *Lolita* is an involuntary repetition of *Beyond the Pleasure Principle*" and expresses his regret that Quilty didn't kill Humbert, which, he suggests, "would have made a better end" (Bloom, *Nabokov's Lolita*, 3, 4). Bloom then notes the "curious revenge of the Freudian death drive upon Nabokov's Humbert" (Bloom, *Nabokov's Lolita*, vii),[29] and sketches a reading of *Lolita* in which Part II of Nabokov's work is a "Freudian allegory" wherein Humbert is Eros and Quilty Thanatos. In his *Anxiety of Influence* Bloom had written how "it is sad to observe most modern critics observing [Milton's] Satan, because they never do observe him. [There is] Eliot who speaks of 'Milton's curly haired Byronic hero' (one wants to reply, looking from side to side: 'Who?') . . ." (Cf. Bloom 1997, 23). At this point in Bloom's description of *Lolita*, the same gesture and question seem in order.

Bloom's remarks here not only cast detail to the wind, they are not in any real sense discursive. He does not support or expand upon the statements cited above, so that if we endeavor to match the details of the plot to his exegeses of its inner meaning, we are left to think, for instance, that the "curious revenge" that Humbert suffers at the hands of the Freudian death drive is, in terms of the book's plot, simply his own death and the drive he takes to it. This is surely not what Bloom wished to convey—what *did* he then wish to convey?

27. Though this is something that Rorty does not discuss, there is a strong possibility that Freud believed that Nietzsche had already written all of *his* best lines—something that Freud was not unaware of and which motivated his refusal to reread Nietzsche later in life, or to approve of projected psycho-analytical analyses of Nietzsche proposed by his students.

28. Bloom repeats his remarks verbatim in a volume he edited that same year on Nabokov's work as a whole (rather than simply *Lolita*) and therein corrects the "recues" of the first version to "reduces."

29. One finds this remark also repeated verbatim in the editor's note to the Chelsea House volume from the same year dedicated to Nabokov (cf. Bloom, *Vladimir Nabokov*, vii).

As Bloom well knew, Freud's death drive, his strangest invention, is not conceived of to explain an individual or cultural running-towards-ruin, but was a *hypothesis* meant to account for a fundamental tendency towards dissolution Freud thought observable in unicellular life, and for which he thought he had found a parallel in human psychology. This is what he expresses in no uncertain terms in the *Beyond the Pleasure Principle* Bloom finds *Lolita* condemned to repeat. The parallel in question is that, so it seemed to Freud, just as on the unicellular level this dispersing or dissolving force needed to be countered by another force to hold it in check, so too did a parallel and opposed force exist within the human psyche to counterbalance a drive lurking therein that would tend towards disintegration and dispersal. Despite its wild sound, Freud's formula did not denote an inner Siren song enticing one towards self-destruction, but, first and foremost, a *biological* force conceived of on an analogy with an—as it turns out, inexistent—property of unicellular life. It could thus take "curious revenge" on, precisely, no one. In a much different work written five years later, Bloom demonstrates an awareness of this fact, telling his reader that "the death drive, while wonderfully suggestive, is either an illusion or a delusion, as is the unconscious or any other major Freudian trope" (Bloom 1992, 35). In this earlier essay, however, the death drive is neither "an illusion" nor "a delusion"—and it is taking its revenge. It is, however, assimilated to nothing, at least in what Bloom chose to set down on paper, other than the fact of human death and, *perhaps*, the presence of violence in society. Humbert, as has many a would-be moralist, wishes to be tried, judged, and punished. Which, indeed, is not the same thing as an organic will-towards-disintegration situated on the biological level of preconsciousness.

If we imagine that Bloom was referring to Freud's celebrated "repetition compulsion," which Freud goes so far as to compare in a passage from *Beyond the Pleasure Principle* to a "destiny compulsion," then the image becomes somewhat clearer (cf. Freud 1968–78, 13:22). The repetition in question might then be seen as Humbert's initial love for Annabel compulsively repeated in his love for Lolita. Though they are closely related in his thought, repetition compulsion and the death drive are, for Freud, not synonyms (either in *Beyond the Pleasure Principle* or elsewhere in his writing), and one cannot be made to stand in for the other. What is more, any repetition compulsion one might wish to find in *Lolita* occurs not in the Part II Bloom notes, but at the opening of Part I. By the outset of Part II, there is little talk of Annabel. Here, however, Bloom might be imagined to be referring to the consequences engendered by that compulsive repetition which in a very extended sense brings about Humbert's death. One must then note, however, that Humbert's story does not conform to the Freudian schema as Freud notes that what is *repeated* is precisely that which cannot be *remembered* (this repetition being a sort of compromise on the part of the ego which, while uncomfortable, is less so than would be a direct recollection of the repressed material—cf. Freud 1968–78, 13:16–17). Humbert, however, remembers very clearly, down to the smallest detail, his earlier, seaside love. (Incidentally, Bloom's reading seems to have not taken the fullest possible cognizance of those scenes in the book that mock such a projected Freudian scenario—as where Humbert offers a mise-en-scène of a seaside tryst with Lolita and how little the repeated surroundings aroused his desire. It is however quite possible that the entire system of Freudian provocations which Nabokov wove into his novel was what provoked Bloom in the first place.)

Resenting what he reads, Bloom punishes Nabokov for the light-heartedness, reflected in light-handedness (mannered and excessive stylistic dexterity), he finds in *Lolita*. He lauds the "sublime temporal pathos" of Proust, and sharply distinguishes it from the reductive "parodistic cunning" of Nabokov (*Nabokov's Lolita*, 2).[30] He declares himself willing to acknowledge the virtuosity of Nabokov's prose, but deems that virtuosity sterile, and, countering Hollander and Trilling,[31] feels that *Lolita*, to its detriment, is not a true "portrayal of human love"—a patent impossibility for him as all the characters are mere "caricatures" (Bloom, *Nabokov's Lolita*, 2). He then chooses the path of greatest violence by assimilating Nabokov to that which Nabokov most detested, and which Bloom most detests in Nabokov. Bloom punishes Nabokov as Dante would have: where he sinned. What better punishment might a critic profoundly influenced by Freud's thought devise than reducing Nabokov's greatest work to a simple "repetition" of a Freudian concept? And what is more, to a repetition of the darkest and most ambiguous of the lot. At the expense of a not inconsiderable incoherence, Bloom thus offers us his one-sentence formulation of the essence of the book: "rejecting Freud is not a possible option in our time, and the whole of part two of *Lolita* is an involuntary repetition of *Beyond the Pleasure Principle*" (Bloom, *Nabokov's Lolita*, 3).[32]

---

30. Bloom repeats these epithets more or less verbatim in his introduction to *Vladimir Nabokov*, 2. This is far and away the most well-founded of Bloom's criticisms.

31. Trilling famously remarked in the October 1958 issue of *Encounter*: "*Lolita* is about love. Perhaps I shall be better understood if I put the statement in this form: *Lolita* is not about sex, but about love" (Trilling 1982, 95). Trilling will note a year later that, for Freud, art is "a sort of inner dishonesty" (Trilling 1957, 44). Hollander's review was to be found in the Autumn 1956 issue of the *Partisan Review*, and was *Lolita*'s very first review (Hollander had borrowed an Olympia Press edition from Nabokov's friend Harry Levin; the review is reprinted in Page, 81–84). As concerns love and the caricatural, Bloom's judgment silently follows that of Nabokov's influential friend and anxious enemy, Edmund Wilson.

32. What might also have spurred Bloom to such dismissiveness was Nabokov's disinterest in influence. Wallace Stevens' remarks on influence, which Bloom cites at the outset of his *The Anxiety of Influence* and which his project therein is to refute, bear close resemblance to Nabokov's own (i.e. Stevens' claim as regards the influence of past poets, "I know of no one who has been particularly important to me" [cited

Bloom's case is indeed only a single one, and an extreme one. It is extreme for its terms and given the fact that, on other more favorable occasions, Bloom's erudition, insight, and commitment to patient literary exegeses have born such remarkable fruit. And it is even extreme in that Bloom has often expressed a profound wariness as concerns Freudian literary criticism (often noting, on the lines of Voltaire's quip about the Holy Roman Empire, that it is neither Freudian, literary, nor criticism). What Nabokov so disliked in Freud and Freudians was that their approach blinded them to particularity, to the particular not as a marker for some other concept, but in and for itself. And if we use Bloom's case as an exemplary one, we would not be able to say that he was entirely wrong.

Bloom 1997, 7]). Nabokov may have found himself in agreement with Bloom's concern that "politiciz-ing literary study has destroyed literary study," though one can hardly imagine him in that same text either finding a study of influence the answer to this problem (Bloom 1997, xvi).

CHAPTER NINE

LEXICOMANIA

NABOKOV'S INSISTENCE on the particularity of perception has as its natural corollary a focus on the words used to convey it. With this in mind, let us look more closely at his language.

In the preface to his finest Russian novel, Nabokov notes that the book's "heroine is not Zina, but Russian Literature" (*Gift*, ii). In the afterword to his finest English novel, he remarks: "an American critic suggested that *Lolita* was the record of my love affair with the romantic novel. The substitution 'English language' for 'romantic novel' would make this elegant formula more correct" (*AL*, 316). The "heroine" of Nabokov's greatest Russian work is thus "Russian Literature," and the real intrigue of his greatest English one is his "love affair" with the English language. It seems clear where his literary interests truly lie.

After discussing various passages with Nabokov, Michael Glenny, the English translator of Nabokov's first novel (*Mary*) labeled the writer "some kind of *lexicomaniac*" (Glenny's remark cited by Schiff, 341; my italics). Had Nabokov heard the epithet, there is every reason to think that he would have been flattered. In a letter from 1924 to the woman who would become his wife, he boasted, "I am prepared to undergo Chinese torture for the discovery of a single epithet" (cited by Schiff, 42). *The Gift*'s Fyodor, who shares many experiences and opinions with his creator, writes to his mother: "If you like I'll admit it: I myself am a mere seeker of *verbal adventures*" (*Gift*, 139; my italics). We evoked Nabokov's riddle earlier. To understand that riddle we must more clearly understand its medium—and to this end we should look more carefully and closely at his language, and at what he thought of it.

Peculiar Language

> "Well," he said, getting up, "I must be going. Good-bye, everybody. Good-bye, Ada. I guess it's your father under that oak, isn't it?"
> "No, it's an elm," said Ada.
> —Vladimir Nabokov, *Ada, or Ardor*

To describe a childhood memory in *Speak, Memory*, Nabokov wanted to note the accordion-like gangways which linked the train cars of his youth. After having sent his wife to consult "every available book on railroads," he decided upon the curious and correct "intervestibular connecting curtains" (the passage is to be found at *SM*, 144; for Nabokov's wife's search for the epithet, cf. Schiff, 135). Here, as elsewhere, there is a rigid principle at work in Nabokov's writing: *les mots justes.*

In *Invitation to a Beheading* the generalization of language is the hallmark of the nightmarish world in which Cincinnatus lives. "Those around him," says Nabokov of Cincinnatus, "understood each other at the first word, since they had no words that would end in an unexpected way . . ." (*IB*, 26). Cincinnatus will thus write:

> . . . the ancient inborn art of writing is long since forgotten . . . I myself picture all this so clearly, but you are not I, and therein lies the irreparable calamity. Not knowing how to write, but sensing with my criminal intuition [criminal in the contorted mirror of that world] how words are combined, what one must do for a commonplace word to come alive and to share its neighbor's sheen, heat, shadow, while reflecting itself in its neighbor and renewing the neighboring word in the process, so that the whole line is live iridescence; while I sense the nature of this kind of word propinquity, I am nevertheless unable to achieve it . . . (*IB*, 93).

Language, left in its habitual form, is inert, and to express the richness of perception and sensation to another, to bridge the gulf of "you are not I," one needs to combine the words of the world in such a radical and creative way that "the whole line" becomes "live iridescence." When this happens, language shrugs off its habitual *generality* and acquires a nuanced richness and individuality all its own.

To obtain the required precision and fidelity Nabokov often has recourse to peculiar perspectives like the one that pervades *Invitation to a Beheading*. In the opening paragraphs of *King, Queen, Knave* it is the station, rather than the train, which is described as departing. In *The Gift*, Fyodor significantly changes his vision of the world by tilting his body backwards (cf. KQK, 1, *Gift*, 332). Years later, Van Veen will make a secret trade of this activity in the form of his literally inverted alter ego "Mascodagama."[1] The inverted view is used, as well, for philological purposes. In his description of Joyce's changing styles in *Ulysses* Nabokov stated:

There is no special reason why this should be—why one chapter should be told straight, another through a stream-of-consciousness gurgle, a third through the prism of a parody. There is no special reason, but *it may be argued that this constant shift of the viewpoint conveys a more varied knowledge, fresh vivid glimpses from this or that side. If you have ever tried to stand and bend your head so as to look back between your knees, with your face turned upside down, you will see the world in a totally different light.* Try it on the beach. . . . Well, this trick of changing the vista, of changing the prism and the viewpoint, can be compared to Joyce's new literary technique, to the kind of new twist through which you see a greener grass, a fresher world (*LL*, 289; my italics).[2]

As was the case for Joyce, Nabokov depicts his greener grass and fresher world through peculiar perspectives and a peculiar language all his own—and this effort to render the personal, peculiar flavor of his own perception accounts, more than any other factor, for the singular strangeness of his style.[3]

1. *Mask-oh-da-gamba* (hide the legs), is what multilingual Van, while walking on his hands, does.

2. One might readily oppose this reading to that of Wilson in *Axel's Castle* where Joyce is not isolated in his visionary singularity, but aligned with other thinkers (such as Proust, Whitehead, and Einstein) attuned to a common change in the historical *air du temps* (cf. Wilson 1961, 177–178). On less personal terrain, we might also compare Nabokov's reading to that of Umberto Eco, whose analysis of *Ulysses* as an "open work" describes "the superimposition of a classical order to a world in disorder [*la sovrapposizione di un ordine classico al mondo del disordine*]" and in doing so "reveals surprising affinities with contemporary culture [*rivela sorprendenti affinità con . . . [la] cultura contemporanea*]" (Eco 1966, 102). As we saw earlier, Nabokov is not in the slightest eager to see any of his cherished works as *symptoms* of larger social, political, or historical forces—and indeed as anything other than essentially *literary* phenomena.

3. George Steiner attributes the peculiar strangeness of Nabokov's style in large part to Nabokov being, like himself, trilingual (cf. Steiner's *Extraterritorial: Papers on Literature and the Language Revolution*). This "extraterritorial" quality of Nabokov's writing, as Steiner calls it, is doubtless an important element. But just as important was Nabokov's search to be unconditionally faithful to his own vision in all its intensity and idiosyncrasy. This defamiliarization of the world offers analogies with the descriptions of the poetic function in the works of Nabokov's countrymen Viktor Shklovsky and the early Russian Formalists where the "making-strange" of poetic language is its essence.

What Nabokov valued above all in art and in life was the absolutely personal appropriation of the world—and the strangeness that accompanies such radically personal vision (opposed to the regularizing, familiarizing support of communality and which, as we saw, is best reflected in his use of the term *reality*). In *Transparent Things* Mr. R., despite his shortcomings, is designated as "a true artist" because he "fought on his own ground with his own weapons for the right to use an unorthodox punctuation corresponding to his singular thought" (*TT*, 24). When Nabokov speaks in his cloaked review of his own *Speak, Memory*, he calls the work "a unique freak as autobiographies go" ("Conclusive Evidence," 124). In *Pale Fire*, Kinbote seems to speak with his maker when he notes: "I trust the reader appreciates the strangeness of this, because if he does not, there is no sense in writing poems, or notes to poems, or anything at all" (*PF*, 207). This strangeness is found in more nuanced and more reliable form in *The Gift*'s Fyodor who relates having a "sense" of "the innate strangeness of human life" transmitted to him by his father (*Gift*, 119). For Nabokov, genius falls under the sign of the strange: "Gogol was a strange creature, but genius is always strange" (*NG*, 55).[4] In *Strong Opinions* Nabokov remarks that "true art deals not with the genus, and not even with the species, but with an aberrant individual of the species" (*SO*, 155). What interested Nabokov, in art and life, was the "unique freak," "the aberrant individual of the species"—the *peculiarity*. There is a problem, however, with expressing this peculiarity in literature and that problem is language.

General Language

In the previous chapter we saw the vehemence of Nabokov's polemic against the symbolic, the allegorical, the mythical, and the *general* as such. We would fail to fully understand this polemic if we did not follow it a step farther than Nabokov explicitly extends it. As Nabokov was well aware, the problem of the general cannot be limited to simple conventional thinking. This is for the simple reason that there is a thing more general than such thinking (which is, according to certain thinkers—such as Nabokov's much-admired Henri Bergson—the *cause* of ready-made, conventional thinking)—and that thing is language itself.

Language, as we all know and which we rarely reflect upon—with good reason—is a system of general signs. Those signs depend for their efficacy on the fact that they denote not a startlingly specific thing, sensation, or perception, but

---

4. Cf. also, "the special touch of [Gogol's] queer genius" and, "that Gogolian gusto and wealth of weird detail" (*NG*, 5, 71).

the most generalizable form of some thing, sensation, or perception. Language is a system which groups under its signs innumerable particular phenomena, but can only function on the condition that it provisionally rob those particular phenomena of their particularity. To retain or to return to such particularity requires talent and effort on the part of the writer. In a certain sense, what runs counter to the essential strangeness of the world which Nabokov saw it as his calling to reproduce is language itself.

Precision

Nabokov was obsessed with precision. In this matter, the first moments of his poetic career seem to have been decisive ones. In describing the composition of his first poem Nabokov reproaches his use of the conventional tag "memory's sting"—"which I had visualized," he says, "as the ovipositor of an ichneumon fly straddling a cabbage caterpillar, but had not dared say so" (SM, 225). Nabokov goes on to relate his subsequent realization that the poem was a banal one, and makes clear that this banality had everything to do with his not daring to say what he thought and to trust in the specificity of his image.[5] As seen in the shiny black rubber of Speak, Memory's "intervestibular connecting curtains," Nabokov learned his lesson and his later search for le mot juste is born of his earlier failure to recognize it.

In The Real Life of Sebastian Knight, Sebastian's mother "left her husband and child as suddenly as a rain-drop starts to slide tipwards down a syringa leaf" (RLSK, 7). In the opening lines of Nabokov's second novel, we find (in the English translation Nabokov worked on with his son), "glossy red strawberries positively crying to be bitten into, all their achenes proclaiming their affinity with one own tongue's papillae," and by the time we get to Lolita we should not be surprised to find not that her prepubertal hips had yet to begin to widen, but that her "iliac crests had not yet flared" [KQK, 1; AL, 65]). Stacy Schiff relates

5. The narrator of The Defense, in relating the efforts of Luzhin, never particularly elegant in verbal expression (though elegance itself in the world of chess thought), to express his childhood recollections, says that, "there were simply no grown-up words for his childish impressions" (Defense, 164). This might be taken as an axiom for Nabokov's world in general. Art in large part is the molding and sculpting of grown-up words into mobile and vivid expressions. The narrator notes a few pages later of Luzhin that "his speech was clumsy and full of shapeless, ridiculous words—but in it there sometimes quivered a mysterious intonation hinting at some other kind of words, which were living and charged with subtle meaning, but which he could not utter" (Defense, 167–168). This "other kind of words" corresponds to the words of the author (half-sensed by his creation): the words of art painstakingly made to burst into vivid life, to form a language which might compare with the vividness, fire and magic of "childish impressions."

Nabokov's advice to a young writer: "memorize the names for everything"—an injunction which obviously included "ovipositor," "achenes," "papillae," and "iliac."

As a matter of taste, Nabokov preferred the obscure to the invented epithet. To invent words was, for him, only permissible in cases where there really was no word to name that thing—and he went to considerable lengths to verify this. But this conservatism knew limits. Inasmuch as the vocabulary existed, Nabokov respected it—but as to the company he placed it in and the contortions he put it through, he was far from conservative. In speaking of Sebastian Knight, his brother refers to the "the terrific vigor of his literary style," and cites Sebastian's proclamation of "innate distrust of what I feel easy to express" (*RLSK*, 5, 25). Nabokov clearly shared this inborn distrust and, like Sebastian, "had no use for ready-made phrases because the things he wanted to say were of an exceptional build and he knew moreover that no real idea can be said to exist without the words made to measure" (*RLSK*, 82). Nabokov's verbal clothes were made from the fabric of the language as he found it—but special tailoring was always required.

And it is this sort of tailoring which Nabokov asked of others. In his book on Gogol, he talks of how the latter went beyond "the hackneyed combinations of blind noun and dog-like adjective that Europe had inherited from the ancients" (*NG*, 86).[6] With pedagogic intent, Nabokov wrote his younger brother Kirill about the latter's poetry, advising him, "as a general rule," to "try to find new combinations of words (not for the sake of this novelty, but because every person sees things in an individual way and must find *his own* words for them)" (*SL*, 8; Nabokov's italics). In an unpublished letter to his mother, Nabokov writes of this same brother's poetry that he saw therein only "parlor metaphysics" which "has not the least relation to life, to poetry—to real birds and real roses" (letter from February 1931; cited by Boyd 1990, 362). In *Bend Sinister*, the greatest contempt is reserved to those who "prefer ideas to words" (*BS*, 107). As we can see, what literature, according to Nabokov, must strive for at all costs is not simply to present the faded roses and flightless birds which language offers every poet, but somehow to evoke "real birds and real roses," to find a magical language where they can bloom and soar. Even closer to home, in Nabokov's last work we find Vadim Vadimirovich (not always so far from Vladimir Vladimorovich Nabokov) stating of his early poetic efforts that "my instrument, however, was still too blunt and immature; it could not express

---

6. In a letter to Wilson Nabokov distinguishes himself from Conrad by saying that though the latter "knew how to handle *readymade* English better than I," Nabokov's own "verbal peaks" could not be reached by the former (*NWL*, 253).

the divine detail, and *her* eyes, *her* hair became hopelessly generalized in my otherwise well-shaped strophes" (*LATH*, 24; Nabokov's italics; my underlining). The artist must develop an instrument rich and strange enough to express *speci-ficity*: the "divine detail"—that is, "*her* eyes" and "*her* hair." From this need is born an inventive English, an English which Vadim refers to elsewhere as "an English I alone would be responsible for, in all its new ripples and changing light" (*LATH*, 124).

Magic, or Language

> It is with good reason that we speak of the magic of art and compare the artist with a magician.
>
> —Sigmund Freud, *Totem and Taboo*

Like his strangest creation, Clare Quilty, Nabokov was "versed in logodaedaly and logomancy" (*AL*, 249–250). In *The Real Life of Sebastian Knight*, Nabokov singles out the great writer by "the magic and force" of his art (*RLSK*, 94). In his *Lectures on Literature*, Nabokov instructs his students as to how they can "bask in that magic" which is a great work of art, refers to the great writer as a "magician" and "enchanter," notes that "a great writer's world" is "a magic democracy," and that an understanding of style is "a magic key" to the authors he studies (*LL*, 6, 5, 124, 113). In *Speak, Memory* Nabokov links his two trea-sured activities—literature and lepidopterology—through magic, telling how he "discovered in nature the nonutilitarian delights that [he] sought in art. Both were a form of magic, both were a game of intricate enchantment and deception" (*SM*, 125). In the afterword to *Lolita* Nabokov tells us: "I happen to be the kind of author who in starting to work on a book has no other purpose than to get rid of that book and who, when asked to explain its origin and growth, has to rely on such ancient terms as Interreaction of Inspiration and Combination—which, I admit, sounds like a *conjurer explaining one trick by performing another*." Nabokov also speaks therein of "the native illusionist" who "can magically . . . transcend the heritage in his own way" (*AL*, 311, 317; my italics). In his notes to *Eugene Onegin*, Nabokov takes us aside from our reading of Pushkin to tell us that "true art is never simple, being always an elaborate, magi-cal deception" (*EO*, 3.498). We even find figures in Nabokov's fiction like "the melancholy, extravagant, wise, witty, magical and altogether delightful Pierre Delalande, whom I invented"; and, the obscure Enricht, "alias Pharsin": a shape-shifter and master "magician" who creates the world of the novel (*IB*, 6; *KQK*, 228). Several of his novels take the form of a magic masque that the conjurer ends with a triumphant trick. Both the Russian novel *Invitation to a Beheading* and the English *Bend Sinister* end with the author entering the world of his creation and declaring that the play is at an end, that all his charms are now overthrown as he takes his protagonists "to [his] bosom" (*SL*, 50). In short, what Demon Veen calls, as we saw, "that third sight (individual, magically detailed imagination) . . ." is called for everywhere in Nabokov's work (*Ada*, 252).

The depth of Nabokov's creative and critical allegiance to magic is perhaps best attested to in a letter from 1951 to John Finley at Harvard University regarding a class Nabokov was to teach there for the coming academic year. Nabokov says of this proposed course that "[it] would deal with questions of structure . . . and imagery and magic and style" (*SL*, 120). What might surprise in such a letter to a curricular official was the use of "magic" as if it were a technical term all students in the field were familiar with. How serious is Nabokov to be taken here? What does he mean by magic? In a letter to Edmund Wilson from 1946, Nabokov remarked: "The longer I live the more I become convinced that the o n l y thing that matters in literature is the (more or less irrational) shamanstvo [shamanism] of a book, i.e., that the good writer is first of all an enchanter" (*NWL*, 177; Nabokov's letter spacing). Does this remark provide us with an answer? Is Nabokov's stress on magic simply a form of irrationalism, a way of saying that the truths of the world cannot be captured in the nets of postulates and propositions? What, in short, is language's magic, magic in language, and the magic of language?

Students of modern literature wishing to explore the relation between language and magic do not have a wealth of resources at their disposal. There is, nevertheless, a line of modern speculation about language and magic which can bring Nabokov's conception of "verbal magic" into relief. In an essay entitled "On Language As Such and the Language of Man," Walter Benjamin wrote that "mediation, which is the immediacy of all mental communication, is the fundamental problem of linguistic theory, and if one chooses to call this immediacy magic, then the primary problem of language is its magic" (Benjamin, 2:142–143). For Benjamin, as for Nabokov, language's fundamental problem is magic. Why? To borrow the terms of Benjamin's formulation: because the *Grundproblem* of the theory of language is that of its medium—and that medium is itself. The fundamental problem of language is that language cannot be rationally described except through language—which must, to borrow Nabokov's phrase, sound like a conjurer explaining one trick by performing another.

In another essay from these same years, Benjamin discussed what he called "the magical side of language" (Benjamin, 2:208). This magic side of language is language considered, strangely enough, independently of its signifying function—it is language viewed not as a medium or messenger, but as a graphic and sonic *thing*. Benjamin immediately notes that this "magical side" of language is never without relation to its "semiotic side" (the side that *signifies* various meanings). The semiotic side of language is the side that bears messages, the magical side is a much stranger and more mysterious thing—it is the side of language which seems to communicate nothing but its capricious self. Might this distinction help us better understand Nabokov's magic?

Nabokov told his students that "real verse music is not the melody of the verse.... Authentic verse music is that mystery which brims over the rational texture of the line" (quoted by Nabokov's student Hannah Green—cf. H. Green, 34). This linguistic mystery is not to be experienced independently of the meaning language carries—it is something that edges just beyond it. For Nabokov, verbal magic as he conceives of it can only be produced through the close and constant intertwining of the two sides of the sign, its semiotic (signifying) side, and its magical side (its sight and sound). Consequently, Nabokov displays distaste for writers who give themselves over to language conceived independently of its signifying function, for language in its riotous sight and sound, and not reined in by the constraints of meaning. For Nabokov, the greatest exemplar of such was the Joyce he, at other moments, so intensely admired. Joyce would refer to words as "quashed quotatoes" and "messes of mottage"—and often treated them as such. Such masses and mixtures did not, however, agree with Nabokov. In his view, after skirting this siren call of singing language in *Ulysses*, Joyce gave himself over in *Finnegans Wake* to the senseless form and flow of language. To express this in the terms Benjamin offers, Joyce's language in his final work has come unmoored from its "semiotic" side, from the side of language which offers more than wild sight and sound. In *Strong Opinions*, Nabokov states: "I detest *Finnegans Wake* in which a cancerous growth of fancy word-tissue hardly redeems the dreadful joviality of the folklore and the easy, too easy, allegory" (*SO*, 102). He described the work elsewhere as a "petrified superpun" and "a formless and dull mass" (*LL*, 122; *SO*, 71). In this same vein, Nabokov wrote to his wife in 1936 of how, "in these new things" of Joyce's," by which he meant the *Work in Progress* which was to become *Finnegans Wake*, "the abstract puns, the verbal masquerade, the shadows of words, the diseases of words" make for a whole which "in the end sinks behind reason, and, while it is setting, the sky is ravishing, but then there is night" (cited by Boyd 1990, 425). The ravishing sky and sinking reason is the same that a number of *Work in Progress*'s most impassioned partisans saw in it, though, of course, with a far different valorization. In Beckett's early essay on Joyce (his first published work), "Dante ... Bruno ... Vico ... Joyce," he informs his, and Joyce's, readers that if they don't understand *Work in Progress* it is not because they are too simple, that they are insufficiently literate or cultivated, but that they're not simple *enough*, that they have become *too* literate and *too* cultivated and that the best way to read the work is by letting oneself *feel* the primal, primitive, illogical magic that the *Work*, according to Beckett, works to evoke. If Nabokov was familiar with the argument, he was not convinced.

Whatever the accuracy of Nabokov's observations about Joyce, his own "verbal magic," his wordplay and wordcraft are in any event more confined, more centripetal than Joyce's titanic dispersion. Such verbal magic as Nabokov practices is a trick of another sort—it is a sleight of mind that allows for any and all combinations and contortions of language on the condition that this *magical* side of language, to employ Benjamin's terminology, not unmoor itself form the *semiotic* side. For all his whimsicality and magical dexterity, Nabokov keeps the magic side of language on a tight leash. For him, a magic trick in language is not merely a sensual explosion of sight, sound, and color, but necessarily involves anticipating and playing upon the expectations of meaning. For Nabokov, the simple giving way to this *magical* side of language leads to nothing grander than the inarticulate logorrhea of Joyce's last work.

Benjamin's theory brings us thus very close to Nabokov's conception of verbal magic, but differs in an essential respect. For Benjamin, the "magic side of language" is language seen or imagined as independent of its signifying function. For Nabokov, "verbal magic" relies not only upon the graceful, barely perceptible oscillation between two meanings (the pun), but also on the graceful, barely perceptible oscillation between two realms of language: those which Benjamin called the semiotic and the magical. For Nabokov, language is magical when and where its meaning fits snugly in its sight and sound. In this, as it seems in many things, Nabokov was an "indivisible monist" (*SO*, 85; cf. also *SO*, 124).[7]

---

7. Wood talks of seeing at times in Nabokov "a writer who cannot hear a word as saying only one thing if there is a chance that it can be got to say more, by whatever contortions of tongue or syntax. Of course, Nabokov is only dabbling in what was the delirious method of *Finnegans Wake*, but the spirit is the same. A commitment to puns, even to lame or laboured puns, signals a language haunted by meanings far in excess of the one in front of us. This is not exactly Benjamin's 'pure language', but there is a philosophical implication here, something like Wittgenstein's 'Whatever we see could be other than it is'. Everything we say is shadowed by a crowd of ghosts, speaking our own language or others. Language, even the most brilliant language, is a kind of shortfall of reason, a leap into graphic or phonetic chaos, the beginning of a story which loves nonsense, but not only nonsense, and (probably) has no end" (Wood, 211). Wood's remark here shows a rare sensitivity to this aspect of Nabokov's writing. Nabokov is indeed "only dabbling" in "the delirious method of *Finnegans Wake*," but we should also recall the contempt in which Nabokov held Joyce's "method" in that work: as merely the surrealistic stutter or babble of a genius carried away by sight and sound.

CHAPTER TEN

THE FINE FABRIC OF DECEIT

. . . but perhaps the most fascinating of all was the fine fabric of deceit . . .
—Vladimir Nabokov, *The Gift*

Deception

ONE OF NABOKOV'S STUDENTS from his lecture class at Cornell relates the following anecdote:

"I want you to copy this down exactly as I draw it on the blackboard," Vladimir Nabokov instructed us, after explaining that he was going to diagram the themes of *Bleak House*. He turned to the blackboard, picked up a piece of chalk, and scrawled "the theme of inheritances" in a weird arching loop. "The theme of generations" dipped and rose and dipped in an undulating line. "The theme of social consciousness" wiggled crazily toward the other lines, then veered sharply away.

Nabokov turned from the blackboard and peered over the rims of his glasses, parodying a professorial twinkle. "I want you to be sure to copy this exactly as I draw it."

After consulting a sheet of paper on the lectern, he turned back to the blackboard and scrawled "The theme of poverty," "the theme of political (chalk snapped under the pressure, he picked up another piece and continued) protest," "the theme of social environment"—all leaping and dipping wildly across the blackboard. Some people simply can't draw a straight line.

Again he peered at us, over his shoulder and over his glasses, in silent reminder to copy this "exactly." And finally he scrawled the last "theme" in a neat dipping curve, a half-moon on its side, "the theme of art"—and we suddenly realized he had drawn a cat's face, the last line its wry smile . . ." (Wetzsteon).

This anecdote illustrates Nabokov's disdain for the study of art as a means of social and political analysis. It tells, however, more—and more even than the student who relates it makes explicit. This added element is the allusion Nabokov's illusion conceals. Nabokov's drawing of art's smile mirrors one of the most famous smiles in English Literature—that of Lewis Carroll's Cheshire Cat. In Carroll's work, which Nabokov had translated into Russian in his youth, the cat's smile is the thing visible when the rest of its body has already disappeared. In Nabokov's inversion, it is the smile which arrives last—and thereby confers a form and a meaning on the preceding. And the meaning in this case is that "the theme of art" is one which is inseparable from the deception which is part of its form.

The Gift's Fyodor remarks that "the most enchanting things in nature and art are based on deception" (*Gift*, 364). The generally misguided Hermann of Nabokov's *Despair* states that "every work of art is a deception" (*Despair*, 178). In this same *Despair*, whose working title was "Notes of a Hoaxer," we find a declaration of purpose as the deceptive—and frequently deceived—narrator states: "Tum-tee-tum. And once more—TUM! I have not gone mad. I am merely producing gleeful little sounds. The kind of glee one experiences upon making an April fool of someone. And a damned good fool I *have* made of someone. Who is he? Gentle reader, look at yourself in the mirror" (*Despair*, 24; Nabokov's italics).

Nabokov's remarks on art swarm with references to mirrors, games, disguises, magic, and the virtues of dissimulation. At a 1943 reading at Wellesley of his short story "The Assistant Producer," he remarked that he liked "to lure the reader this way and that and then tickle him behind the ear just to see him whirl around" (Boyd 1991, 71). In all of Nabokov's critical and fictional works deception is imperative. In *Strong Opinions*, Nabokov states that "a good combination should always contain a certain element of deception"; that "art at its greatest is fantastically deceitful and complex"; that "all art is deception and so is nature" (*SO*, 12, 11, 12).[1] In the same interview from which these remarks come, Nabokov continues his speculations by integrating them into a myth of the origin of poetry. After asking his interviewers whether they knew "how poetry started," he furnishes them with an answer: "I always think that it started

1. The same formulation is found in Nabokov's *Lectures on Literature*: "all art is deception" (*LL*, 146).

when a cave boy came running back to the cave . . . shouting as he ran, 'Wolf, wolf,' and there was no wolf. His baboon-like parents, great sticklers for the truth, gave him a hiding, no doubt, but poetry had been born"—which is to say that poetry began in deception (*SO*, 11).

This deceptiveness is fantastically concentrated in some of Nabokov's most famous characters—such as the indifferently cruel Axel Rex of *Laughter in the Dark* and the outrageously blithe Clare Quilty from *Lolita*. Axel, who earns his living as a caricaturist and forger of paintings, cherishes a love of "fooling people," and is goaded by an "itch to make fools of his fellow men," that "amounted almost to genius" (*LD*, 143;182). He is said to have an, "innate conviction that everything that had ever been created in the domain of art, science or sentiment, was only a more or less clever trick" (*LD*, 22).[2] Quilty's monstrously mischievous merrymaking and its reliance on diabolically complicated deception is familiar enough that it requires no documentation.

In Nabokov's autobiography, he goes so far as to present deceptive problems as *gifts*, as things "lovingly prepared," for the would-be solver: "deceit, to the point of diabolism, and originality verging on the grotesque, were my notions of strategy. . . . a great part of the [chess] problem's value is due to the number of 'tries'—delusive opening moves, false scents, specious lines of play, astutely and *lovingly prepared* to lead the would-be solver astray" (*SM*, 289–290; my italics). As he often linked and likened the composing of chess problems to the composing of literary works, it should come as no surprise that in his introduction to *Poems and Problems* Nabokov writes: "Chess problems demand from the composer the same virtues that characterize all worthwhile art: originality, invention, conciseness, harmony, complexity, and splendid insincerity (*PP*, 15).[3] But why should there be something "lovingly prepared" about deceptive problems—be they literary or other? They are certainly not all of this sort—Axel and Quilty, among others, bear clear enough witness to this. Nevertheless, there are clearly *some* sorts of deception that *are* charmed.

2. Axel's perspective on Albinus' sad travails was that Albinus was at the heart of a "roaring comedy" the "stage-manager" of which was neither God nor the devil, but "an elusive, double, triple, self-reflecting magic Proteus of a phantom, the shadow of many-colored glass balls flying in a curve, the ghost of a juggler on a shimmering curtain" (*LD*, 182, 183).

3. Nabokov notes in a letter to Wilson from 1941 how he "hate[s] so intensely the way 'sincerity' is considered by some critics to be the main *quality* of a writer" (*NWL*, 51; Nabokov's emphasis). Given his fondness for deception, Nabokov's dislike of "sincerity" need come as no surprise. In an annotation bearing the heading "books and people," *Pale Fire*'s Kinbote reports the poet Shade saying, "when I hear a critic speaking of an author's sincerity I know that either the critic or the author is a fool"—and it is abundantly clear that at least here Nabokov felt with him (*PF*, 156). Nabokov's pointed disdain for the term *sincerity* seems to owe something to his pointed disdain of a person who used it prominently. In *Strong Opinions*, Nabokov remarks upon how often his students had been taught before entering into his intellectual orbit that "art is simple, art is sincere," and he tells himself: "Someday I must trace this vulgar

What is singular about Nabokov's deception is its seriousness. For him, the deceiving artist is not merely following his own playful whims, he is following *Nature*. "All art is deceptive, and so is nature," says Nabokov in *Strong Opinions*, where we also read that "deception is practiced even more beautifully by that other V.N., Visible Nature" (*SO*, 11, 153). In *Lectures on Literature*, V.N. sees the relation between Nature and deception as causal: "every great writer is a great deceiver, but so is that arch-cheat Nature. Nature always deceives . . . *The writer of fiction only follows Nature's lead*" (*LL*, 5; my italics). This deception which Nabokov finds in art—and above all in his own—is nothing less than a reflection and a consequence of a deceptiveness present in Nature itself.[4]

The analogy that Nabokov establishes between the two V. N.'s leads him to postulate that Nature, like art, is not governed by a principle of utility. Polemics against the idea that literature should fit in an economy of social *utility* can be found, of course, in a number of places—and all the more starting in the nineteenth century, from the pastoral tones of the English Romantics, to the metropolitan vehemence of Baudelaire, to the Russian Silver Age poets who shaped Nabokov's artistic youth, and to his cherished novelists Flaubert and Proust. But whatever Nabokov's points of agreement or divergence with those writers and movements, the idea he most fundamentally shared with them was that "Fancy is fertile only when it is futile" (*NG*, 76).[5] This strong opinion was not limited to literature, however, and it leads Nabokov to vocally oppose Darwin's theory of evolution. In general, Nabokov was careful to separate the two spheres of his specialized interest. There is, however, one point at which Nabokov's interests in the arts dovetail with those in the sciences—in the question of mimicry. "The mysteries of mimicry had a special attraction for me," he remarked in *Speak, Memory*, "its phenomena showed an artistic perfection usually associated with man-wrought things" (*SM*, 125). Later in this memoir he speaks of "the highest enjoyment of timelessness," and finds it "when I stand among rare butterflies

---

absurdity to its source. A schoolmarm in Ohio? A progressive ass in New York? Because, of course, art at its greatest is fantastically deceitful and complex" (*SO*, 33). Later it seems as though Nabokov has in part succeeded in tracing the "absurdity." In unpublished notes on Eliot's essay on Baudelaire (from *Selected Essays 1917–1932*), Nabokov cites a passage from Eliot followed by the exclamation "What nonsense!" and gives himself a page reference to "Eliot's cult of 'sincerity'" (Berg Collection, Notes on Various Subjects). Though he nowhere quotes it, Nabokov was likely aware of Eliot's remark from his most famous essay, "Tradition and the Individual Talent," where he states that "there are many people who appreciate the expression of sincere emotion in verse" (Eliot 1951, 22). Nabokov's distaste for Eliot's writing and person is evidenced in both a number of unfavorable remarks in interviews, as well as the pastiches of Eliot included in *Lolita* (cf. *AL*, 16, 299–300).

4. Nabokov thus presents Nature in a manner not unlike that in which Emerson presents her in his famous essay "Experience": "Nature does not like to be observed, and likes that we should be her fools and playmates" (Emerson, 95).

5. Cf. also his remark, "all art is inutile [*sic*]," in *Poems and Problems* (*PP*, 15).

and their food plants. This is ecstasy, and behind the ecstasy is something else, which is hard to explain. It is like a momentary vacuum into which rushes all that I love. A sense of oneness with sun and stone. A thrill of gratitude to whom it may concern—to the contrapuntal genius of human fate or to tender ghosts humoring a lucky mortal" (*SM*, 139).

In 1942, Nabokov gave a talk at the Cambridge Entomological Club on the topic. It enchanted his audience (of ten). All that remains of the talk, is the secretary of the club's summary: "The scientific program of the evening was in the hands of Dr. [*sic*] Vladamir [*sic*] Nabokov who read from his as yet unpublished book a chapter entitled 'Mimicry in Theory and Practice'—a reading, the entertaining informativeness and clarity of which these prosaic minutes could hardly attempt to capture. After considerable stimulating discussion the meeting adjourned at 9:15" (*Nabokov's Butterflies*, 278). The reader interested in Nabokov's deception might have wished that Nabokov had finished the essay he claimed to have been preparing on animal mimicry, and which, as he stated in a letter to Aldanov from 1941, was to contain "furious refutations of 'natural selection' and 'the struggle for life'" (letter from October 20, 1941; cited in Boyd 1991, 37). Some form of this essay was put to paper in 1942 under the title "The Theory and Practice of Mimicry," and was shown to Wilson as well as to a number of zoology students at Harvard. Neither the essay, nor any detailed account of its contents, survived—except for a curious fragment. This fragment is to be found in *Speak, Memory*, where Nabokov attacks Darwinism on the grounds that Darwin's theories are unable to account for the fineness of deceptive devices on butterflies' wings which, according to Nabokov, exceed the merely utilitarian. "When a butterfly has to look like a leaf," says Nabokov, "not only are all the details of a leaf beautifully rendered but markings mimicking grub-bored holes are generously thrown in. 'Natural selection,' in the Darwinian sense, could not explain the miraculous coincidence of imitative aspect and imitative behavior, nor could one appeal to the theory of the 'struggle for life' when a protective device was carried to a point of mimetic subtlety, exuberance, and luxury far in excess of a predator's power of apperception" (*SM*, 125). He continues, "I discovered in nature the non-utilitarian delights that I sought in art. Both were a form of magic, both were a game of intricate enchantment and deception" (ibid.). This position finds earlier expression in *The Gift*, where Fyodor's father tells him "about the incredible artistic wit of mimetic disguise, which was not explainable by the struggle for existence (the rough haste of evolution's unskilled forces), was too refined for the mere deceiving of accidental predators, feathered, scaled and otherwise . . . and seemed to have been invented by some waggish artist precisely for the intelligent eyes of man" (*Gift*, 110). Elsewhere in his memoir he scoffs, "'Struggle for life' indeed! The curse of battle and toil leads man back to the boar" (*SM*, 298). In a posthumously published addendum to that work he refers to the theory of "protective mimicry" as an "illusory theory" (*Nabokov's Butterflies*, 222). In *Strong Opinions*, Nabokov more laconically remarks of animal mimicry that its "refinement transcends the crude purpose of mere survival" (*SO*, 153).

This interest in animal mimicry was anything but peripheral. "The question of mimicry is one that has passionately interested him all his life," wrote Nabokov's wife Véra in 1952, "and one of his pet projects has always been the compilation of a work that would comprise all known examples of mimicry in the animal kingdom" (cited by Schiff, 218). Given his interests, it is not surprising that Nabokov nurtured such a Herculean aspiration. And given his view of mimicry—a term he uses in a loose, but completely acceptable sense which includes the phenomena usually referred to as crypsis and camouflage (cf. Zimmer 2001, 51)—it is no wonder that he never wrote the work. As a view of nature—above all on the part of a naturalist—his assertion that animal mimicry exceeds the perceptive powers of its predators and therefore cannot be explained through natural selection is one of the extremely rare cases where one might say that he lacked imagination. To judge the utilitarian, survival-enabling value of the physical or behavioral characteristics of organisms would necessitate a knowledge of nature—its past interconnectedness (the evolution of its species and their environment) as well as its present interconnectedness—which goes far beyond that available to the sciences. One might easily imagine that for a given butterfly with what Nabokov might have judged unnecessarily elaborate deceptive markings that what might have made such markings seem *superfluous* ("transcend[ing] the crude purpose of mere survival") is simply the fact that we do not understand enough about the dangers that butterfly faces or has faced, which elements act, or have acted, upon its morphology. To isolate a single possibility, one might easily imagine that deceptive wing markings which might seem unnecessary even to trained eyes are simply avatars of earlier marking formations which may indeed have ceased to offer survival benefits and, now vestigial, are gently effacing themselves with the passage of time. But they might just as well be protecting the butterfly in question from dangers unseen by, or unknown to, even the best-trained eyes amongst those who study it. What might seem like excessive camouflaging markings might be the fruit of our ignorance of the butterfly's evolutionary present (the perceptive powers of its known predators, as well as those of predators not yet known), just as of its evolutionary past.

As I mentioned earlier in connection with Freud, Marx, and generalization, Nabokov implied that Darwinian evolutionism betrayed the singular flower and finch in favor of general substitutes, that it did not do justice to the particular, and that it was for this reason that Nabokov's criticisms of Darwin so resemble his criticisms of those other sinners against Particularity, Freud and Marx. On the one hand, this could not be more unfair. Darwin did not invent evolutionism: the idea was present from well before—from, at the latest, Lamarck's theories of progressive adaptation in his *Philosophie zoologique* (1809), and had found powerful and influential expression in Herbert Spencer's *Principles of Psychology* (1855) (where the other term Nabokov singles out for "furious refutation," "struggle for life" is to be first found). Where Darwin differed from—and innovated upon—the evolutionists who preceded him was in observing carefully and closely the particulars of this evolution—the flowers and the finches. Perhaps Nabokov recalled this many years later when, in one of the final interviews he gave, he referred to Darwin as a "true scientist" and someone who possessed an "acute imagination" (Laansoo, 44). Darwin developed a theory based not on remaining at the level of the species, characterizing and classifying the general, but on observing individual organisms until their individuality began to win out over their generality. It should be remembered that *On the Origin of Species* (1859) is also a book on the *insufficiency* of species, the insufficiency of seeing the natural world in terms of such static, general forms as, precisely, *species*. What Darwin was convinced of was that species were mutable things and his studies of the flight and foraging of the finches proved this to him. It would be wrong, however, to see Nabokov's antipathy to Darwin as being principally a charge against Darwin's generalizing influence. Nabokov planned to offer his reader, as we saw, furious refutations of natural selection. The term is well chosen as it is precisely natural selection which infuriates Nabokov. It should be remembered that, like Nabokov, Darwin too had reservations about the term "natural selection," and even regretted at times having employed it. This regret was born from his feeling that the term was misleading in that it implied that some intelligent intention and Intelligent Intender lay behind the process, that some entity or force, some supranatural intelligence, was *selecting* traits. For Darwin, this process evolved much more through blind chance. For Darwin, "natural selection" implied too much intelligence in the origin and evolution of species;[6] for Nabokov, it implied too little.

Critics and scientists have sought to be conciliating on this matter—each in deference to the other. The problem here is that it has yet to be widely

---

6. In the autobiography which Darwin began in 1876 for his children he notes how when he first set off on the *Beagle* he made himself a laughing stock through his habit of quoting the *Bible* to arbitrate difficult moral situations. He claims that at the time of penning *On the Origin of Species* he was a "theist," but that the consequences of his theories vitiated his belief and he was forced to call himself in this autobiography an "Agnostic."

recognized that Nabokov's position is fundamentally unsound for fundamental reasons. The point is, naturally, not one of condemnation or exoneration, but lies in why Nabokov came to such surprising positions in the first place. To say, however, as do the authors of *Nabokov's Blues*, that Nabokov was "simply honest enough to admit that he could not understand how the theory [of natural selection] as it was developed in his day could account for phenomena like mimicry," is to see only one side of the question (Coates and Johnson, 328).

Though neither he nor any of his critics have stated the matter in these terms, it is clear that what Nabokov objected to in Darwin's "natural selection" and Spencer's "struggle for life," what made him long to furiously refute them was that their view of evolution precluded an Intelligent Designer. Darwin's most famous opponent in the years directly following the publication of *On the Origin of Species* was Louis Agassiz, the founder, in 1859, of the institution where Nabokov would conduct the majority of his lepidopterological investigations, Harvard's Museum of Comparative Zoology, and, two years later, of the library at Harvard which bore his name. What Agassiz could under no circumstances accept was the absence in Darwin's theory of a Creator. Neither could Nabokov, though understandably he did not say so. But his asserting that natural selection and the struggle for life did not account for the mimicry he found in nature was clearly a means of reasserting a form, albeit singular, of intelligent design. For Nabokov, the wings of butterflies which he had examined scale by scale had too fine a form not to be the work of a Creator. He did not believe that any great or grand message could be read on those wings, that any precepts or postulates to live by were inscribed there, but he did believe that he glimpsed an intricacy and a fineness in those designs which must be lost upon all predators but man. With the development of more and more advanced studies of genetic populations, Nabokov's Harvardian nemesis Ernst Mayr's "modern synthesis" has carried the scientific day. No better proof of Mayr's defense of natural selection in the face of those defending the doctrine of intelligent design can be found, perhaps, than the utilitarian one reflected in the rededication in 1995 of the Agassiz Library at Harvard where Nabokov worked as the Ernst Mayr Library of Comparative Zoology.[7]

7. Nabokov lodged a second complaint against Darwin's theory, and one which is particularly stressed in this same posthumously published addendum to *The Gift* referred to above: that the world was too young to have produced the variations it had produced. Corollary to this objection lay another: that there would not have been enough time for the intermediary forms separating species to have disappeared—that there were too many leaps between related organisms which were impossible to account for on the basis of gradual mutation and evolution (cf. *Nabokov's Butterflies*, 223). This gradualism with its remarkable and unexpected exceptions and leaps has since been explained, but it was a stumbling block for a great many naturalists of the first part of the century. In 1942, the same year that Nabokov announced his intention to furiously refute natural selection and the struggle for life, Ernst Mayr

The incompletion or erroneousness of Nabokov's theory *as a scientific theory* takes nothing, of course, from his art, just as Goethe's essentially erroneous theory of colors took nothing from his. The contrary might, in fact, be asserted. Nabokov's bewailing of the short-sightedness of Darwinian natural selection is ultimately only explicable in light of an image and idea of *deception* which he drew from elsewhere than the scientific. Attacking natural selection was a way of attacking the utilitarianism of his age. But it was also something more. In the addendum to *The Gift*, we read that "Nature found it amusing, or artistically valid, to retain, near a selected species, an elegant corollary" (*Nabokov's Butterflies*, 226). The principal source of Nabokov's dissatisfaction with natural selection lay, in fact, in the analogy he established between the creator of a fictional work and the Creator of the created world—the two "V.N.",s, "Vladimir Nabokov" and "Visible Nature," we met earlier. It should begin to become clear to us why Nabokov never finished his "furious refutation"—and why such a refutation might have been furious in the first place. Just as in the case of Goethe, what motivated Nabokov's scientific claim regarding deception and mimicry was an aesthetic—or, perhaps, a theological—question. What he wished to demonstrate—and perhaps to no one less than himself—was a fundamental analogy between the Book of the World and the book of the artist—and not just any artist, but himself.[8] What Goethe wished for was a scientific theory that would purge scientific investigation of its abstracting tendency and return that investigation to the realm of lived experience. Goethe's theory of colors is scientifically untenable because, in his wish to combat a Newtonian utilitarian worldview which he saw taking hold of his age, he sacrificed facts for desires. For Nabokov, things do not stand so very differently. It is not felt or lived experience which is at issue in his speculations on natural selection, but his sense of a world more and more ruled by the veneration of utility. It should then come as no surprise that he attacked that tenet of modern thought which most concisely and comprehensively expresses this veneration of the useful: Darwin's natural selection. Natural selection is, in fact, utility itself: traits and behaviors have no better, brighter or larger reason for being than precisely

---

published a work in which he proposed that Darwin's theory of natural selection could in fact explain all of evolution, including why genes evolve at the molecular level. The question of the origin of such disparate species as the earth knows, and of the existence of such developmental gaps between species, was answered in Mayr's work with an explanation of how a population of organisms becomes separated from the main group by time or geography and eventually evolves different traits to the point that it can no longer interbreed. Nabokov bitterly opposed Mayr (and his "modern" or "neo-Darwinian synthesis").

8. The theological inflection of this belief is reflected in Nabokov's early poem "Mother" (from 1922), where he reads this book of nature on the pages of the wings of butterflies, speaking of, "fragrant, dry glass drawers, / like the leaves of big, folded Bibles" (*Nabokov's Butterflies*, 107).

their usefulness in aiding the organism to survive. Nabokov's repudiation of Darwinian morphological analysis is a structural element in the ivory tower in which Nabokov wished to protect art and its practitioners from the devotees of the useful laying siege to it.

The role of deception in Nabokov's vision of the world is then twofold: he is both a creature in a deceptive creation, and a creator of deceptive creations. In his unpublished "Notes for a second volume (twenty years in America) of *Speak, Memory*," Nabokov begins his introductory remarks by stating: "Two—and only two—critical remarks really distress and anger me. One is the accusation of my liking or loving 'to pull the reader's leg'; and the other is the bland assumption that I am a 'satirist.'"[9] Nabokov's dislike of satire and refusal to be branded as a satirist is well documented in his works and is easily understandable in light of the fact that one tends to see satirists as bitter people working in a derivative genre. The question of "leg-pulling" is less evident. Nabokov seems to have prided himself on being deceptive—and thus something of a "leg-puller." Continuing to respond to these two things which anger and distress him, he writes: "There are writers . . . whose way of seeing and recreating the world has so little in common with the accepted way, that their unusual approach is mistaken for a more or less insulting piece of tomfoolery" (Nabokov Archive, Berg Collection, New York Public Library, folder "Notes for Work in Progress," card D). He states that he is saying "all these rather obvious things" as he would be "distressed and angry" should this projected continuation of his memoirs be seen as such a piece of "tomfoolery." Nabokov's deceptive practices are for him the furthest thing from simple "leg-pulling" and "tomfoolery"—beneath them lay a deeper commitment.

9. Folder "Notes for Work in Progress," card A, Nabokov Archive, Berg Collection, New York Public Library.

CHAPTER ELEVEN

THE FIGURE IN THE MAGIC CARPET

Let us ... Expatiate free o'er all this scene of man;
A mighty maze! but not without a plan.
—Alexander Pope, *An Essay on Man*.

Patterns

EZRA POUND CLAIMED to have heard sometime in 1921 or 1922 that members of the British wartime censorship authorities believed they had discovered that James Joyce's *Ulysses* was, in fact, a German code. Though the British authorities also met Nabokov's *Lolita* with skepticism, no such suspicion seems to have arisen as concerns his complicated and coded work. Nevertheless, Nabokov was at no small pains to indicate to his better readers and critics that there *was* more in his works than they had found, that there were hidden patterns therein, and while it seems unlikely that he meant anything like a secret code destined for foreign agents, no consensus has been reached as to what, precisely, these patterns *are*.

To orient our search, let us turn to a bird. Vladimir Nabokov's literary aviary is dominated by a single, signal bird: the waxwing. As we have seen, Nabokov adhered to no principle as rigorously, and defended no principle as insistently, as that which asserts the sovereignty of the particular, and the necessity, in the reading and writing of literature, of attending to the details of the work of

art. And no belief of Nabokov's was so strong as that which asserted that such attention paid to the particulars of life and art offered rich rewards for the observer. This being the case, we would do well to attend to the particular bird that inaugurates the poetic speculations of one of Nabokov's most patterned and complex creations—*Pale Fire*.

The well-known first lines of John Shade's 999-line poem from Nabokov's *Pale Fire* offer us the shadow of this curious bird: "I was the shadow of the waxwing slain/By the false azure of the windowpane . . ." (*PF*, 1). The problem that the impertinent-looking bird poses is that of the nature and purpose of *deception* in Nabokov's work. And a glance at its leads us to ask, with *Lolita's* Humbert, an important question: "Is 'mask' the keyword?" (cf. *AL*, 53).

The waxwing, emblem and shadow of deception, played an essential role in the novel from Nabokov's earliest plans. In a letter to Jason Epstein from March 1957, the exiled (and, initially, heterosexual) "King of Thule" (who will become the king of another northern place, Nova Zembla, in the final version) "lives more or less incognito, with the lady he loves, somewhere on the border of Upstate New York and Montario [*sic*] . . . and from the picture window of my creature's house one can see the bright mud of a private road and a leafless tree all at once abloom with a dozen waxwings" (SL, 213). The reader familiar with the bird quickly sees that the detail is not simply a picturesque one. "A leafless tree all at once abloom with a dozen waxwings" conveys concealment, intrepid observation, and the paranoia provoked by a belief in an unfathomable menace. Such a telling detail seems in Nabokov's letter to be sign of the real or imaginary persecution to which Kinbote will fall prey. In the final version of the novel, no such tree is to be found—the image has sunk deeper into the story. This masked and mirroring bird crashes to its death, as we saw, in the opening lines of Shade's poem—and from beyond its mirrory grave it serves to signal shadows, concealment, deception, paranoia—and something lying beyond.

On the last page of *Pale Fire*, in the index which forms its strange climax, one finds a reference to the waxwing under the Latin name *Bombycilla shadei* (PF, 315). Kinbote refers to this index entry as an "interesting association belatedly realized" (ibid.). Why should such an association be, for Kinbote, interesting? To begin with, the species name is a literary one. Waxwings do belong to the family *Bombycillidae*, but none of the three known species of waxwings carries this name (which is Shade's own—*shadei*). The Bohemian waxwing's classificatory name is *Bombycilla garrulus*; that of the cedar waxwing, *Bombycilla cedrorum*; and of the Japanese waxwing, *Bombycilla japonica*. The photo here is of a cedar waxwing, the species that Nabokov himself might have seen slain in the false azure of a window pane in the environs of Ithaca, New York, where he wrote Shade's ghostly lines. It would not be excluded, if one wishes to remain in the context of what the author might have seen while composing the work, that Nabokov caught sight in upstate New York of a rare Bohemian waxwing, which unlike the cedar waxwing is also found in Europe and which breeds largely in an area farther north, from Alaska to northern Idaho, but can be found as far east as the Hudson Bay. This bird's Latin name, as we saw above, is *Bombycilla garrulus*. Given Kinbote's pathological garrulousness, one might be inclined to think this was the waxwing therein slain—that Kinbote himself, fooled by a reflection, slays his critical sense against the false azure of Shade's poem "Pale Fire." What is more, if the bird were a Bohemian waxwing, it would then be common to both continents, could theoretically have lived in the frigid climes of the semi-fictional Nova Zembla, and thus have been an apt reflection of Kinbote's crazed consciousness in the New World. As the difference in aspect is slight between the two species, and as Nabokov's work is one of poetry and fiction, not ornithology, nothing requires that a distinction be made. Shade's precise geographical location (which is imaginary) excludes any determination of what waxwing he might have seen. As the three waxwings species all share the masked aspect that interests us here, we might assume that *Bombycilla shadei* does so as well.

The emblematic force of the waxwing's mask-like stripe is important because it is a mask provided by nature herself. In addition to this mask, the waxwing also possesses two other special characteristics of note which might account for its prominent place in Nabokov's novel of deception: a crest that is raised only in alarm—and there is both a lot of crest-raising and a lot of alarm in Kinbote's wild words—and the titular spots of red that ornithologists first compared to drops of sealing wax on the tips of its wing feathers—conjuring a mixture of blood and sealed words. Michael J. Seago notes in his *Birds of Britain*: "My diaries record one memorable occasion at Hickling where 20 [waxwings] were engaged in aerial flycatching. After executing rapid bat-like flights all returned to sun themselves-wings half-opened-in a leafless oak. Two waxwings repeatedly performed a gift-passing ceremony, a choice berry constantly passing back and forth. This display was accompanied by drooping and quivering wings and raised and lowered crests. Later the party, after a chorus of trills, swooped down to a hawthorn hedge rapidly swallowing berry after berry."[1] The waxwing's "gift-passing ceremony" might too be of some relevance for the understanding of the bird's presence in *Pale Fire*. What is more—a fact that Nabokov may or may not have known—in flight, the waxwing's triangular wing shape can cause it to be mistaken for the similarly sized starling. The relevance of such a detail would be the waxwing's connection to another famous novelistic bird from a work Nabokov had a special affection for—Laurence Sterne's *A Sentimental Journey*—where the starling speaks out requesting that it be freed from its cage. And what is Shade's text for him if not a cage?

The importance of the waxwing does not, however, stop here. The bird's bandit aspect (its mask) evokes the central and titular theme of *Pale Fire*: theft. To understand in what sense this claim is true, we might ask to what the title refers. It refers first to the title of the 999-line poem written by the (fictional) poet John Shade, stolen or saved by the (fictional) critic Charles Kinbote after the former's sudden death and copiously and, it seems, dementedly, annotated by the latter. These same notes rail against the idea of choosing the title of a work of art from one of the great poets (Shakespeare, Milton, etc.) and at once bemoans and suspects that the title "Pale Fire" is a citation from some work of Shakespeare's, though Kinbote concedes that he cannot ascertain from which work as he is preparing his notes in seclusion, has no access to a library and has with him only a Zemblan (his native language) translation of *Timon of Athens*. It is indeed apt that this is the only work he has with him as he, like Shakespeare's Timon, has closed himself off from the world in a rascally fashion. It is doubly apt as the phrase "pale fire" is, in fact, from that very play. "But in which of

1. Http://www.birdsofbritain.co.uk/bird-guide/waxwing.htm.

the Bard's works did our poet cull it?" asks Kinbote of the title "Pale Fire," "My readers must make their own research. All I have with me is a tiny vest pocket edition of *Timon of Athens*—in Zemblan! It certainly contains nothing that could be regarded as an equivalent of 'pale fire' (if it had, my luck would have been a statistical monster)" (*PF*, 285). This statistical monster, in fact, lives—a fact not disclosed in Nabokov's novel and which readers must discover for themselves.[2]

The titular phrase is to be found in *Timon of Athens* Scene 3, Act 4: "the moon's an arrant thief,/And her pale fire she snatches from the sun" (3.4.437–438). The words are Timon's own and are to be found in a speech, or rather an invective: he is in a bad mood and some few lines earlier has given vent to his irascibility by saying to the philosopher Apenantus, "I am sorry I shall lose a stone by thee. [*Throws a stone at him.*]" (3.4.370). His speech and the pale fire in it is prompted by the arrival of three thieves at his cave. This gives him occasion to denounce *theft* as the guiding and universal principle of the universe, as he states that "all is theft," and concludes with the summary judgment that "each thing's a thief" (3.4.442). In any case, the moon's stolen "pale fire" sheds no small light on the work of the same name. The book, being a book about the theft of literary fire by the pale critic—a subject which Nabokov had ample time and space to reflect on in his preparation of the voluminous notes he was preparing for his translation of *Eugene Onegin* at the same time as he was writing *Pale Fire*—does well to inscribe itself under the sign or suspicion of generalized theft.

Timon of Athens' relevance for tracing the patterns Nabokov wove into his text does not, however, stop there. Shakespeare's play has generally been held to be his weakest, and with the notable exception of Hazlitt, critics have not often sung its praises. More germane for the question at hand is that various theories have held various degrees of currency about the text being the fruit of collaboration or revision and at various points in the play's reception there has

---

2. Nabokov will have Kinbote inadvertently quote the passage in question, but his translation from the Zemblan to the English produces "silvery light"—which is not easily recognizable as "pale fire." Nabokov, not one to go easy on his creations, has Kinbote involuntarily echo this same epithet again elsewhere by stating: "in many cases I have caught myself borrowing *a kind of opalescent light* from my poet's fiery orb" (*PF*, 81; my italics). Concerning Nabokov's own predilection for embedded Shakespearean citations, we should note his short story from 1958, " 'That in Aleppo Once. . .' " Here, the title is helpfully placed in quotation marks and is taken from a far more famous speech in a far more famous play than *Timon of Athens*, Othello's final one (*Othello* 5.2.352–356). The story that takes from this its title has the form of a letter to a certain "V" enjoining him to transform the true story recounted in the letter into a fictional one. The letter writer tells "V" not to use the title "That in Aleppo Once . . ." if he, the letter-writer, is still alive, saying, after the death of his Desdemona, "it may all end in *Aleppo* if I am not careful. Spare me, V.: you would load the dice with an unbearable implication if you took that for a title" (*Stories*, 568). Only when no dice were left to load can it serve as the story's title and in so doing supply the final piece of information in the story: the letter writer's suicide.

reigned a consensus, or near consensus, that Shakespeare was not the play's only, or final, author. What is more, we can note that Shakespeare (and/or his dark collaborator) borrowed for its plot elements from Plutarch's *Life of Antony*, such as certain names and the idea of the retreat into the wilderness (which is not found in accounts of Timon's life, but is attributed to Antony after his defeat at Actium). Nabokov declared that "the verbal poetical texture of Shakespeare is the greatest the world has known," and as he was an avid reader and rereader of Shakespeare's works these facts would not be new to him (cf. *SO*, 89).

Advancing farther towards speculation, we might note that the Greek noun *timoria*, which is at the base of Timon's name, means both "assistance" and "vengeance"—precisely how one might describe Kinbote's behavior towards Shade's text. And yet, in noting this we are far from having exhausted the field of possible meanings for the title, nor even the field of possible Shakespearean references, as this is not Shakespeare's only "pale fire."

In *Hamlet*, we read: "The glow-worm shows the matin to be neer, / And 'gins to *pale* his uneffectual *fire*" (1.5.90; my italics). This Hamletian "pale fire" is found in the mouth of a ghost come back from the beyond to urge his son to avenge the wrongs committed against him and that have led to his suffering the less ineffectual fires of purgatory. The shining of this "pale fire" (betokening the dawn) indicates to him that he must return beyond the pale of the living. Given the place occupied elsewhere in *Pale Fire* of visitations from beyond the grave (such as those of Shade's daughter Hazel), is it not plausible to find here an evocation of the visitations of wandering shades? Might the title than not also refer, in the context of the Hamletian "pale fire," to the central importance of communication with that which is shining palely from the beyond?

Though the reference to Shakespeare is certainly of the greatest relevance, and indeed is the solution to part of the riddle Nabokov presents to his reader, we might note a final pale flickering of sense in the title. One derivation of "pale" is from the Latin *palus*, stake. A pale fire might thus be a fire or burning at the *palus*, or stake. With a bit of imagination might we see this evoking the fate of the poet John Shade martyred by his deranged editor? "Pale," derived from another meaning (the pale beyond which one is not meant to go), can also mean "fence, boundary, barrier." It could thus refer to the burning or overstepping of boundaries which the voyeuristic and decidedly beyond the pale Kinbote repeatedly infringes upon. He does so both literally (he is Shade's neighbor and frequently crosses without permission the boundary separating their estates) and also metaphorically—overstepping the boundaries of neighborly friendliness, overstepping the bounds of tact and tastefulness in nearly every thing he does, overstepping the boundaries of editorial and even juridical propriety in absconding with Shade's text, and finally overstepping the bounds of a critic and editor in the notes he accompanies Shade's poem with. Going a step farther into the realms of speculation, we might also point out the darkly glimmering possibility that "pale fire" is a heraldic reference. "Pale" is also a heraldic term denoting a vertical stripe or band (a fact which Nabokov, who took a heraldic description for the title of his first novel written in America, *Bend Sinister*, would not have been ignorant of). In such a context, one might see in Nabokov's title a reference to a family crest in flames of the sort necessarily seen in the revolution which Kinbote either hallucinates or escapes from, and which forms the central theme of his notes.

Here we are in the shadowy realms of speculation. What this foray illustrates is that Nabokov, like the bird which flies through his work, masks himself and takes pleasure in that masking. And this is something clear from the reader's doing nothing more complicated or ambitious than trying to understand the work's title.

Hiding and Finding

The question then arises of what meaning, if any, we should attribute to such playful coding and encoding, as well as what Nabokov's ambition was in weaving such patterns into his works. Are they meant to disclose a hidden meaning or message to the careful reader, or are they just one aspect of an impish wish to keep literary critics busy and befuddled, as Joyce proclaimed that he wished to do, for at least three hundred years? In *Bend Sinister*, Nabokov writes that "the glory of God is to hide a thing, and the glory of man is to find it" (*BS*, 106). How are we to understand this glorious hiding and finding? What is hidden and what is there to find under the surface of Nabokov's texts? Does this hiding and finding simply involve the solving of a puzzle or a riddle engaged in for its own sake and meant only to exercise the agility, dexterity, and erudition of the reader? Or does it belong instead to a larger system or sphere of speculation?

The encrypting of a parallel, often concealed, content in a work of art has known a rich and long tradition. Before we place Nabokov in this tradition we should recall that there are few things that he railed against with more vehemence than, precisely, this tradition. Allegory is a method of reading where the work is read not merely for its more or less simple story, but as a vessel for the expression of another story running alongside of it, full of social, political, religious, and metaphysical meaning. As we saw earlier, Nabokov loathed allegory and was eager to tell his readers such. If we are to believe Nabokov, then, the patterns he weaves into his works are not allegories in the sense of being signs pointing towards another story or sense of which his narrative is but a cipher.

Nabokov felt so strongly about this point that he actually went to the trouble of sprinkling his stories with reminders. One finds in his works various mocking invitations to read allegorically. To name just a single member of this family, we might think of the weird insertions of sexualized objects in his works, such as *Ada*'s "enormous purple pink plums, one with a wet yellow burst-split" (*Ada*, 62). These details seem to be placed along the reader's way principally as a means of dissuasion, through their crass excess, from seeking a meaning for the work elsewhere than in the work (i.e. in this case, in systems of sexual symbolism of a more or less psychoanalytical sort). One of the types of patterning included in Nabokov's works is then patterning that is to remind the reader not to go seeking meanings in symbolic signs or systems. But there are many more.

Nabokov described life as rich, varied, alive, and fantastically important in every one of its moments. For him, every moment in every place offered something for the gifted and dedicated observer to observe and cherish. A writer with such a belief coupled with an exceptionally retentive memory must thus find some criterion of selection, some means or method by which to uncover a pattern and progression in the multiform heterogeneity of what one perceives. Without such a pattern, all experience would swim before one's eyes, would dissolve into an unceasing, senseless series, a concatenation of the unconnected.

In his first novel, Nabokov's protagonist talks in a moment of depression of how "the whole of life seemed like a piece of film-making where heedless extras knew nothing of the picture in which they were taking part" (*Mary*, 22). Later in that same work we read:

> And as he [Ganin] stared at the sky and listened to a cow mooing almost dreamily in a distant village, he tried to understand what it all meant—that sky, and the fields, and the humming telegraph pole; he felt that he was just on the point of understanding it when suddenly his head would start to spin and the lucid languor of the moment became intolerable. (*Mary*, 47).

This entrancing and nearly intolerable moment where a blessed instant seems so rich in promise that it cannot but reveal its secret—and then that secret slips away—is a telling one. Nabokov was well familiar with the passage in Proust's *Recherche* where young Marcel relates, in a similar setting, how he was suddenly gripped in the midst of a seemingly unexceptional adventure by a sense of importance and meaning, of a riddle about to unveil itself—that then recedes from view (cf. Proust 1987–89, 1:177–179). This pattern, about to resolve itself, is what the narrator of Proust's novel will follow until its very end—which

riddle turns out to be nothing more or less than the creation of a work of art
and the pattern proper to that work. For Nabokov, from his first work to his
last, nothing less is at stake.

In the final section of Nabokov's last Russian novel, *The Gift*, we read of
Fyodor:

> He was in a troubled and obscured state of mind which was incomprehensible to
> him, just as everything was incomprehensible, from the sky to that yellow tram
> rumbling along the clear track of the Hohenzollerdamm . . . but gradually his an-
> noyance with himself passed and with a kind of relief—as if the responsibility for
> his soul belonged not to him but to someone who knew what it all meant—he
> felt that all this skein of random thoughts, like everything else as well—the seams
> and the sleaziness of the spring day, the ruffle of the air, the coarse, variously in-
> tercrossing threads of confused sounds—was but the reverse side of a magnificent
> fabric, on the front of which there gradually formed and became alive images
> invisible to him (*Gift*, 314).

Just when the teeming and disparate world is too much with him, Fyodor finds
in it the promise of a pattern, a magnificent fabric that began gradually to reveal
the images and forms which it concealed.

Just as we find such a moment in Nabokov's final Russian novel, we find
one as well in his final English one. In *Look at the Harlequins!* we learn of the
narrator's waking nightmares. Of the observation in the dark of night of points
of light constituting one instance of such, we read:

> Those dots corresponded, perhaps, to my rapid heartbeats or were connected
> optically with the blinking of wet eyelashes but the rationale of it is inessential; its
> dreadful part was my realizing in helpless panic that the event had been stupidly
> unforeseen, yet had been bound to happen and was the representation of a fatidic
> problem which had to be solved lest I perish and indeed might have been solved
> now if I had given it some forethought or had been less sleepy and weak-witted at
> this all-important moment. The problem itself was of a calculatory order: certain
> relations between the twinkling points had to be measured or, in my case, guessed,
> since my torpor prevented me from counting them properly, let alone recalling
> what the safe number should be. Error meant instant retribution—beheading
> by a giant or worse; the right guess, per contra, would allow me to escape into
> an enchanting region situated just beyond the gap I had to wriggle through in
> the thorny riddle, a region resembling in its idyllic abstraction those little land-
> scapes engraved as suggestive vignettes—a brook, a *bosquet*—next to capital letters
> of weird, ferocious shape such as the Gothic *B* beginning a chapter in old books

for easily frightened children. But how could I know in my torpor and panic that *this* was the simple solution, and the brook and the boughs and the beauty of the Beyond all began with the initial of Being? (*LATH*, 16; Nabokov's italics).

Finding a pattern is that which is able to forestall the anxiety caused by the strangeness, suddenness, and disparateness of perception. It is the way out of the labyrinth of fear, the thread that will lead in *Look at the Harlequins!* to "the simple solution" of life's language: ". . . and the brook and the boughs and the beauty of the Beyond all began with the initial of Being." For Nabokov and his creations, the tracing of patterns combats anxiety—from the rationalized anxiety engendered by a sense that the world lacks an intrinsic order (one that we saw earlier in Nabokov's discussion of "reality") to the irrational anxieties of sleepless nights and their whirling images.

The search for a pattern presents a danger, however, of which Nabokov was well aware. In Nabokov's early novel *The Defense*, Luzhin, the young chess genius at the heart of that novel, is hiding in the attic of his house: "After a few minutes Luzhin grew bored, as when one's throat is wrapped in flannel and one is forbidden to go out. He touched the gray dusty books in the open box, leaving black imprints on them. Besides books there was a shuttlecock with one feather, a large photograph (of a military band), a cracked chessboard, and some other not very interesting things" (*Defense*, 23). Both for the reader and for Luzhin, one of those things does prove rather interesting (not the shuttlecock). The military band has no suite in the story, but the cracked chessboard does as the gifted player runs aground on his obsessive reliance on the forms and patterns of the game that has become his life. Luzhin's "chess obsession" consists precisely in the ultimately annihilating search for a certain type of pattern—patterns in life like those found in chess—that spread out ever further across the spaces of his life. The trick of the novel is that though within its world Luzhin is quite mad (it seems to the reader that he hallucinates the chess pattern he finds), in the world of the reader's perception of patterns, he is not at all mad as those patterns are to be found in the novel. As Nabokov himself made clear in the preface to the English translation, the novel unfolds following the rules and form of a game of chess ending in the baroque sui-mate situation whose correlate in the world of the novel is Luzhin's suicide.[3]

Later, in his introduction to *Bend Sinister*, Nabokov points out to his reader a "peculiar code message" transmitted to the protagonist by "an anthropomorphic deity impersonated by me" we encountered earlier (*BS*, xviii). "In the last chapter

3. Nabokov noted in the foreword to *Despair*: "my story was difficult to compose, but I greatly enjoyed taking advantage of this or that image and scene to introduce *a fatal pattern* into Luzhin's life" (*Defense*, 8; my italics). He also refers therein to Luzhin's suicide as a "sui-mate" (ibid.).

of the book," says Nabokov, "this deity experiences a pang of pity for his creature and hastens to take over. Krug, in a sudden moonburst of madness, understands that he is in good hands: nothing on earth really matters, there is nothing to fear, and death is but a question of style, a mere literary device, a musical resolution" (*BS*, xviii–xix). This coded message through which "a nameless, mysterious genius" communicates takes the form of a recurrent pattern: a puddle. "The puddle thus kindled and rekindled in Krug's mind," says Nabokov, "remains linked up with the image of his wife not only because he had contemplated the inset sunset from her death-bedside, but also because this little puddle vaguely evokes in him my link with him: a rent in his world leading to another world of tenderness, brightness and beauty" (*BS*, xv). That rent, or as he calls it in another story, "hole" in the "world" of one of his characters leads directly to him (cf. *Stories*, 595). *Pnin* proceeds along analogous lines where similar signs and wonders are announced in the unprepossessing form of a squirrel. And there too "the key of the pattern" unlocks a door leading into the room in which the work was written (*Pnin*, 23).

Luzhin, Krug, Pnin, and others are confronted with similar patterns—patterns that are the signs of their maker. As concern the first two, the difference is that the chess genius is not able to see beyond them, while the philosopher, Krug, is—if only faintly. Luzhin's unique but fatal error is in believing that the opposing force wishes to beat him. That he is wrong can be seen in the book's last lines, where "the window reflections gathered together and leveled themselves out, the whole chasm was seen to divide into dark and pale squares, and at the instant when Luzhin unclenched his hand, at the instant when icy air gushed into his mouth, he saw exactly what kind of eternity was obligingly and inexorably spread out before him" (*Defense*, 256). Of *Bend Sinister* Nabokov was to write, "I, the Author, take Krug to my bosom and the horrors of the life he has been experiencing turn out to be the artistic invention of the Author" (*SL*, 50). Luzhin too returns to the bosom of his maker—it is only that he realizes his destination a moment later.

This danger involved in perceiving or misperceiving the hidden connections in the world, and the world of words, is not limited to characters *in* Nabokov's works—it is also one confronted by his critics. In the first work to explicitly approach Nabokov's writing from this angle, *Nabokov's Deceptive World*, Rowe states that "Nabokov's world breathes with a teasing and unseen deception" (Rowe, 161). Though Nabokov himself was to take Rowe to task for the latter's adventurous analysis of sexual symbols, Rowe's claim here is one that Nabokov would have doubtless seconded. Elsewhere in that work, Rowe notes "the more one reads Nabokov, the more each individual word seems a purposeful participant in the total, uniquely calculated world of this works" (Rowe, viii). Similarly, M. H. Abrams once remarked: "I think that Nabokov was one of the most deliberate and self-conscious of writers; hardly a detail in his prose is accidental. Even syllables" (cf. Abrams, 219). Sensitive to the idea that each word seems a purposeful participant and the idea that, as Abrams suggests, not even a single syllable is left to change, Gavriel Shapiro has undertaken a study of anagrammatic patterns, or as he calls it "anagrammatic encoding" in Nabokov's fiction (primarily *Invitation to a Beheading*). Shapiro found what he was looking for: "anagrammatically encoded" instances of proper names, such as Nabokov's own name, his Russian pen name, his father's name, his wife's name, his painting teacher Dobuzhinsky's, and others—the only question is whether what he found had been left for him, or whether he had brought it with him; whether what he found was chance or choice. As noted earlier, Nabokov wrote in *Ada* that, some law of logic should fix the number of coincidences, in a given domain, "after which they cease to be coincidences, and form, instead, the living organism of a new truth" (*Ada*, 361). This was a number that Shapiro set out to calculate. Fellow critic Alexander Dolinin undertook an analytical examination of Shapiro's findings, confirming that the anagrams in question could be formed following Shapiro's method, but added, "I checked the fragments suggested by Shapiro in his writings and easily discovered in them Vladimir Ilich Ulianov-Lenin, Leo Nikolaevich Tolstoi and Alexander Alexeevich Dolinin" (Dolinin 2000, 99).

A similarly eccentric search for pattern can be found in Priscilla Meyer's book on *Pale Fire* where she pursues a series of dating parallels such as the identical birthdays of *Eugene Onegin*'s Tatyana and Lolita (if one takes into account the distance between the Gregorian and the Julian calendars); the fact that Humbert meets Annabel precisely one hundred years after Pushkin started work on *Eugene Onegin*; and that Pushkin ceased working on *Eugene Onegin* in 1835 and thus one hundred years before Lolita's birth. On their basis she argues that "underlying both [*Pale Fire* and *Lolita*] is the theme of the development from literature from its earliest oral stages through migration and metamorphosis" (Meyer, 38, 215). Meyer's suggestion is as provocative as Shapiro's, and given Nabokov's exceptional interest in deception and patterning, few hypotheses can be ruled out as simply too far-fetched. Philological method must guide the reader's search, and yet nonetheless philology is not an exact science and the danger of mistaking one's own patterns for those of the text is ever-present. The prudent critic is tempted to speak with Humbert when he writes, "as undoubtable clues *per se* but baffled me in respect to their finer points I do not care to mention many since I feel I am groping in a border-land mist with verbal phantoms turning, perhaps, into living vacationists."[4]

4. Or, as Rowe not only observed but also experienced: "Following distant stars that glow only for him, the persevering critic of Nabokov sometimes fails to notice, upon his triumphant arrival, that someone has quietly tilted the sky" (Rowe, x).

Within Nabokov's fictions, the search for patterns is a defense against the anxiety engendered by the disparate plenitude of perception, and the discovery of pattern is an alternately reassuring and alarming sign that beyond that disparate plenitude lies a Creator. For his critics, the activity is a more uncertain one, with bravura feats of philological deduction as well as forays onto more uncertain terrain as in the above examples. With these ideas of the pleasures and sorrows of pattern in mind, let us turn to a more personal realm: what Nabokov has to say about the patterns he has been able to trace in his own existence.

In his autobiography, Nabokov refers to "the supreme achievement of memory," which is "the masterly use it makes of innate harmonies when gathering to its fold the suspended and wandering tonalities of the past" (*SM*, 170). Memory's "supreme achievement" is the ordering of the chaotic richness of perception, full of loose ends and half-sketched movements ("the suspended and wandering tonalities of the past"), into a form which allows the "innate harmony" underlying those "suspended and wondering tonalities" to be heard. In a proposed sixteenth and last chapter of his memoir (which took the playful form of a review of the preceding fifteen chapters) a disguised Nabokov says the following: "Nabokov's method is to explore the remotest regions of his past life for what may be termed thematic trails or currents" ("Conclusive Evidence," 124). In the work itself, relating the seemingly chance connections between the matches with which his father's friend General Kuropatkin performed a trick for Nabokov as a child, and the match a disguised Kuropatkin later asked of Nabokov's father on a railway platform—which in turn links up with a theme of trains relating to his toys and to the Russo-Japanese War in which Kuropatkin commanded the Russian forces—Nabokov remarks that "the following of such thematic designs through one's life should be, I think, the true purpose of autobiography" (*SM*, 27). This searching for "thematic design" in life ceases here to be a *method* that Nabokov observes in his writing and becomes a *vocation*—the "true purpose of autobiography."[5]

When one examines *Speak, Memory* with an attentive eye, one finds a rich array of such patterns. The memoir begins with a "cradle," and ends with a "coffin"—indicating in a luminous abbreviation the path every life must follow. And yet this, like the match-train-war thematic pattern noted above, never tells a larger overarching story, never amounts to another story, but instead reflects the principal theme of the story itself in a different way. In the final lines of

5. One should note that Nabokov confides this same task to drama. In the Stanford Lecture notes from 1940 we read of Nabokov's aspirations for drama, that it consist, in its method, in "the selective and harmonious intensification of the loose patterns of chance and destiny, character and action, thought and emotion, existing in the reality of human life" (cited by Boyd 1991, 31).

Speak, Memory, Nabokov, his wife, and his young son are walking towards the boat which is to take them to America, when they at last see "a splendid ship's funnel, showing from behind the clothesline as something in a scrambled picture—Find What the Sailor Has Hidden—that the finder cannot unsee once it has been seen" (*SM*, 310). Here we at last see, and cannot then unsee, that the structure of the book is an evocation of, and farewell to the Europe, and the Russia, of Nabokov's life up to that point: the hidden rebus of exile. But what that rebus discloses is nothing other than the same theme which had been seen in more wandering and disparate form from the memoir's opening pages.

In the *Apostrophes* interview Nabokov speaks openly of employing such a technique for his novels: "My best novels do not have one, but instead several specially interwoven stories. My *Pale Fire* employs this counterpoint technique, as does *Ada*. I like to see the principal theme not simply radiate throughout the novel, but to also develop small secondary themes. Sometimes it is a digression become dramatic in an out of the way corner of the story, or the metaphors from a developed discourse linking up to form a new story." [Mes meilleurs romans n'ont pas une mais plusieurs histoires qui s'entrelacent d'une certaine façon. Mon *Feu pale* possède ce contrepoint et Ada de même. J'aime voir le thème principal non seulement rayonner à travers le roman mais encore développer des petits thèmes secondaires. Quelquefois c'est une digression qui tourne au drame dans un coin du récit, ou bien les métaphores d'un discours soutenu se joignent pour former une nouvelle histoire.] Nabokov himself offers no examples here, but it is not difficult to fill in the blanks. In *Ada, or Ardor*, for instance, we find a diamond necklace theme that not only accords perfectly with Nabokov's description, but functions in a similar way as does the match theme of *Speak, Memory* seen above. *Ada* first presents a real diamond necklace, then a quote from Chekhov about diamonds which segues into a story that is a transmogrification of Maupassant's diamond necklace tragedy, "*La Parure*," and which story then foreshadows the violent breaking of the initial necklace that then follows—and which figure returns in Demon's "demented diamonds" of the latter half of the book (cf. *Ada*, 189, 193, 509). In the extra (and excised) chapter cited above, a disguised Nabokov says of *Speak, Memory*: "The reader will surely enjoy finding for himself the convolutions, the stepping stones, the various smiling disguises of this or that thematic line running through the book"—and he clearly did not mean that book alone ("Conclusive Evidence," 124).

This patterning, or as Nabokov calls it here, "counterpoint technique," does not tell a separate story, but instead allows "the principal theme" to radiate more fully through the book—and to shape it. In *The Real Life of Sebastian Knight*, we are told that Sebastian enjoyed "juggling with themes, making them clash or blending them cunningly, making them express that hidden meaning, which could only be expressed in a succession of waves" (*RLSK*, 174). "The glory of god," as we saw, "is to hide a thing, and the glory of man is to find it." But in Nabokov's works, what is hidden is not another meaning, but that same meaning more artfully *signed*. Or in the words of Nabokov's first English novel, "the intricate pattern of human life turns out to be monogrammatic" (*RLSK*, 177).

Lolita is particularly rich in such signatures. Therein we find an excerpted passage from a "Who's Who in the Limelight" from 1946 which wryly evokes the various raveling and unraveling thematic threads one will later find in the work (*AL*, 31–32). A similar usage of a seemingly innocuous detail ostensibly offered only to lend the narrative the disparate flow and feel of life can be found in Lolita's class list, which contains many a wink and nod for the attentive rereader—not least in the person of the mysterious pupil "Aubrey McFate" (cf. *AL*, 51–52). Thinking of toilets and telephones in the unfolding of his fate, Humbert remarks that "we all have such fateful objects—it may be a recurrent landscape in one case, a number in another—carefully chosen by the gods to attract events of special significance for us" (*AL*, 211). The principal instance in this work, however, of such patterning seems surely to be the one that shrouds "Clare the Obscure"—Lolita's lover and abductor whom the narrative carefully cloaks and reveals—and in so revealing shows that many a seemingly unimportant detail provided earlier was pointing precisely to Mr. Quilty.[6]

At the moment when Humbert at last learns from Lolita's lips who his rival and vanquisher is, we read:

> Quietly the fusion took place, and everything fell into order, into the pattern of branches that I have woven throughout this memoir with the express purpose of having the ripe fruit fall at the right moment; yes, with express and perverse purpose of rendering . . . that golden and monstrous peace through the satisfaction of logical recognition, which my most inimical reader should experience now (*AL*, 272).

For Humbert, even the reader most strongly disposed against him must credit the formal discipline and craftsmanship involved in reproducing the stations of his discovery. Dozens of details in his narrative show how this face and form flickered at the edges of Humbert's consciousness over a period of years without his ever being able to resolve it into a single, recognizable image. When it

6. To cite a single instance, one might think of the strange letter that Lolita's friend and partner in deception Mona Dahl writes to her. Therein she reminds Lolita: "Ne manque pas de dire à ton amant, Chimène, comme le lac est beau car il faut qu'il t'y mène. Lucky beau! Qu'il t'y—What a tongue-twister!" (*AL*, 223). It would require a very patient reader to find Quilty's name nestled in that strange twist of Mona's French grammar "il faut *qu'il t'y* mène."

does, following Humbert, it should not fail to produce a "golden and monstrous peace."

Humbert's account of this process evokes one of the passages in *Speak, Memory* which tell us most about Nabokov's veneration of deception and discovery. "It occurs to me," he writes, "that the closest reproduction of the mind's birth obtainable is the stab of wonder that accompanies the precise moment when, gazing at a tangle of twigs and leaves, one suddenly realizes that what had seemed a natural component of that tangle is a marvelously disguised insect or bird" (*SM*, 298). Deceptive pattern and its revelation mimic nothing less than the initial movements of consciousness, nothing less than the "mind's birth." Nabokov notes elsewhere in *Speak, Memory* that "coincidence of pattern is one of the wonders of nature" (*SM*, 157). As a young man, Nabokov began to look very closely, as his remarkable gifts allowed him to do, into the book of Nature. Therein he began to see something akin to signs and symbols of a Creator in the created world—in, to chose the example he chooses, the excessively, extravagantly elaborate markings on the wings of butterflies. Mirroring nature, for him, means mirroring the patterns it reveals to the careful observer. By doing so, he reproduces an experience like that which he claims to have of the world. What is most singular about this revelation is that what is revealed when the deception is discerned and deciphered is not a hidden message or meaning, but, so to speak, the process of discovery itself. That which is revealed is not another story, but a deeper interconnection of elements in that same story—all its hidden winks, nods, clues, and codes tell the same story more finely perceived. Many of the signs encoded in Nabokov's works are better characterized as signatures, denoting principally the conscious and willed fact of their signing. Many can be traced to their signifying lair, many cannot, and still more wander between the two regions.

A Divinity that Shapes Our Ends

In *The Gift* we read:

Beyond the bridge, near the small public garden, two elderly postal workers, having completed their check of a stamp machine and grown suddenly playful, were stealing up from behind the jasmine, one behind the other, one imitating the other's gestures, toward a third—who with eyes closed was humbly and briefly relaxing on a bench before his working day—in order to tickle his nose with a flower. Where shall I put all these gifts with which the summer morning rewards me—and only me? Save them up for future books? Use them immediately for a practical handbook: *How to Be Happy*? Or getting deeper, to the bottom of things: understand what is concealed behind all this, behind the play, the sparkle, the thick, green greasepaint of the foliage? For there really is something, there is something! And one wants to offer thanks but there is no one to thank. The list of donations already made: 10,000 days—from Person Unknown (*Gift*, 328).

One does not know whom to thank for the donation of the gift of works and days, but the tracing of patterns is a way of ordering one's gifts, and this ordering is called for because, for Nabokov, there *is* "something" "concealed behind all this." In a similar vein he also states that his "highest enjoyment of timelessness" was "a sense of oneness with sun and stone. A thrill of gratitude to whom it may concern—to the contrapuntal genius of human fate or to tender ghosts humoring a lucky mortal" (*SM*, 139). As noted by Nabokov's son, from the date of Nabokov's father's assassination in Berlin in 1922, the word *God* disappeared from his poetry.[7] Nabokov was a member of no organized religion and voiced no faith in organized religion. He stresses, on the contrary, that he was an "indivisible monist" and seems to speak with his creation Shade when the latter writes, "Theolatry I found / Degrading, and its premises unsound" (*PF*, 32). Elsewhere he remarks that "since, in my metaphysics, I am a confirmed non-unionist and have no use for organized tours through anthropomorphic paradises I am left to my own, not negligible devices when I think of the best things in life" (*SM*, 297).

Nevertheless, in Chapter 2 of *Speak, Memory*, Nabokov says of his mother:

> her intense and pure religiousness took the form of her having equal faith in the existence of another world and in the impossibility of comprehending it in terms of earthly life. All one could do was to glimpse, amid the haze and the chimeras, something real ahead, just as persons endowed with an unusual persistence of diurnal cerebration are able to perceive in their deepest sleep, somewhere beyond the throes of an entangled and inept nightmare, the ordered reality of the waking hour (*SM*, 39).

This chapter of Nabokov's memoir is written under the sign of motherly love (it was originally titled "Portrait of My Mother") and finds a symmetry between the discovery of this world and life (in childhood), and the intuition, the intimation of some other form of life beyond this one. It treats of first and last things and ends in artistic lucidity. Nabokov tells us that it is not in dreams,

---

7. Dmitri Nabokov, interview with the Spanish journal *Joyce*, submitted (in English) to the NABOKOV-L Listerve by Dmitri Nabokov, October 12, 2003.

"but when one is wide awake, at moments of robust joy and achievement, on the highest terrace of consciousness, that mortality has a chance to peer beyond its own limits, from the mast, from the past and its castle tower. And although nothing much can be seen through the mist, there is somehow the blissful feeling that one is looking in the right direction" (*SM*, 50). This highest terrace of consciousness, this robust joy and achievement, seems to be none other than that of creation—the creation of a work of art.[8]

Earlier in *Speak, Memory*, Nabokov tells us that "neither in environment nor in heredity can I find the exact instrument that fashioned me, the anonymous roller that pressed upon my life a certain intricate watermark whose unique design becomes visible when the lamp of art is made to shine through life's foolscap" (*SM*, 25). For Nabokov, this "intricate watermark" stamped upon our life becomes visible first with the aid of "the lamp of art." It is through the specific form of creation that is art that he is able to first glimpse the sign and signature of his own creation. The watermarks he so carefully stamps on the pages of his works are not just the means through which he discovers his own "intricate watermark," but are also reflections of the ones he himself saw in creation—the signs and signatures he saw shining through the translucent wings of the butterflies—and through himself. The work of art, for him, was then a means not just to shine a light into the darkness of his origin, but to pay homage to the greater creation of which he felt himself a part.

Nabokov's lover Irina Guadanini related a remark he made in 1937: "the novelist [is] God's translator" (cf. Schiff, 87). In Nabokov's *Lectures on Literature*, we read of "the real writer" that he "sends planets spinning and models a man asleep and eagerly tampers with the sleeper's rib" (*LL*, 2). In *Bend Sinister*, he wrote, as we saw, of "an anthropomorphic deity" that he "impersonated" (*BS*, xviii). In an interview from 1963, he told his readers that "a creative writer must study carefully the works of his rivals, including the Almighty" (*SO*, 32). These are conceits and need not be seen as directly contradicting Nabokov's "non-unionist" vision of a world beyond this one. There is every indication from remarks made both in his fiction and elsewhere that he conceived of a

---

8. For Savely Senderovich, one of the critics who has most perceptively and reflectively followed Nabokov's patterns, Nabokov's "game" of "deliberately . . . pointing to the hidden and concealing it . . . constructs a metapoetic likeness of the fundamental, ultimate figure of concealment" (Senderovich, 30). Senderovich goes on to say of this figure of concealment that it "not only demonstrates the workings of concealment, but also both *signifies and conceals the concealment of a different order, that which encompasses the genuine, uncontrolled process of the psyche's self-discovery, a process that taps into the unconscious*" (ibid.; Senderovich's italics). This idea is sensitive and sound, but one might object to it that there is no reason to think that for Nabokov what was at stake in hiding and finding was a voyage "that taps into the unconscious." It seems, rather, that it was a pattern first visible from this "highest terrace of consciousness."

Creator for this world, and that he did not see this Creator along traditional Judeo-Christian lines, or along the lines of any religion whatsoever. This does not remove an element of reverence from his writing nor its importance for understanding his view of the relation of art to life.

To return to the remark made above, just as that Almighty deceptively signed his works, leaving a "watermark" in his Creation, so too must the creator who would be his translator. A watermark, however, does not communicate a message—it signs and seals a sheet's authenticity and provenance. Do Nabokov's patterns not function in precisely this way? Do they not, instead of communicating a message, sign and seal a provenance? Nabokov's Creator was, without question, a *Deus absconditus*. As His translator, what could be more appropriate than that he become, in His wake, a *scriptor absconditus*?

The Figure in the Magic Carpet

> I like to fold my magic carpet, after use, in such a way as to superimpose one part of the pattern upon another. Let visitors trip.
>
> —Vladimir Nabokov, *Speak, Memory*

In "The Figure in the Carpet," Henry James tells the story of a writer who speaks deceptively of his works. He does this by speaking quite openly about them. In James' tale, the mysterious and acclaimed author Hugh Vereker allures and perplexes the story's protagonist by giving him more and less cryptic clues as to the nature of his carefully wrought works. Vereker tells his avid reader of how the meaning of his works lies therein like a "complex figure in a Persian carpet" (James 1964, 289). Of this figure in the carpet, Vereker tells him that "it's exactly as palpable as the marble of this chimney . . . the thing's as concrete there as a bird in a cage, a bait on a hook, a piece of cheese in a mouse-trap" (James 1964, 282–284). Vereker's string of teasing and tantalizing metaphors point in a single direction. This "thing," this meaning to and in his works, "as palpable as the marble of this chimney," is nothing more or less than the textured text of Vereker's works themselves. Considered in themselves, they could not be more evident, could not be more "concrete." But for the reader who seeks a meaning beyond or above this concrete one, Vereker's texts deepen into something dizzying and dangerous. They become lures ("a bait on a hook, a piece of cheese in a mouse-trap") and once readers in search of a meaning beyond the work bite down, they are held fast ("a bird in the cage").

Though, as we saw, Nabokov did not like James, he shares something of his vision—and his metaphor. In a poem from 1944 Nabokov writes, "In this life, rich in patterns . . . / no better joy would I choose than to fold / its magnificent carpet in such a fashion / as to make the design of today coincide / with the past, with a former pattern" (*PP*, 123). "I like to fold my magic carpet, after use," Nabokov tells us in *Speak, Memory*, "in such a way as to superimpose one part of the pattern upon another. Let visitors trip" (*SM*, 139). In *Ada, or Ardor* we find a less metaphorical magic carpet, and in *Invitation to a Beheading*, Cincinnatus talks of an imaginative realm where "time takes shape according to one's plea-sure, like a figured rug whose folds can be gathered in such a way that two designs will meet—and the rug is once again smoothed out, and you live on, or else superimpose the next image on the last, endlessly, endlessly . . ." (*IB*, 94).

   Pale Fire is Nabokov's work which most concerns itself with patterns. It is not only itself densely and intricately patterned, it graphically portrays charac-ters in search of patterns both earthly and divine. In Shade's poem "Pale Fire," the poet relates his search for such patterns. He describes how the decision to seek out patterns of the most varied sort in his own experience was a response to his frustrated attempts to locate clear signs of a Beyond: he is tricked by a misprint in a newspaper article into believing that he had shared a vision of the afterlife—or at least of its forecourt—with a stranger. He writes:

> But all at once it dawned on me that *this*
> Was the real point, the contrapuntal theme;
> Just this: not text, but texture; not the dream
> But topsy-turvical coincidence,
> Not flimsy nonsense, but a web of sense.
> Yes! It sufficed that I in life could find
> Some kind of link-and-bobolink, some kind
> Of correlated pattern in the game,
> Plexed artistry, and something of the same
> Pleasure in it as they who played it found. (*PF*, 62–63; Nabokov's italics)[9]

Like Nabokov in his autobiographical writings, Shade finds his vocation in lo-cating and lyricizing patterns of "coincidence." As we saw earlier, *Ada*'s Van notes that, "some law of logic should fix the number of coincidences, in a given do-main, after which they cease to be coincidences, and form, instead, the living organism of a new truth" (*Ada*, 361). Nabokov was much concerned with the fixing of this number, as were his creations. Both as a writer and a man, he was fascinated, and—at times—haunted, by coincidences, and proved highly sensitive to recurrent images, fatidic dates, chance optical or auditory hallucinations, curi-

9. One finds a related remark in the occluded final chapter of *Speak, Memory* where a cloaked Nabokov refers to "the way his [Nabokov's] life had been planned by unknown players of games" ("Conclusive Evidence," 126).

ous dreams, and any other perceptions which seemed to suggest a faint pattern leading beyond the limits of consciousness. He went about trying to follow those perceptions by cataloguing his dreams, and kept a dream diary to this end where he endeavored to catch sight of a space beyond time (both inspired and guided in this by the eccentric British scientist J. W. Dunne—whose theories on time's illusory nature are reflected in *Ada*). Goethe once wrote that: "Supersition is the poetry of life, and for that reason it does the poet no harm to be superstitious [*Der Aberglaube ist die Poesie des Lebens; deswegen schadet's dem Dichter nicht, abergläubisch zu sein*]" (Goethe 12:.494). In Nabokov's case, not only did his superstition not harm his poetry, it gave specific shape to his prose.

For Shade, these patterns of coincidence noted above are his proof that all is not "flimsy nonsense," but woven instead into "a web of sense." These patterns are, however, of a peculiar character. They are intricate, imbricated, but nonetheless recognizable. That recognition does not lead, however, to their simple translation or transformation into a *message*. The "real point" is "not text, but texture." The patterns found by Shade and his peers are signs of provenance, signatures of intent, but a clear summary of that intent is not to be had. To create, however, analogous patterns is what gives Shade at least a "faint hope" (*PF*, 63).

In the final canto of "Pale Fire," he writes:

> Maybe my sensual love for the *consonne*
> *D'appui*, Echo's fey child, is based upon
> A feeling of fantastically planned,
> Richly rhymed life.
>
> I feel I understand
> Existence, or at least a minute part
> Of my existence, only through my art,
> In terms of combinatorial delight;
> And if my private universe scans right,
> So does the verse of galaxies divine . . . (*PF*, 68–69)

Nabokov's Shade calls the patterns he sees "richly rhymed life," and finds that the poet's "private universe scans right" through his creating of his own patterns, so too does the "verse of galaxies divine."

This is an idea which is far from exclusive to Shade (who ranks, however, amongst those of Nabokov's creations with whom he shares the most positions and perceptions[10]). In Nabokov's preface to *The Eye*, he notes that "the texture

---

10. In *Strong Opinions*, Nabokov notes: "It is true that some of my more responsible characters are given some of my own ideas. There is John Shade in *Pale Fire*, the poet. He does borrow some of my own opinions" (*SO*, 18).

of the tale mimics that of detective fiction," but that "the stress is not on the mystery but on the pattern" (*Eye*, iv). In the foreword to *Speak, Memory*, Nabokov notes that his initial choice of title for that work was "The Anthemion": "which is the name of a honeysuckle ornament, consisting of elaborate interlacements and expanding clusters, but nobody liked it" (*SM*, 11). Doubtless with this passage in mind, Appel wrote in one of his proposed annotations for the *Annotated Lolita*: "A grand anthemion has been laid across Humbert's narrative, like some vast authorial watermark . . ." When Appel submitted his notes to Nabokov for counsel and approval, the latter penciled in a correction: ". . . has been laid *into*."[11] Nabokov's correction is slight but decisive. As it reflects, Nabokov envisioned the patterning in his texts not as something which would be writ large over and across them, not a template or a palimpsest which would be "laid *across*" them, but which would instead be imbedded into their fiber and substance; they would not be separate text, but integral texture. In *Strong Opinions*, Nabokov remarks that "in my memoirs, quotable ideas are merely passing visions, suggestions, mirages of the mind. They lose their colors or explode like football fish when lifted out of the context of their tropical sea" (*SO*, 147).[12]

This, as well as many of Nabokov's patterns, is not visible at first glance. And both the complexity of his compositions and the emotional intensity they convey have led a number of Nabokov's readers to call him cruel. This charge had much to do with Nabokov's relation to his readers. He made no secret of his relative indifference to them. While Nabokov was indeed not especially dependent upon outside approval, his remarks on the subject are playful, provocative, and, as more private communications show, not entirely what he meant. Though they were not to influence the work in its inception and composition, he did envision at least a restricted group of readers for his works. But these readers were anything but pampered. The perception Nabokov had of the world and which he endeavored to reflect in the creation of his fictional worlds was one where no precepts or prescriptions could prevail, where to learn one needed to perceive with fantastic energy and attention even—and especially—the finest details in nature and art, and to study these details with insight, intelligence, and imagination. In his works, the anthropomorphic deity he said he was impersonating reproduced this experience, dissimulating signs,

11. Photostat, Nabokov Archive, Berg Collection, New York Public Library, 26; my italics. Appel's notes to *The Annotated Lolita* are an invaluable resource. Composed as they were with the help of Nabokov himself, they offer a rare insight into Nabokov's conception of his work and what the reader needs to know to understand it, in addition to being witty, urbane, and informative. The Nabokov Archive in the Berg Collection of the New York Public Library contains two typescripts submitted by Appel to, and corrected by, Nabokov.

12. Interestingly enough, the image Nabokov chooses here is one that he silently lifts out of the sea of an earlier work—*Invitation to a Beheading* (cf. *IB*, 94).

signals, and signatures in the details of his works. The difficulty and complexity of the hidden patterns these details formed, and Nabokov's insistence that these patterns were not of the order of a moral or allegorical message, brought him the charge from certain readers of a gratuitousness verging on the cruel. What shaped Nabokov's novelistic patterns, and distinguished them from what he dismissively called "the traditional patterns of fiction," was more than anything else his belief in the inviolability of the particular, and what he professed to loathe above all else in art and life was the loose-fitting generality (*LL*, 2). If ethics is the province of the individual, and that individual must make judgments without the benefit of an overarching law, the individual decisions arrived at could not be approximatively expressed in the generalizing form of a precept or prescription. Such a morality would be inexpressible in the form of a proposition which would confine in the tiny coffin of a prescriptive phrase the manifold morality of life.

Nabokov says of his lectures on literature that he envisioned them as "a kind of detective investigation of the mystery of literary structures" (*LL*, 89). The remark remains puzzling so long as we do not look to where in that same lecture Nabokov defines what he means by the term "structure." He says that it is "the planned pattern of a work of art" (*LL*, 113). We saw earlier Nabokov's surprising insistence on "style" in the work of art, his insistence that style and only style truly mattered. In the same passage cited here, Nabokov tells his audience what style is. It means "how does the structure work" (*LL*, 113). If the structure is planned pattern in a work of art, style is how that planned pattern laid into the work of art works. Style is then not an arid concern with language and nothing but language which excludes all moral intent or effect, but, to adopt Nabokov's phrase, an indivisibly monistic approach to the work of art. To express in art a morality other than prescriptive, and to signal the existence of a Creator, required a density and a complexity which became Nabokov's passion—and which required of his readers a patience and a persistence which to many of them seemed too great. And thus the charge of cruelty. But might he not have been cruel to be kind?

Conclusion

Style

AT THE END OF "Good Readers and Good Writers," Nabokov notes that "the three facets of the great writer—magic, story, lesson—are prone to blend in one impression of unified and unique radiance, since the magic of art may be present in the very bones of the story, in the very marrow of thought" (*LL*, 6). Now that we have examined something of the bones of Nabokov's stories and the marrow of his thought, let us return to the magic, the story, and the lesson of *Lolita*.

The question this study has endeavored to ask is a simple one: How are we to read *Lolita*? To better approach and more carefully define this question other intermediate questions have been posed. One of these was how we are ultimately meant to view Humbert Humbert at the end of his entrancing tale. If Nabokov found that Humbert was "a vain and cruel wretch," "a foreigner and an anarchist,"[1] why was he to be granted a yearly stroll at dusk in a green lane in Paradise? This question is a different formulation of the question posed as to the role the "mournful monsters" Nabokov exiled from art's inner sanctum to its façade play in his work, what message they offer, and what pattern they form.

To understand the reprieve Nabokov grants his creation, it is necessary to identify the sin that precedes it. This was not merely what Humbert himself calls it ("nympholepsy"). It was something more sweeping involving not only what

---

1. "My creature Humbert is a foreigner and an anarchist, and there are many things, besides nymphets, in which I disagree with him" (*AL*, 315).

he does but how he does it—and how he justifies it. Though Humbert is graced with gifts that would have allowed him to do so, he fails to see from the standpoint of his Lolita. He fails to exercise the empathy that Nabokov stressed must balance and temper artistic gifts that tend of themselves towards sovereign independence, isolation, and even, in some cases, cruel indifference to the standpoint of others. Entranced by his senses and pursuing his image of Lolita as if she were an inspiring image of art, Humbert fails to see that "there was in her a garden and a twilight, and a palace gate." These "dim and adorable regions" are forbidden to him because of the intensity and the single-mindedness with which he occludes them, with which he concentrates on "another Lolita," an "image" created in his sensual haze that his desperation and desire lead him to call "more real" than the little girl in his charge. In this, Nabokov has Humbert fail to observe the line that divides art from life—that same line that Nabokov's compatriot Khodasevich identified decades before *Lolita* as lying at the heart of the burgeoning writer's aesthetics.

In works early and late—and nowhere more spectacularly than in *Lolita*— Nabokov asked how the artist was to live in the world, how to balance fierce independence of vision with the necessity of seeing the world from the standpoint of others. This is a question of judgment: the question of how to balance the aesthetic with the ethical, the disinterested remove of aesthetic judgment with the interested proximity of moral judgment. To understand this balance better, we need to turn to what preceded *Lolita*: its inspiration.

Inspiration, or the Artist and the Ape

> *Qui fait l'homme, fait le singe.*
>
> —Pascal

In "On A Book Entitled *Lolita*," Nabokov offers something he normally kept to himself—his inspiration:

The first little throb of *Lolita* went through me late in 1939 or early in 1940, in Paris, at a time when I was laid up with a severe attack of intercostal neuralgia. As far as I can recall, the initial shiver of inspiration was somehow prompted by a newspaper story about an ape in the Jardin des Plantes, who, after months of coaxing by a scientist, produced the first drawing ever charcoaled by an animal: this sketch showed the bars of the poor creature's cage (*AL*, 311).

Nabokov was not the first great writer to find inspiration in what went on in the Jardin des Plantes. In his diary entry for January 2, 1871, Victor Hugo wrote: "They killed the elephant at the Jardin des Plantes. It wept. They're going to eat it." Thirty years later, another poet, Rainer Maria Rilke, paid a gentler and more poetically fruitful visit to the Jardin des Plantes. What captured *his* eye was a panther. For Rilke's cat, like Nabokov's ape, captivity was the central fact of his existence. "It seems to him," wrote Rilke, that, "there are / A thousand bars; and behind the bars, no world" (Rilke 1.469). What Rilke found at the zoo was, however, far different from what Nabokov found there. What interested the wandering poet was how impenetrable, how full of incommunicable will, strength, and silence the animal was; what awakened Rilke's poetic sensibilities was how closed-off that animal's world was, how deeply it was entrenched in its inner jungle. Nabokov's ape, by contrast, is singled out for doing something normally seen as intrinsically human—seeking to express its sorrow through art—or something like it. Rilke's proud panther would never deign to draw aside the veil of its impenetrable perception.[2] Nabokov's ape, on the other hand, freely offers a sign of what most colors its world—the dark bars of its confinement.

Lolita is the tale of a man who, much more so than Joyce's Leopold Bloom, "is too beastly awfully weird for words." Humbert will describe himself as "attractively simian" and Quilty, in mortal danger, will cry out to him, "Show me your badge instead of shooting at my foot, you ape, you" (*AL*, 106, 298). For this and other crimes he is, as he tells his reader, writing behind bars—having begun his "confession" as a document to be presented to the court convened to judge him. By the end of its composition he has recognized that what he has written is far too personal to be paraded before the world and asks that it not be published until after his—and his Lolita's—deaths. Is the inspiration for such a final document to be drawn from an ape?

When led to do so, the ape's first attempt at self-expression expresses the most fundamental fact of its existence: imprisonment. While those who come to see the ape may, in following the creature's movements, begin to see through or around the bars of its cage, the ape looking back has no such freedom of vision. Did Nabokov's inspiration merely consist in his being moved by the poignancy of the ape's effort to express something of his caged world? Did he find inspiration in this newspaper account because the beast behind bars conjured to this mind another beast behind another set of bars?

To understand what Nabokov was trying to express in this account of the work's inspiration, we would do well to turn to the particular article that inspired the bedridden author and ask whether it can teach us something about

---

2. In a singular act of poetic justice, Ted Hughes will free Rilke's panther's poetic descendant. Hughes' jaguar "spins from the bars, but there's no cage to him / More than to the visionary his cell: / His stride is wildernesses of freedom" ("The Jaguar," in *Hawk in the Rain*, 9). J. M. Coetzee has his Elizabeth Costello turn to these same poems in *The Lives of Animals* (37).

the book it led to. As such, it may not. In the note to this passage in the *The Annotated Lolita*, Appel stresses the importance of this "prison trope" but of the literal source he says nothing (*AL*, 311n). And it seems that there is a good reason for this: it does not exist. The newspapers for those years have been combed and recombed and the article has not been found. The most definitively annotated edition of Nabokov's works in any language is (at present) the German critical edition of Dieter Zimmer. In Zimmer's exhaustive note to this passage in Nabokov's afterword, he lists the various researches undertaken by himself and others to find any such article in the newspapers of those years. Zimmer notes that the celebrated zoologist Desmond Morris published an exhaustive list of all known experiments conducted with primates involving drawing or sign making and that nothing resembling Nabokov's ape is to be found anywhere therein.[3] More recently, Dmitri Nabokov noted that he knew nothing of the article's whereabouts and confirmed that neither himself nor anyone else had to his knowledge ever seen it.[4] In summary, writes Zimmer, "this article about the incident in Paris's Zoo has despite extensive efforts never been uncovered and is perhaps a fiction" (Nabokov, *Lolita* [*Gesammelte Werke*, vol. 8], 686–687).

To all appearance Nabokov's inspiration was a "fiction." Was it then a hoax? Was it merely a stylistic flourish or flash of impish wit, or was there something more behind it, deceptively concealed therein? "On a Book Entitled *Lolita*" was not the only instance where Nabokov offered his inspiration. "I remember with special limpidity," he writes in the foreword to the English translation of *The Defense*, "a sloping slab of rock, in the ulex- and ilex-clad hills, where the main thematic idea of the book first came to me" (*Defense*, 7). Though Nabokov wryly follows this indication by remarking that "some curious additional information might be given if I took myself more seriously," the remark deserves to be taken seriously enough for us to examine the thematic relation between this sloping slab and the complicated chess patterns woven into that work (ibid.). Nabokov states of this especially limpid moment of inspiration that this was "*where* the main thematic idea of the book first came to me"—and not "*when*." "*When*" would have led us to dismiss the following as local color while we awaited the *what*. At first sight, it seems that Nabokov recounts the setting for his inspiration without its content or nature. But might he not be doing both? Nabokov may have seen a slab of stone amid an arrangement of

---

3. Nabokov, *Lolita* (*Gesammelte Werke*, vol. 8), 686–687. Cf. Morris, *The Biology of Art*. Zimmer also directs his reader's attention to the claims of the primatologist David Premack in his *The Mind of an Ape* that though apes do not lack the motor skills to produce drawings, they seem to lack the mental skills for such complex depictions (Premack, 108 ff.; Nabokov, *Lolita* [*Gesammelte Werke*, vol. 8], 686–687).

4. Email of Wednesday, November 13, 2002 5:51 AM. Nabokov List-Serve: http://listserv.ucsb.edu.

ilex and ulex that suggested to him the backdrop and the pieces of that novel, just as he may have felt that the slab of stone evoked a primitive chessboard—or an isolated one. The idea of a chessboard seen in an improbable or impossible natural setting may have led Nabokov to imagine someone so obsessed or possessed by a given passion (such as chess) that they begin to see the forms and patterns that make up that passion elsewhere—and everywhere. Luzhin's world becomes ever more colored, and divided, by his chess obsession, and he begins with mounting regularity to see natural forms and human interactions in chess patterns and chess terms. We might even conjecture that something more verbal than visual may have set Nabokov's mind in motion, the alternating ilex and ulex resembling in their paired similarity the black and white figures and squares on a board. This is all tantamount to saying that what seemed like mere mischief or coquetry (in Nabokov revealing the *when* but not the *what*) might have been a carefully concealed revelation full of sense and meaning. These are questions impossible to answer definitively, but the direction they point towards is that the inspirational core of Nabokov's *Defense* may indeed have found apt expression in the deceptive description Nabokov offered. And that the careful if "fictional" account of inspiration he offered as regards *Lolita* may have served a similar purpose. Nabokov was much interested in cages in art, and in his *Lectures on Literature* put special emphasis upon the centrality of caged birds in the work of Sterne and Dickens—"Cages, bird cages, their bars, the shadow of their bars striking out, as it were, all happiness" (*LL*, 74). It seems that Nabokov invented just such a cage for the occasion of a text to accompany *Lolita's* publication.

Nabokov has his Humbert see a set of bars and Wood is doubtless right to claim that Humbert "has drawn not the world but what separates him from the world" (Wood, 108).[5] This portrait of separation, however, takes a turn as it nears its end—as Nabokov was to tell Appel (cf. *SO*, 73). Humbert realizes that in Lolita "there was in her a garden and a twilight, and a palace gate—dim and adorable regions which happened to be lucidly and absolutely forbidden to me" (*AL*, 284). This change is Humbert glimpsing the garden he will never enter and the gate which, as he gazes upon it, slowly becomes the cage he will painfully, painstakingly draw—and which drawing is the memoir he leaves at his death.[6]

5. In a similar vein, Rothstein remarks in an article published six years later, "like the ape, [Humbert] can draw only the traces of his own and Dolores's confinement, a tale of continual cross-continental motion in the blue cage of his car or stops in motel rooms he sees as paradisal prison cells" (Rothstein, 49).

6. In her essay on the figure of the monster in Nabokov's fiction, Dawson sees in this passage a lesson in curiosity and empathy: "In *Lolita*, Nabokov will call upon a pedophile (the most monstrous and ape-like human he could imagine) to ask his reader to consider what it must be like to be this poor creature" (Dawson, 121).

The Conspiratorial Dagger

Returning to the question of how we are to ultimately view Humbert, we should recall that Nabokov once remarked that "Humbert Humbert in his last stage is a moral man because he realizes that he loves Lolita like any woman should be loved. But it is too late, he has destroyed her childhood" (quoted by Rampton, 202 n. 34). This change in Humbert's heart that makes of him, in Nabokov's final words, a "moral" man, is also the one that leads to his annual reprieve.

Humbert is offered the special grace of a yearly stroll, however, not only because of the lesson he learns, if too late, but also because of one he imparts. Nabokov has Humbert employ the methods destined for art to life, has him move in his world as if that world were but a work of art where the kindling of the senses and the pursuing of inspiring images were what should come before all else. This is how someone graced with his powers of perception and sensitivity could act with such callousness towards someone he claimed to love. And it is this lesson learned too late which spurs him on to a special undertaking: the writing of his "confessions."

The first part of Nabokov's formal challenge was the one we noted in the introduction: making the abhorrent appealing. The second part was to have the appealing unmask itself as abhorrent—but at the right time and in the right fashion. Nabokov has Humbert compose a memoir in which he narrates not from the point of view of the repentance and bitter resignation that is his own at the time of writing, but from that of the euphoria and haunted rapture that preceded it, from the perspective that had been his own and through which he gradually persuaded himself that what he was doing to young Dolores Haze could be explained, could be justified, could not be avoided. This device allows for the fine "pattern of remorse daintily running along the steel of his conspiratorial dagger" to remain, for the better part of the book, invisible. When it is revealed, when Humbert ceases to recreate and relate his coldness for the sake of what he calls "retrospective verisimilitude," we understand why he chose to call that dagger "conspiratorial" in the first place. Against whom was it turned? Against whom did he conspire? "Tum-tee-tum. And once more—TUM! I have not gone mad. I am merely producing gleeful little sounds. The kind of glee one experiences upon making an April fool of someone. And a damned good fool I *have* made of

---

Frosch is especially attentive to this passage, but interprets it in a much different light: as a parable about parody and authenticity. He stresses the traditional idea that apes are mere mimics and consequently reads this passage in that light: "So Humbert, the ape, the parody, gives us a picture of his emotional and moral imprisonment and enchantment. To be free is to be original, not to be a parody" (Frosch, 46).

someone. Who is he? Gentle reader, look at yourself in the mirror" (*Despair*, 24).
Humbert's conspiracy is against his reader, and it is, like all successful conspira-
cies, so effective because it is so well concealed.

Nabokov once said of two other books named after the women who lose
their lives in them—*Madame Bovary* and *Anna Karenina*—that they were "delightful explosions admirably controlled" (*LL*, 10). The description might apply
with equal justice to *Lolita*. It is precisely this mechanism that led so many of
the work's finest readers to note an insidious unease in reading his tale and to
detect a cruelty in Nabokov's undertaking that went beyond the acts described
therein. Humbert's eloquence is powerful and profoundly deceptive, and what
is more deceptive than all else is his purpose. Nabokov has Humbert make the
worse appear the better reason in the first part of his memoir so that he can
show how he came to so mistreat the girl he pretended to so dearly love. By the
time the light hits the pattern and his reader sees his "conspiratorial dagger,"
it is too late to parry and all that is left is to admire the design—an experience
that fifty years of critical reception admirably testifies to.

Much of *Lolita*'s poignancy then comes from Humbert and his artistic
gifts—gifts put into practice too late to stop him from "destroying [Lolita's]
childhood," but not too late to put them to use in telling an "entrancing" tale.
The gifts of perception and persistence that are the artist's bring with them
a charge: the moral duty that, as we saw, an "old poet" reminds us that mortals
must pay on art. This moral duty is nothing other than vigilance—vigilance as
regards the danger of art, the threat that in its single-minded pursuit of its goal,
in its heat and hurry it might trample the tenderness that the artist, more than
any other, should know to prize and to protect. In his *Defense of Poetry*, Shelley
claimed that "the greatest instrument of moral good is the imagination" (Shelley, 488). Nabokov may have felt similarly, but he found the matter far from
simple as, for him, the imagination and the senses that fire it must be reined in,
must learn to limit themselves to the artistic sphere so that they may remain
an instrument of widening and deepening perception, not of pain and loss.

The Death of Art

The answer to the question of how we are to view and understand
Humbert—both "a vain and cruel wretch" and, ultimately, "a moral man"—leads
us directly to another element essential to our answering of the question of
how we are to read *Lolita*. If, for Nabokov, *Lolita* was a "moral" book, why
didn't he simply come out and say so? An initial answer is that, on occasion,

he did come out and say so. This is, however, only a partial answer as it does not explain why he also seemed to say the opposite, or why he so vehemently stressed that *Lolita*—like his other books—had "no moral in tow." To answer the question as to why, if Nabokov had written *Lolita* with something of a moral intention he did not come out and say so, that he did come out and say so, would be to misrepresent the facts. What Nabokov on occasion did was to offer reminders that his work was neither written nor meant to be read in the moral vacuum he seemed to advocate in his more polemical public statements. Nevertheless, from his earliest to his latest remarks on the topic, he claimed that the pronouncing of precepts for the propagation of proper moral conduct lay far from the heart of literature, and that when literature reduced itself to being *merely* such pronouncement and propagation, it mortally endangered its own essence.

For both more and less practical reasons, all having to do with how he envisioned his works to be read, Nabokov was extremely wary about stressing the moral import of his works in the public domain. As we saw earlier, his reasoning is all too easy to understand. Stressing this moral import brought with it the real and significant risk of being misunderstood. As it seemed to him that his age and its readers were more inclined to err on the side of placing the work of art—and, especially, the novel—in too immediate and intimate contact with everyday reality, and were inclined to identify an artist's creations with their creator, he stressed the other side: the distance of work from world and the corresponding autonomy of the work of art.

This is seen with remarkable clarity in a letter from October 1945. Therein, Nabokov replied to a reader's reproach that in his recently published *Nikolai Gogol* he had presented Gogol, and art itself, as fundamentally amoral. "I never meant to deny," wrote Nabokov, "*the moral impact of art which is certainly inherent in every genuine work of art.* What I do deny and am prepared to fight to the last drop of my ink is the deliberate moralizing which to me kills every vestige of art in a work however skillfully written" (*SL*, 56–57; my italics). By separating "moral impact" from "moralizing," Nabokov is trying, in compressed form, to express the essence of his aesthetics: that his vision of the morality of art is one where that morality is absolutely inseparable from the work.

Nabokov claims here as elsewhere that conceptions of art that ask of the work to transport social, moral, or political messages endanger it by reducing it to the mere carrier of an ideological freight that would, in any event, have been more efficiently transported—or towed—by another vessel. For Nabokov, what happened when literary content came to be prized over literary form was, even in the case of his most treasured authors, a disaster. In this same letter, he reminds his correspondent of Tolstoy's *Kreutzer Sonata* and *Power of Darkness*, works written, following Nabokov, "with a deliberate moral purpose," which, he claims, "largely defeats their purpose, *killing the inherent morality of uninhibited art*" (*SL*, 56–57; my italics).

Of Part 2 of Gogol's *Dead Souls*, Nabokov will say that, "good as some passages are, the author's spiritual message is felt to be gradually killing the book," and that "ethical and religious considerations could only destroy the soft, warm, fat creatures of [Gogol's] fancy" (*NG*, 161, 103). As in the letter from 1945, his terms are categorical and could hardly be more extreme: art is "destroyed" or "killed" when it attempts to tote or tow ethical, religious, or political content. Both works by Tolstoy mentioned in the above letter are from a period in the latter's literary production that Nabokov refers to elsewhere as his "hyperethical stage," and which he will describe as Tolstoy's "surrender[ing] the writing of his novels to the ethical, mystical, educational urge,"—where the baseness of the surrender is clearly identified in Nabokov's relegating what Tolstoy saw as a high calling to a low "urge" (cf. *NG*, 40, 117). More epigrammatically, Nabokov will borrow, years later, an expression from Verlaine to stress the mortal danger at issue and inveigh against the use of "la pointe assassine, that is introducing an epigrammatic or moral point at the end of a poem, and thereby murdering the poem" (*SO*, 124). Stendhal famously proclaimed that "politics in a literary work is like a shot fired in the middle of a concert."[7] Nabokov seems to go a step farther in such remarks: in his view, politics in a work of art is not merely a shot fired during a concert which distracts and even frightens its audience, it is the shooting of the musicians themselves.

No Moral in Tow, or a Moral Book

These positions seem to indicate a paradox: If *Lolita* has "no moral in tow," how could Nabokov claim that it is a "moral" book? To answer the question we might begin by bracketing Nabokov's own claim that the work was a moral one and recalling that to ascertain that the book is a moral book we need no recourse to Nabokov's own claims about it. The novel itself richly suffices to make this clear. *Lolita* is a moral novel not in the rather abstract sense that every document of human expression inevitably contains, expressed in one fashion or another, an ethical element. Nor is it a moral novel merely for the fact that Nabokov called it one—just as little as it is an amoral novel because he also called it that. Such questions can only lead the reader into a hazy area of authorial intention

---

7. "*La politique dans un oeuvre littéraire, c'est un coup de pistolet au milieu d'un concert . . .*" Stendhal. *De l'amour.* Texte etabli, avec introduction et notes, par Henri Martineau. Paris: Garnier, 1959, 236.

from which little is to be learned. *Lolita* is a moral book in the simple sense that from its first page to its last it explicitly treats moral questions. Morality in the form of the persistent question of whether it is ethically acceptable for Humbert to do what he does when and how he does it is one of the novel's central themes—one that is constantly alluded to and addressed therein. Morality, moral choices, moral falterings, faults, failings, and failures make up the matter of the work and in this sense Nabokov's reminder that the book was a "moral" one is perfectly clear. The work may have the same compositional virtues and complexity as a chess problem, but to view the movement of more and less powerful and versatile figures across its board independent of any moral considerations is to read against the book's clearly ingrained purpose.

In his early review of the novel (from 1957), Nemerov stressed that "*Lolita* is . . . a moral work, if by morality in literature we are to understand the illustration of a usurious rate of exchange between our naughty desires and virtuous pains, of the process whereby pleasures become punishments . . . Humbert Humbert . . . gets punished . . . in the end. Also in the middle. Also in the end" (Nemerov, 320). Nemerov is immediately concerned here with showing that the work is not a salacious and not an amoral or immoral one. He stresses that Lolita is "a moral work" because its thematic concern is intrinsically moral, focusing as it does upon the relation of desire to attainment and on what routes are acceptable to move from the one to the other. But there is also an added element to *Lolita*'s morality concerning artistic means and ends. Humbert encourages his reader to view his memoir in its initial stages through the lens of art. In its second stage, he encourages his reader to view his memoir through another lens—the lens of life. This opposition is one whose dividing line is drawn with a moral pen—one of many ways in which the novel brings the question of the relation of art to life and how to make the necessary moral distinctions between the two to the forefront.

That *Lolita* incited a public scandal concerning the social and moral effects of works of art on society at large does not make it a moral book. That fact makes it, instead, a document having served as a social or cultural touchstone at a given point in time. But its *thematic* occupation with moral questions—and the tension between artistic impulses and moral imperatives—makes it unambiguously moral. In Nabokov's (and Nemerov's) words, *Lolita* is "a moral book" for the simple reason that it directly and thematically engages moral questions.

In this light we can see that Nabokov is not simply contradicting himself, or being cunningly deceptive, when he on the one hand says that *Lolita* has "no moral in tow" and on the other that it is a "moral book." The seeming contradiction arises because of the special sense in which Nabokov understood the relation of morality to the work of art. A "moral in tow" would be something separate and separable from the work of art—a moral to the story that lies outside it and that is pulled along in its wake. In the terms he used in his letter above, this would be "moralizing." In this light, only failed novels, only ones where matter and manner fail to fuse, "moralize"—only they have "a moral in tow" as they must tow behind them what they could not bring on board. A truly "moral book" is not merely prescriptive, does not bluntly or blandly offer ethical precepts or maxims but presents a more integral vision of the relation of morality to art. When Nabokov claimed that *Lolita* was "a moral book" he clearly meant "moral" in the sense of "an inherent morality of uninhibited art"—a "moral impact" so intimately bound up with the individual elements of the story as to be inseparable from it. Nabokov's position on the importance of the particularity of the work of art and his vehement opposition to generalities and generalizing schemata such as those offered by modern master-thinkers like Freud, Marx, and Darwin is of a piece with his position on the moral tenor of the work of art. The moral element of the work of art is inseparable from individual elements of a story, from its "quiddity." We saw earlier Nabokov pointing out "the fatal flaw in Mr. Rowe's treatment of recurrent words, such as 'garden' or 'water,'" in the latter's "regarding them as abstractions, and not realizing that the sound of a bath being filled, say, in the world of *Laughter in the Dark*, is as different from the limes rustling in the rain of *Speak, Memory* as the Garden of Delights in *Ada* is from the lawns in *Lolita*" (*SO*, 36). There is an ethical element in *Lolita*, but it is one indissociable from its losses, lures, loves, and lawns.

For this reason the last word on the subject is reserved for what Nabokov revered above all else in art: *style*. Style, however, is a word he used in a special sense: not merely smooth and elegant form, but a moral stance reflected in formal choice. Style was, for Nabokov, an idea of art where moral form and moral content were indissoluble, and thus could be expressed in no fewer and no other words than those of the work.

Style *Is* Matter

Of *Madame Bovary*, Nabokov once remarked, "the subject may be crude and repulsive. Its expression is artistically modulated and balanced. This is style. This is art. This is the only thing that really matters in books" (*LL*, 138). This claim is a crucial one and should be understood in its full import. It is indeed striking and peremptory after the fashion of many of Nabokov's remarks concerning those books and authors he most treasured (and whose essence he sought to defend against those he saw as seeking to appropriate it for their own critical ends), but this should not lead us to miss its polemical target: a facile and prescriptive "realism."

We saw earlier the special issues Nabokov had with the term "reality." In this light, we can more readily understand the problems he had with the term "realism" and the normalizing element it implies. Accused of obscenity, Flaubert replied, "obscene books are immoral because untruthful. When reading them, one says: 'That's not the way things are' . . . Mind you, I detest what is convention-ally called 'realism,' although I have come to be regarded as one of its pontiffs" (Flaubert/Sand, 365–366). Even if no one regarded him as one of its pontiffs, Nabokov found himself in an equally uneasy relation to "realism." He had no time or patience for doctrinaire adhesion to a movement or literary guide-lines, just as he had no patience with the idea that a work of art needed to be measured by the yardstick of what he elsewhere contemptuously referred to as "the myth of the average audience" (Boyd 1991, 30). Nevertheless, Nabokov passionately believed in fidelity to detail and fidelity to a reality perceived with clarity and imagination, and that, as we saw earlier, led him in *Lolita* "to use my combinatorial talent *to make it real*" (*SO*, 15; my italics). The discipline he asked of his readers—whether reading his own works or those he treasured—was pre-cisely of this sort. And yet alongside of this attention and fidelity to detail he encouraged his readers to remember to draw the fine line between art and life. The ethical matter and manner of *Lolita* are difficult to understand—and to judge—not because the ethical question therein is a difficult one to decide upon, but because that ethical matter is so closely wedded to and so tightly interwoven with its artistic matter and manner, with the question of the limits of art.

In this light, it makes all the more sense that the only morality that had a place in Nabokov's conception of art was "an inherent morality" embodied and expressed in every word of the work. In an unpublished Wellesley lecture from the same period as the letter about Gogol, Nabokov will state that "art has been too often turned into a tool to convey ideas," but conditions this observation by noting:

> I am not telling you that art does not improve and enlighten the reader. But it does this in its own special way and it does it only then when its own single purpose remains to be good, excellent art, art as perfect as the creator can make it. The moment this only real and valuable purpose of art is forgotten, the moment it is replaced by a utilitarian aim . . . art . . . loses not only its sense and its beauty but also the very object to which it has been sacrificed: bad art neither teaches nor improves nor enlightens . . . (cited by Boyd 1991, 111).

Of the most pathetic passage in Dickens' *Bleak House* Nabokov reminded his students not to get carried away, admonishing them that "this is a lesson in *style*, not in participative emotion" (*LL*, 94; my italics). In *Nikolai Gogol*, he wrote that "the real plot (as always with Gogol) lies in the *style*" and the tone of such passages makes clear that these remarks might be equally well applied to his own style and his own plots (*NG*, 144; my italics).[8] Years later, he offered a particularly programmatic description of purpose, telling Katharine White, "for me, 'style' *is* matter" (*SL*, 116; Nabokov's italics).

Nabokov says that "style *is* matter," for the same reason that he says, "art and thought, manner and matter, are inseparable" (*LL*, 252). "Style," says Nabokov, "is not a tool, it is not a method, it is not a choice of words alone. Being much more than all this, style constitutes an intrinsic component or characteristic of the author's personality. Thus when we speak of style we mean an artist's peculiar nature" (*LL*, 59–60). Here we can begin to glimpse the full scope Nabokov ascribed to style. For him, it is not an instrument, nor is it simply the author's more or less felicitous choice of words. It is a global conception touching every aspect of the work of art: the inseparability of manner and matter and the full and final expression of the author's particular vision and "peculiar nature." Nabokov once claimed that, "philosophically," he was, "an indivisible monist" (*SO*, 85). It seems that what he had in mind was less an assertion of the unity of matter and mind—the meaning first and most often given to the term—than something that applied to the philosophy of his own works and the only adequate name he found for which was *style*.[9]

In light of this special article of artistic faith, we can understand an element of Nabokov's response to the furor his most famous book caused. In the heat of the scandal surrounding *Lolita*, Nabokov curtly informed its first publisher, Maurice Girodias, "my moral defense of the book is the book itself" (*SL*, 210). In the preface to *David Copperfield* Dickens wrote, "all that I could say of the Story, to any purpose, I have endeavored to say in it" (Dickens, i). Nabokov is saying something similar. To say that his moral defense of *Lolita* was *Lolita* is to say that the work, when carefully read, was more than capable of defending itself. This did not mean, of course, that there was nothing to say about the question of morality therein or that it was sheerly irrelevant to his undertaking.

8. Consequently, separating or abstracting out a series of events from the full flow of the work seemed to Nabokov absurd. This was best reflected in his numerous refusals of his editor James Laughton's courteous requests to include plot summaries of Gogol's works in his biography.

9. Boyd will write that, "Although Nabokov would write differently in all sorts of ways if his metaphysics and ethics were thinner and poorer, we would still read Nabokov without them" (Boyd 2005, 31). He then asks the rhetorical question, "*Why* would we?" and the answer he offers is: "style" (ibid.). In one sense this is doubtless the case as Nabokov's stylistic virtuosity is such that he would likely find appreciative readers no matter his topic, but in another sense it is misleading as it suggests that metaphysics, ethics and style are separable elements in Nabokov's work—or, in other words, that had his metaphysical and ethical ideals been different, his style might have somehow remained the same.

Instead, it was to say that the work itself was intensely and integrally concerned with moral questions—in a fashion inseparable from the manner and the matter of the work itself.

Understanding what Nabokov meant by style presents a challenge to his readers, but, once met, it is not without its rewards. In his finest English poem, Nabokov claims that what poetry can reflect is the intricate, imbricated immanence he saw in the world— "because all hangs together—shape and sound, / heather and honey, vessel and content" ("An Evening of Russian Poetry," *PP*, 158). This conception of the identity of shape and sound, vessel and content, heather and honey allows us to understand a remark he made in an interview from 1961 to the effect that "the intention of art is always pure and always moral" (interview with Anne Guérin, 27). In the introduction to this study, we saw Nabokov speak of *Lolita*'s "purity" and how he associated that qualification with how "carefully contrived" the work was. Here this same epithet ("pure") is immediately and intimately linked to the "moral" element in art. This is not a contradiction born of the bustle, haste, or inaccuracy of an interview (an impossibility given his strictures). For him, there was no paradox in conceiving of a work of art as at once sincere and contrived, no paradox in seeing it as at once art for art's sake and fundamentally moral. For this reason he spoke of "the inherent morality of uninhibited art"—and for this reason he more laconically referred to this as, simply enough, *style*. This word proved his last on the matter. Ultimately, it was only through such style that those three facets of the great writer, "magic, story, lesson," were, as he said, "prone to blend in one impression of unified and unique radiance."

Acknowledgments

My first thanks go to Jonathan Culler who guided this study with kindness and care from beginning to end. Walter Cohen provided invaluable encouragement and assistance throughout. Alongside Professors Culler and Cohen, I warmly thank Professors Richard Klein and Natalie Melas for their direction of this work in its earlier incarnation as a doctoral dissertation at Cornell University. I thank Kevin Ohi and Leah Shafer for reading sections of this work in its first stages and my colleagues in Harvard University's Department of English and American Literature and Language for listening to parts of it in its final ones. I thank my students at Cornell University, Harvard University, the Ecole Normale Supérieure, and the Université de Paris XIII, without whom it would never have been written. Lily Xiao-Lei Huang's lucid and insightful reading of the manuscript did much to pare away the inessential and clarify what remains; Moira Gallagher Weigel helped proofread the final text. I thank John Ackerman for his interest in the project and his help in carrying it to completion; I also thank his colleagues at Cornell University Press, Karen Laun and Susan Barnett, as well as Gavin Lewis for his patient and professional editing of the manuscript. Marjorie Garber, James Engell, Werner Sollors, and Louis Menand all helped me find a title for the work, but none of them should be blamed for the one chosen.

This study would not have been possible without the generous support of Cornell University, the Andrew Mellon Foundation, the Fulbright Foundation, the Deutscher Akademischer Austauschdienst, the Woodrow Wilson

Foundation, Harvard University's Literature Concentration, and its departments of Comparative Literature and English and American Literature and Language. I thank the staffs of Olin, Uris, and Kroch Libraries at Cornell University, Stephen Crook and the staff of the Berg Collection of the New York Public Library, as well as the staff of the Bibliothèque nationale de France in Paris, the Staatsbibliothek in Berlin, and the libraries of Harvard University for their assistance. I thank Tilo Richter for his kind and timely assistance in obtaining the rights to the cover photo.

Finally, I would like to thank Gordon Teskey for the initial idea behind the work. Running into Professor Teskey one day near the beginning of my graduate studies, I responded to his polite and innocuous question about what I planned to write my dissertation on with a list of authors roughly corresponding to the European canon. He nodded kindly, paused briefly, and asked, "Why not just write on a single writer?"

Some material in the Introduction and in chapters 1, 6, and 8 originally appeared, in altered form, in "Vladimir Nabokov and Sigmund Freud, or a Particular Problem," *American Imago* 62, no. 1 (Spring 2005): 59–73; "Eichmann, Empathy, and *Lolita*," *Philosophy and Literature* 30, no. 2 (2006): 311–328; and "The Pattern of Cruelty and the Cruelty of Pattern in Vladimir Nabokov," *The Cambridge Quarterly* 35 (2006): 301–326. The illustration of the cedar waxwing on page 158 is copyrighted by photographer Bruce Macqueen/Agency Dreamstime.

Bibliography

Works by Vladimir Nabokov

Ada, or Ardor: A Family Chronicle. 1969; reprint, New York: Vintage International, 1990.

"Anniversary Notes." Supplement to *TriQuarterly* 17 (1970).

The Annotated Lolita. Edited with preface, introduction, and notes by Alfred Appel Jr., 1970. Revised and updated edition: New York: Vintage, 1991.

Apostrophes: Bernard Pivot rencontre Vladimir Nabokov (Apostrophes: Bernard Pivot meets Vladimir Nabokov). May 30, 1975. Interviewer: Bernard Pivot. Live broadcast by: Antenne 2, Paris. Video version (VHS SECAM): Visions Seuil, Paris.

Bend Sinister. 1949; reprint, New York: Vintage, 1990.

"Conclusive Evidence." *New Yorker,* December 28, 1998, 124–133.

Correspondance: 1940–1971. Edited by S. Karlinsky. Paris: Rivages, 1988.

The Defense. Translated by Michael Scammell in collaboration with the author. 1964; reprint, New York: Vintage, 1989.

Despair. 1966; reprint, New York: Vintage, 1989.

"L'écrivain et l'époque." *Le Mois* 6 (June/July 1931): 137–139.

The Enchanter. Translated by Dmitri Nabokov. 1986; reprint, New York: Vintage, 1991.

Eugene Onegin. A Novel in Verse by Aleksandr Pushkin. Bollingen Series 72. Translated with commentary by Vladimir Nabokov, 4 vols. 1964; rev. ed., Princeton, N.J.: Princeton University Press, 1975.

"An Evening of Russian Poetry." *Poems and Problems,* 158–163.

The Eye. Translated by Dmitri Nabokov in collaboration with the author. 1965; reprint, New York: Vintage, 1990.

Foreword to Mihail Lermontov's *A Hero of Our Time,* in *Nabokov's Congeries,* 247–259.

The Gift. Translated by Michael Scammell with the collaboration of the author. 1963; reprint, New York: Vintage, 1991.

Glory. Translated by Dmitri Nabokov in collaboration with the author. 1971; reprint, New York:Vintage, 1991.

Interview with Guy de Belleval. "Buvant du xérès chez monsieur Nabokov." *Journal de Genève*, March 13–14, 1965, iv.

Interview with Gerard Clarke. "Checking in with Vladimir Nabokov." *Esquire*, July 1975, 67–69.

Interview with Pierre Dommergues. *Les langues modernes*, no. 1 (January–February 1968): 92–102.

Interview with Anne Guérin. *L'Express*, January 26, 1961, 26–27.

Interview with Claude Mercadié. "Sur la promenade des Anglais,Vladimir Nabokov, le père de *Lolita*, a planté sa tente de nomade . . ." *Nice-Matin*, April 13, 1961, 5.

Interview. *Les Nouvelles Littéraires*, October 29, 1959, 17–18.

Interview with Robert Robinson. "The Last Interview." In Quennell, 119–125.

Interview. *Die Zeit*, April 17, 1959.

Invitation to a Beheading. Translated by Dmitri Nabokov in collaboration with the author. 1959; reprint, New York:Vintage, 1989.

King, Queen, Knave. Translated by Dmitri Nabokov in collaboration with the author. 1968; reprint, New York:Vintage, 1989.

Laughter in the Dark. 1938; reprint, New York:Vintage, 1989.

Lectures on Literature. Edited by Fredson Bowers. New York: Harcourt Brace Jovanovich, 1980.

Lectures on Russian Literature. Edited by Fredson Bowers. New York: Harcourt Brace Jovanovich, 1981.

Lolita. In *Vladimir Nabokov: Gesammelte Werke*. Edited and translated into German by Dieter E. Zimmer.Vol. 8. Reinbeck bei Hamburg: Rowohlt, 1989.

Lolita: A Screenplay. In Vladimir Nabokov, *Novels, 1955–1962*. New York: Library of America, 1996.

Look at the Harlequins! 1974; reprint, New York:Vintage, 1990.

The Man from the USSR and Other Plays. Translated and edited by Dmitri Nabokov. New York: Harcourt Brace Jovanovich, 1984.

Mary. Translated by Michael Glenny in collaboration with the author. 1970; reprint, New York:Vintage, 1989.

Morris, Desmond. *The Biology of Art*. New York: Knopf, 1962.

"Mr. Masefield and Clio." *New Republic*, December 9, 1940, 808–809.

Nabokov's Butterflies: Unpublished and Uncollected Writings. Edited and annotated by B. Boyd and R. M. Pyle; new translations from the Russian by Dmitri Nabokov. Boston: Beacon Press, 2000.

Nabokov's Congeries. Edited by Page Stegner. New York:Viking, 1968.

The Nabokov-Wilson Letters: Correspondence between Vladimir Nabokov and Edmund Wilson, 1941–1971. Edited, annotated, and with an introductory essay by Simon Karlinsky. New York: Harper and Row, 1979. Corrected edition, with same pagination, Harper Colophon, 1980.

Nikolai Gogol. 1944; corrected edition, New York: New Directions, 1961.

"On a Book Entitled *Lolita*." In *The Annotated Lolita*, 311–317.

Pale Fire. 1962; reprint, New York:Vintage, 1989.

"Perfection." In *Tyrants Destroyed*, 185–202.

"Playwriting." In *The Man from the USSR and Other Plays*, 315–321.

Pnin. 1957; reprint, New York: Vintage, 1989.
Poems and Problems. New York: McGraw-Hill, 1970.
"Postscript to the Russian Edition of *Lolita*." Translated by Earl D. Sampson in Rivers and Nicol, 188–194.
"Pouchkine ou le vrai et le vraisemblable." *Nouvelle Revue Française* 25 (March 1937); reprint, *Nouvelle Revue Française* 282 (September 1999): 78–95.
The Real Life of Sebastian Knight. 1941; reprint, New York: International, 1992.
Selected Letters 1940–1977. Edited by Dmitri Nabokov and Matthew J. Broccoli. New York: Harcourt Brace Jovanovich, 1989.
Speak, Memory: An Autobiography Revisited. 1967; reprint, New York: Vintage, 1989.
Stories of Vladimir Nabokov. New York: Knopf, 1996.
Strong Opinions. 1973; reprint, New York: Vintage, 1990.
"The Tragedy of Tragedy." In *The Man from the USSR*, 323–342.
Transparent Things. 1972; reprint, New York: Vintage, 1989.
Tyrants Destroyed and Other Stories. Translated by Dmitri Nabokov in collaboration with the author. New York: McGraw Hill, 1975.
"What Faith Means to a Resisting People." *Wellesley Magazine* 26, no. 4 (April 1942): 212.

Archives

Morris Bishop Collection of Nabokov Letters at Cornell. Kroch Library, Cornell University.
Nabokov Collection. Kroch Library, Cornell University.
Nabokov Archive. Berg Collection, New York Public Library.

Other Works

Abercrombie, N. J. "Reviews." *French Studies* 5 (1951): 73–74.
Abrams, M. H. *The Mirror and the Lamp.* Oxford: Oxford University Press, 1953.
———. "Remembering Nabokov." In Gibian and Parker, 218–221.
Adorno, Theodor Wiesengrund. *Gesammelte Schriften.* Twenty volumes. Herausgegeben von Rolf Tiedemann unter Mitwirkung von Gretel Adorno, Susan Buck-Morss, und Klaus Schultz. Frankfurt am Main: Suhrkamp, 1973–1986.
Albee, Edward. *Lolita: A Play by Edward Albee, Adapted from the Novel by Vladimir Nabokov.* New York: Dramatists Play Service, 1979.
Anonymous. "Vladimir Nabokoff-Sirine, L'amoureux de la vie." *Le Mois* 6 (June/July 1931): 140–142.
Alexandrov, Vladimir E., ed. *The Garland Companion to Vladimir Nabokov.* New York: Garland, 1995.
———. *Nabokov's Otherworld.* Princeton, N.J.: Princeton University Press, 1991.
———. "Nature and Artifice." In Alexandrov, ed., 553–556.
———. "A Note on Nabokov's Anti-Darwinism; or, Why Apes Feed on Butterflies in *The Gift*." In *Freedom and Responsibility in Russian Literature: Essays in Honor of Robert Louis Jackson.*

Edited by Elizabeth Cheresh Allen and Gary Saul Morson. Evanston, Ill.: Northwestern University Press, 1995, 239–244.

Amis, Kingsley. Review of *Lolita*. *Spectator*, June 11, 1959.

Amis, Martin. "Introduction." In Vladimir Nabokov, *Lolita*. New York: Everyman's Library, 1992, vii–xxv.

Anderson, Douglas. "Nabokov's Genocidal and Nuclear Holocausts in *Lolita*." *Mosaic* 29 (June 1996): 73–90.

Andrews, David. *Aestheticism, Nabokov and Lolita*. Lewiston: Edwin Mellen, 1999.

——. "Varieties of Determinism: Nabokov among Rorty, Freud, and Sartre." *Nabokov Studies* 6 (2000–2001): 1–33.

Appel, Alfred, Jr. "*Lolita*: The Springboard of Parody." *Wisconsin Studies in Contemporary Literature* 8 (Spring 1967): 204–224; reprinted in Dembo, Bloom.

——. "Nabokov: A Portrait." *Atlantic*, September 1971, 77–92.

Appel, Alfred, Jr. and Charles Newman, eds. *Nabokov: Criticism, Reminiscences, Translations, and Tributes*. Evanston, Ill.: Northwestern University Press, 1970.

Arendt, Hannah. *Eichmann in Jerusalem: A Report on the Banality of Evil*. Rev. and enl. ed. New York: Penguin, 1964.

Augustine. *Confessions*. Translated by William Watts. Loeb Classical Library. 2 vols. Cambridge, Mass: Harvard University Press, 1988.

Bacon, Francis. *The Advancement of Learning*. New York: Modern Library, 2001.

Bader, Julia. *Crystal Land: Artifice in Nabokov's English Novels*. Berkeley: University of California Press, 1972.

Ballestrini, Nassim. "Nabokov Criticism in German-Speaking Countries: A Survey." *Nabokov Studies* 5 (1998–99): 184–234.

Baudelaire, Charles. *Œuvres complètes*. Edited by Claude Pichois. 2 vols. Paris: Gallimard, 1975–76.

Belletto, Steven. "Of Pickaninnies and Nymphets: Race in *Lolita*." *Nabokov Studies* 9 (2005): 1–17.

Benjamin, Walter. *Gesammelte Schriften*. Edited by Rolf Tiedemann and Herman Schweppenhäuser. 7 vols. Frankfurt am Main: Suhrkamp, 1974–1989.

Berman, Jeffrey. *The Talking Cure: Literary Representations of Psychoanalysis*. New York: New York University Press, 1985.

Bethea, David M. "Nabokov and Khodasevich." In Alexandrov, ed., 452–462.

——. "Style." In Alexandrov, ed., 696–704.

Bishop, John. *Joyce's Book of the Dark: Finnegans Wake*. Madison: University of Wisconsin Press, 1986.

Bishop, Morris. "Nabokov at Cornell," In Appel and Newman, eds., 234–239.

Blake, William. *The Complete Poetry and Prose of William Blake*. Edited by Harold Bloom. Commentary by David Erdman. Second Edition. New York: Anchot, 1997.

Blanchot, Maurice. *L'espace littéraire*. Paris: Gallimard, 1955.

Bloom, Harold. *The American Religion: The Emergence of the Post-Christian Nation*. New York: Simon and Schuster, 1992.

——. *The Anxiety of Influence*. 2d ed. Oxford: Oxford University Press, 1997.

——. "Editor's Note." In Bloom, ed., *Vladimir Nabokov's Lolita*, vii–viii.

——. "Introduction." In Bloom, ed., *Vladimir Nabokov's Lolita*, 1–4.

——, ed. *Vladimir Nabokov*. New York: Chelsea House, 1987.

——, ed. *Vladimir Nabokov's Lolita*. Modern Critical Interpretations Series. New York: Chelsea House, 1987.

Blum, Virginia L. "Nabokov's *Lolita*/Lacan's Mirror." In *Hide and Seek: The Child Between Psychoanalysis and Fiction.* Urbana: University of Illinois Press, 1995, 201–245.

Booth, Wayne. *The Rhetoric of Fiction.* Chicago: University of Chicago Press, 1961.

Borges, Jorge Luis. *Ficciones.* Translated by Anthony Kerrigan. New York: Grove Weidenfeld, 1962.

——. *Labyrinths.* ed. Donald A. Yates and James E. Irby. New York: New Directions, 1964.

——. *This Craft of Verse: The Charles Eliot Norton Lectures 1967–1968.* Cambridge, Mass.: Harvard University Press, 2000.

Boyd, Brian. "'Even Homais Nods': Nabokov's Fallibility, or, How to Revise *Lolita*." *Nabokov Studies* 2 (1995): 62–86.

——. "Nabokov as Storyteller." In *The Cambridge Companion to Vladimir Nabokov.* Edited by Julian Connolly. Cambridge: Cambridge University Press, 2005, 31–48.

——. *Nabokov's Ada: The Place of Consciousness.* Ann Arbor, Mich.: Ardis Press, 1985.

——. *Nabokov's Pale Fire: The Magic of Artistic Discovery.* Princeton, N.J.: Princeton University Press, 1999.

——. *Vladimir Nabokov: The Russian Years.* Princeton, N.J.: Princeton University Press, 1990.

——. *Vladimir Nabokov: The American Years.* Princeton, N.J.: Princeton University Press, 1991.

Bradley, A. C. "Poetry for Poetry's Sake." In *Oxford Lectures on Poetry.* London: Macmillan, 1920. 24.

Bruss, Elizabeth. *Autobiographical Acts: The Changing Situation of a Literary Genre.* Baltimore: Johns Hopkins University Press, 1976.

Burgess, Anthony. Interview. *Paris Review* 14, no. 56 (Spring 1973): 119–163.

Calvino, Italo. *Saggi 1945–1985.* Edited by Mario Barenghi. 2 vols. Milan: Arnoldo Mondadori, 1995.

Carroll, William. "Nabokov's Signs and Symbols." In *A Book of Things About Vladimir Nabokov.* Ed. by Carl R. Proffer. Ann Arbor, Mich.: Ardis, 1974, 203–217.

Cassirer, Ernst. *Kants Leben und Lehre.* Berlin: B. Cassirer, 1921.

Cicero. *Brutus*, trans. G. L. Hendrickson; *Orator*, trans. H. M. Hubbell. Loeb Classical Library. Cambridge, Mass.: Harvard University Press, 1962.

Clifton, Gladys M. "Humbert Humbert and the Limits of Artistic License." In *Nabokov's Fifth Arc: Nabokov and Others on His Life's Work.* Edited by J. E. Rivers and Charles Nicol. Austin: University of Texas Press, 1982, 153–171.

Coates, Steven L. and Johnson, Kurt. *Nabokov's Blues: The Scientific Odyssey of a Literary Genius.* Cambridge, Mass.: Zoland Books, 1999.

Coetzee, J. M. *The Lives of Animals.* Princeton, N.J.: Princteon University Press, 1999.

Coleridge, Samuel Taylor. *Biographia Literaria, or Biographical Sketches of My Literary Life and Opinions.* Edited by James Engell and W. Jackson Bate. Princeton, N.J.: Princeton University Press, 1983.

——. *The Notebooks of Samuel Taylor Coleridge.* Edited by Kathleen Coburn. 3 vols. New York: Pantheon, 1957.

Constant, Benjamin. *Journaux intimes.* Edited by A. Roulin and C. Roth. Paris: Gallimard, 1952.

Connolly, Julian. "'Nature's Reality' or Humbert's 'Fancy'? Scenes of Reunion and Murder in *Lolita*." *Nabokov Studies* 2 (1995): 41–61.

——. "Nabokov's Dialogue with Dostoevsky: *Lolita* and 'The Gentle Creature.'" *Nabokov Studies* 4 (1997): 15–36.

——, ed. *Nabokov and His Fiction: New Perspectives.* Cambridge, UK: Cambridge University Press, 1999.

Corliss, Richard. *Lolita*. London: British Film Institute, 1995.

Cousin, Victor. *Cours de philosophie professée à la faculté des letters pendant l'année 1818 par M. V. Cousin sur le fondement des idées absolues du vrai, du beau et du bien publié avec son autorisation et d'après les meilleures rédactions de ce cours par M. Adolphe Garnier*. Paris: L. Hachette, 1836.

Couturier, Maurice. "Introduction." *Oeuvres romanesques complètes*. Vol. 1. Paris: Gallimard, 1999.

——. "The Magician's Doubts and the Risks of Fiction." *Nabokov Studies* 3 (1996): 215–222.

——. "Nabokov and Flaubert." In Alexandrov, ed., 405–411.

——. *Nabokov, ou la tyrannie de l'auteur*. Paris: Editions du Seuil, 1993.

——. "Narcissism and Demand in *Lolita*." *Nabokov Studies* 9 (2005): 19–46.

Cwagenbaum, Bernard, with Pierre Dommergues. *Vladimir Nabokov est un joueur d'échecs*. Film documentary. Collection Nouveau dimanche: Images et idées. Paris: ORTF, 1967.

Dawson, Kellie. "Rare and Unfamiliar Things: Vladimir Nabokov's 'Monsters.'" *Nabokov Studies* 9 (2005): 115–131.

Deleuze, Gilles and Guattari, Félix. *L'Anti-Œdipe*. Paris: Minuit, 1973.

——. *Mille Plateaux*. Paris, Minuit, 1980.

Dembo, L. S., ed. *Nabokov: The Man and his Work*. Madison: University of Wisconsin Press, 1967.

Derrida, Jacques. *De la grammatologie*. Paris: Editions de Minuit, 1967.

De Vries, Gerard. "'Perplex'd in the Extreme': Moral Facets of Vladimir Nabokov's Work." *Nabokov Studies* 2 (1995): 135–152.

Dickens, Charles. *David Copperfield*. Oxford: Oxford University Press, 1999.

Diment, Galya. "Uncollected Critical Writings." In Alexandrov, ed., 733–739.

Dolinin, Alexander A. "Nabokov's Time Doubling: From *The Gift* to *Lolita*." *Nabokov Studies* 2 (1995): 3–40.

——. "Of some anagrams in the work of Vladimir Nabokov." In *Culture of Russian Diaspora: Vladimir Nabokov—100*. Tallinn, 2000, 99; translated from the Russian by Savely Senderovich, Nabokov List Serve, November 3, 2000.

——. "What Happened to Sally Horner?: A Real-Life Source of Nabokov's *Lolita*." *TLS*, September 9, 2005.

duCille, Ann. "The Shirley Temple of My Familiar." *Transition* 73 (1997): 10–32.

Eco, Umberto. *Le poetiche di Joyce: Dalla "Summa" al "Finnegans Wake."* Milan: Bompiani, 1966.

——. "Postille a *Il nome della rosa*, 1983." In *Il nome della rosa*. Milan: Bompiani, 2000.

Egan, Rose Francis. "The Genesis of the Theory of 'Art for Art's Sake' in Germany and England." *Smith College Studies in Modern Languages* 2, no. 4 (July 1921): 5–61.

Eliot, T. S. *Selected Essays 1917–1932*. 3d ed. London: Faber & Faber, 1951.

Ellis, Havelock. *Etudes de psychologie sexuelle*. Vol. 3. Paris: Le Livre précieux, 1964.

Emerson, Ralph Waldo. *Essays and Lectures*. Ed. Joel Porte. New York: Library of America, 1983.

Epstein, Jason. *Book Business*. New York: Norton, 2001.

Ferger, George. "Who's Who in the Sublimelight: 'Suave John Ray' and *Lolita*'s 'Secret Points.'" *Nabokov Studies* 8 (2004): 137–198.

Fiedler, Leslie. *Love and Death in the American Novel*. Rev. ed. New York: Stein and Day, 1975.

Field, Andrew. *Nabokov: His Life in Art*. Boston: Little, Brown, 1967.

——. *Nabokov: His Life in Part*. New York: Viking, 1977.

——. *VN: The Life and Art of Vladimir Nabokov.* New York: Crown, 1986.

Flaubert, Gustave. *Correspondance.* Edited by Jean Bruneau. Vol. 2. Paris: Gallimard, 1973.

——. *Madame Bovary.* Collection Classiques Garnier. Paris: Garnier, 1971.

——. *Les Pensées suivies du Dictionnaire des idées reçues.* Edited by Jean-Yves Clément. Paris: Cherche Midi, 1993.

——. *Préface à la vie d'écrivain.* Paris: Seuil, 1963.

Flaubert, Gustave and Sand, Georges. *The George Sand–Gustave Flaubert Letters.* Translated by A. L. McKenzie. Chicago: Academy Chicago, 1979.

Fletcher, John. *Novel and Reader.* London: Marion Boyars, 1980.

Fowler, Douglas. *Reading Nabokov.* Ithaca, N.Y.: Cornell University Press, 1974.

Freud, Sigmund. *Gesammelte Werke.* 18 vols. Frankfurt am Main: Fischer Verlag, 1968–78.

Leonardo da Vinci and a Memory of His Childhood. In *The Standard Edition of the Complete Works of Sigmund Freud.* 24 vols. Edited by by James Strachey et al. London: The Hogarth Press and the Institute of Psychoanalysis, 1953–74.

——. *Das Unbehagen in der Kultur.* Frankfurt am Main: Fischer, 1994.

Freud, Sigmund and Andreas-Salomé, Lou. *Sigmund Freud, Lou Andreas-Salomé.* Translated by Elaine and William Robinson-Scott. London: Hogarth, 1970.

Freud, Sigmund and Jung, Carl. 1974. *The Freud/Jung Letters: The Correspondence between Sigmund Freud and C. G. Jung.* Edited by William McGuire. Translated by Ralph Manheim and R. F. C. Hull. Princeton, N.J.: Princeton University Press, 1974.

Frosch, Thomas R. "Parody and Authenticity in *Lolita.*" In Pifer, ed., 39–56.

Frye, Northrop. *The Anatomy of Criticism.* Princeton, N.J.: Princeton University Press, 1957.

Gardiner, Muriel, ed. *The Wolf-Man by the Wolf-Man.* New York: Basic Books, 1971.

Gay, Peter. *Freud: A Life for Our Time.* New York: Anchor Books, 1988.

Gibian, George and Stephen Jan Parker, eds. *The Achievements of Vladimir Nabokov.* Ithaca, N.Y.: Cornell Center for International Studies, 1984.

Goethe, John Wolfgang von. *Werke. Hamburger Ausgabe (14 Bände).* Herausgegeben von Erich Trunz. Hamburg: C.H. Beck, 1999.

Goldman, Eric. "'Knowing' Lolita: Sexual Deviance and Normality in Nabokov's *Lolita.*" *Nabokov Studies* 8 (2004): 87–104.

Gombrich, E. H. *The Story of Art.* 16th ed. New York: Phaidon, 1995.

Grabes, Herbert. *Fictitious Biographies: Vladimir Nabokov's English Novels.* Translated in collaboration with Pamela Gliniars. The Hague: Mouton, 1977.

Grayson, Jane. Review of Alexandrov, ed. *Nabokov Studies* 3 (1996): 210–215.

Green, Geoffrey. *Freud and Nabokov.* Lincoln: University of Nebraska Press, 1988.

——. "Visions of a 'Perfect Past': Nabokov, Autobiography, Biography, and Fiction." *Nabokov Studies* 3 (1996): 89–100.

Green, Hannah. "Mister Nabokov." *New Yorker,* February 14, 1977, 32–35.

Gregory, Robert. "Porpoise-iveness without Porpoise: Why Nabokov Called James a Fish." *Henry James Review* 6, no. 1 (Fall 1984): 52–59.

Haven, Cynthia. "The Lolita Question." *Stanford,* May/June 2006, 70–75.

Hegel, G. W. F. *Werke in zwanzig Bänden.* Theorie-Werkausgabe. Frankfurt: Suhrkamp, 1970.

Hollander, John. Review of *Lolita. Partisan Review,* Autumn 1956; reprinted in Page, 81–84.

Holt, Terry. "Shades of Nabokov." *Cornell Reports* 17, no. 3 (Summer 1983): 2–33.

Housman, A. E. *The Name and Nature of Poetry.* Cambridge, UK: Cambridge University Press, 1933.

Hughes, Ted. *Hawk in the Rain.* London: Faber & Faber, 1957.

Hugo, Victor. *Choses vues.* 2 vols. Paris: Editions de la Librairie Ollendorf, 1913.

Hume, David. *An Enquiry Concerning Human Understanding.* Edited by L. A. Selby-Bigge and P. H. Nidditch. 3d. ed. Oxford: Clarendon Press, 1975.

Jakobson, Roman. "Closing Statement: Linguistics and Poetics." In *Style in Language.* Edited by Thomas A. Sebeok. Cambridge, Mass.: Technology Press and John Wiley, 1960, 350–377.

James, Henry. *Complete Tales of Henry James.* Edited by Leon Edel. Vol. 9. Philadelphia: Lippincott, 1964.

——. *Literary Criticism.* New York: Library of America, 1984.

Johnson, D. Barton. "The Nabokov-Sartre Controversy." *Nabokov Studies* 1 (1994): 69–81.

Johnson, D. Barton and Brian Boyd. "Prologue: The Otherworld." In *Nabokov's World*, vol. 1: *The Shape of Nabokov's World.* Edited by J. Grayson, A. McMillin, and P. Meyer. New York: Palgrave, 2002, 19–26.

Joyce, James. *Portrait of the Artist as a Young Man.* New York: Bantam, 1992.

Kant, Immanuel. *Critique of Judgment.* Translated by Werner S. Pluhar. Indianapolis: Hackett, 1987. *Die drei Kritiken* Bd. 11. Ed. Alexander Ulfig. Köln: Parkland Verlag, 1999.

Karlinsky, Simon. "Nabokov and Chekhov: The Lesser Russian Tradition." *TriQuarterly* 17 (Winter 1970): 7–16.

Kauffman, Linda. *Special Delivery: Epistolary Modes in Modern Fiction.* Chicago: University of Chicago Press, 1992.

Khodasevich, Vladislav. "On Sirin." Translated Michael H. Walker, Edited by Simon Karlinsky and Robert P. Hughes. In Appel and Newman, eds., 96–101.

Krafft-Ebing, Dr. R. von. *Psychopathia Sexualis, with Special Reference to Contrary Sexual Instinct: A Medico-Legal Study.* Translated by Charles Gilbert Chaddock, M.D. Philadelphia: The F. A. Davis Company, 1895.

Laansoo, Mati. "An Interview with Vladimir Nabokov for the CBC." *Vladimir Nabokov Research Newsletter* (Lawrence, Kansas) 10 (Spring 1983): 39–48.

Maar, Michael. "Curse of the First Lolita: Heinz von Lichberg and the Pre-history of the Nymphet." *TLS*, April 2, 2004, 13–15.

——. *The Two Lolitas.* Translated by Perry Anderson. New York and London: Verso, 2005.

——. "Was wußte Nabokov?" *Frankfurter Allgemeine Zeitung*, March 19, 2004, 37.

Machen, Ernest. "Sources of Inspiration for *Lolita.*" *TLS*, November 27, 1998, 17.

Maclagan, Eric. "Leonardo in the Consulting Room." *Burlington Magazine* 42 (1923): 54–57.

McHale, Brian. "The Great (Textual) Communicator, or, Blindness and Insight." *Nabokov Studies* 2 (1995): 277–289.

McNeely, Trevor. "Lo and Behold: Solving the *Lolita* Riddle." *Studies in the Novel* 21, no. 2 (Summer 1989): 182–200.

Megerle, Brenda. "The Tantalization of Lolita." *Studies in the Novel* 11, no. 3 (1979): 338–348.

Mercanton, James. "The Hours of James Joyce." In *Portraits of the Artist in Exile: Recollections of James Joyce by Europeans.* Edited by Willard Potts. Seattle: University of Washington Press, 1979), 206–252.

Meyer, Priscilla. *Find What the Sailor Has Hidden: Vladimir Nabokov's Pale Fire.* Middletown, Conn.: Wesleyan University Press, 1988.

Milton, John. *The Complete Poetical Works of John Milton.* Edited by Douglas Bush. Boston: Houghton Mifflin, 1965.

Mizruchi, Susan "*Lolita* in History." *American Literature* 75, no. 3 (2003): 629–652.

Mouchard, Claude. "Doctor Froid." In Roth, ed., 130–133.

Moynahan, Julian. "Nabokov and Joyce." In Alexandrov, ed., 433–444.

Nabokov, Dmitri. "On Revisiting Father's Room." In Quennell, ed., 126–136.

——. "Translating with Nabokov." In Gibian and Parker, eds., 145–177.

Nabokov, Véra. "Predislovie." In *Stikhi,* by Vladimir Nabokov, 3–4. Ann Arbor, MI: Ardis, 1979.

Nafisi, Azar. *Reading Lolita in Tehran: A Memoir in Books.* New York: Random House, 2003.

Naiman, Eric. "A Filthy Look at Shakespeare's *Lolita.*" *Comparative Literature* 58, no. 1 (Winter 2006): 1–24.

Nemerov, Howard. "The Morality of Art." *Kenyon Review* 19 (1957): 313–321.

Nicol, Charles. "Politics." In Alexandrov, ed., 625–628.

Nietzsche, Friedrich. *Sämtliche Werke: Kritische Studienausgabe.* Edited by G. Colli und M. Montinari. 15 vols. Berlin: De Gruyter, 1980.

Nivat, Georges. "Speak, Memory." In *The Garland Companion to Vladimir Nabokov.* Edited by Vladimir E. Alexandrov. New York: Garland, 1995, 672–685.

Oates, Joyce Carol. "A Personal View of Vladimir Nabokov." *Saturday Review.* January 1973; reprinted in Roth, ed., 104–108.

Obholzer, Karin. *The Wolf-Man: Conversations with Freud's Patient—Sixty Years Later.* Translated by Michael Shaw. New York: Continuum, 1982.

Ohi, Kevin. "Narcissism and Queer Reading in *Pale Fire.*" *Nabokov Studies* 5 (1998–1999): 153–178.

Packman, David. *Vladimir Nabokov: The Structure of Literary Desire.* Columbia: University of Missouri Press, 1982.

Page, Norman, ed. *Nabokov: The Critical Heritage.* London: Routledge, Kegan & Paul, 1982.

Parker, Dorothy. "Sex—Without the Asterisks." *Esquire,* October 1958, 102–103.

Pater, Walter. *The Renaissance: Studies in Art and Poetry. The 1893 Text.* Edited by D. Hill. Berkeley: University of California Press, 1980.

Pera, Pia. *Lo's Diary.* Translated by Ann Goldstein. New York: Foxrock, 1999.

Pfister, Oskar. "Kryptolalie, Kryptographie und Unbewußter Vexierbild bei Normalen." *Jahrbuch für psychoanalytische und psychopathologische Forschungen* 5 (1913): 146–151.

Pifer, Ellen. "*Lolita.*" In Alexandrov, ed., 305–321.

——. "Nabokov and the Art of Exile." In Roth, ed., 215–221.

——. *Nabokov and the Novel.* Cambridge, Mass.: Harvard University Press, 1980.

——. "Nabokov's Novel Offspring: Lolita and Her Kin." In Pifer, ed., 83–110.

——, ed. *Vladimir Nabokov's Lolita: A Casebook.* New York: Oxford University Press, 2003.

The Collected Dialogues of Plato, including the Letters. Edited by Edith Hamilton and Huntington Cairns. Translated by Benjamin Jowett. New York: Pantheon Books, 1961 (Bollingen Series LXXI).

Poe, Edgar Allen. *Essays and Reviews.* New York: Library of America, 1984.

Pope, Alexander. *Essay on Man.* Edited by John Butt. New York: Methuen & Co. Ltd., 1982.

Premack, David and Ann James Premack. *The Mind of an Ape.* New York: W. W. Norton, 1984.

Proffer, Carl. *Keys to* Lolita. Bloomington: Indiana University Press, 1968.

Proust, Marcel. *Correspondance.* Edited by Philip Kolb. 21 vols. Paris: Plon, 1970–93.

——. *A la recherche du temps perdu.* Edited by Jean-Yves Tadié. 4 vols. Paris: Gallimard, 1987–89.

Quennell, Peter. ed. *Vladimir Nabokov: A Tribute.* New York: William Morrow, 1980.

Rampton, David. *Vladimir Nabokov: A Critical Study of the Novels.* Cambridge, UK: Cambridge University Press, 1984.

Rayfield, Donald, ed. *The Confessions of Victor X*. New York: Grove Press, 1985.

Raymond, Marcel. *Jean-Jacques Rousseau: La quête de soi et la rêverie*. Paris: José Corti 1962.

Rilke, Rainer Maria. *Werke: Kommentierte Ausgabe*. Edited by Manfred Engel, Ulrich Fülleborn, Horst Nalewski, and August Stahl. 4 vols. Frankfurt am Main: Insel Verlag, 1996.

Rivers, J. E. "Proust, Nabokov and *Ada*." *French-American Review* 1 (Fall 1977); reprinted in Roth, ed., 134–157.

Rivers, J. E. and Charles Nicol, eds. *Nabokov's Fifth Arc: Nabokov and Others on His Life's Work*. Austin: University of Texas Press, 1982.

Roazen, Paul. "Oedipus at Versailles: New Evidence of Freud's Part in a Study of Woodrow Wilson." *TLS*, April 22, 2005, 12–13.

Robbe-Grillet, Alain. "Notes sur la notion d'itinéraire dans *Lolita*." *L'Arc* (Aix-en-Provence) 7, no. 24 (Spring 1964): 35–36.

Rorty, Richard. *Contingency, Irony, Solidarity*. Cambridge, UK: Cambridge University Press, 1989.

Roth, Phyllis A., ed. *Critical Essays on Vladimir Nabokov*. Boston: G. K. Hall, 1984.

Rothstein, Eric. "'Lolita': Nymphet at Normal School." *Contemporary Literature* 41, no. 1 (Spring 2000): 22–55.

Rousseau, Jean-Jacques. *Confessions*. Vol. 1 of *Œuvres complètes*. Edited by B. Gagnebin et M. Raymond with Robert Osmont. Paris: Gallimard, 1959.

———. *Emile*. Translated by Allan Bloom. New York: Basic Books, 1979.

Rowe, William Woodin. *Nabokov's Deceptive World*. New York: New York University Press, 1971.

Schapiro, Meyer. "Leonardo and Freud: An Art-Historical Study." *Journal of the History of Ideas* 17 (1956): 147–178.

Schickert, Katharina. *Der Schutz literarischer Urheberschaft im Rom der klassischen Antike*. Tübingen: Mohr Siebeck, 2005.

Schiff, Stacy. *Véra (Mrs. Vladimir Nabokov)*. New York: Random House, 1999.

Schiller, Friedrich. *Sämtliche Werke*. Edited by Gerhard Fricke und Herbert G. Göpfert. Rev. ed. Munich: Carl Hanser Verlag, 1993.

Senderovich, Savely. "Dickens in Nabokov's *Invitation to a Beheading*: A Figure of Concealment." *Nabokov Studies* 3 (1996): 13–32.

Shakespeare, William. *A Midsummer Night's Dream*. New York: Penguin, 2000.

Shapiro, Gavriel. "Setting His Myriad Faces in His Text: Nabokov's Authorial Presence Revisited." In Connolly, ed., 15–25.

Shelley, Percy Bysshe. *The Prose Works of Percy Bysshe Shelley*. Edited by E. B. Murray. Oxford: Clarendon Press, 1993.

Shute, Jenefer. "Nabokov and Freud." In Alexandrov, ed., 412–420.

Spector, Jack J. *The Aesthetics of Freud: A Study in Psychoanalysis and Art*. London: Allen Lane, 1972.

Stegner, Page. *Escape Into Aesthetics: The Art of Vladimir Nabokov*. New York: Dial Press, 1966.

Steiner, George. *Extraterritorial: Papers on Literature and the Language Revolution*. New York: Atheneum, 1971.

Stevens, Wallace. *Collected Poetry and Prose*. New York: Library of America, 1997.

Tamir-Ghez, Nomi. "The Art of Persuasion in Nabokov's *Lolita*." In Pifer, ed., 17–38.

Tekiner, Christina. "Time in *Lolita*." *Modern Fiction Studies* 25 (1979): 463–469.

Toker, Leona. "Nabokov and Bergson." In Alexandrov, ed., 367–373.

———. *Nabokov: The Mystery of Literary Structures*. Ithaca, N.Y.: Cornell University Press, 1989.

Trilling, Lionel. "The Last Lover—Vladimir Nabokov's 'Lolita.'" *Encounter*, October 1958, 9–19; reprinted in Page, ed., 92–102.

———. *The Liberal Imagination*. New York: Doubleday, 1957.

Updike, John. *Assorted Prose*. New York: Knopf, 1965.

Vidal, Gore. "Professor V. Nabokov." *The Observer* (London), May 12, 1974; reprinted in Vidal's *United States. Essays. 1952–1992*. New York: Abacus, 1994.

Wetzsteon, Ross. "Nabokov as Teacher." In Appel and Newman, eds., 240–246.

———. "A Student's Recollection." *Village Voice,* November 30, 1967; reprinted in *Cornell Alumni News*, February 1968, 12–15.

White, Duncan. "'(I have camouflaged everything, my love)': *Lolita*'s Pregnant Parentheses." *Nabokov Studies* 9 (2005): 47–64).

White, Edmund. "Nabokov: Beyond Parody." In Gibian and Parker, 5–28.

Wilcox, John. "The Beginnings of *l'art pour l'art.*" *Journal of Aesthetics and Art Criticism* 11, no. 4 (June 1953): 360–377.

Wilde, Oscar. *The Complete Works of Oscar Wilde*. Vol. 4. New York: Doubleday, Page. 1923.

Wilson, Edmund. *Axel's Castle*. London: Collins, 1961.

———. *Upstate: Records and Recollections of Northern New York*. New York: Farrar, Straus and Giroux, 1971.

Wind, Edgar. *Art and Anarchy*. London: Faber & Faber, 1963.

Wittgenstein, Ludwig. *Philosophical Occasions: 1912–1951*. Indianapolis: Hackett, 1983.

———. *Tractatus Logico-Philosophicus: German Text with English Translation*. Translated by C. K. Ogden. London: Routledge, 1999.

Wood, Michael. *The Magician's Doubts: Nabokov and the Risks of Fiction*. London: Chatto & Windus, 1994.

Woolf, Virginia. *To the Lighthouse*. New York: Harvest, 1989.

Wordsworth, William. "Preface to *The Excursion*" (1814). In *The Poetical Works*. Edited by Thomas Hutchinson and Ernest de Selincourt. London: Oxford University Press, 1961.

Zimmer, Dieter E. "Zeittafel zur Entstehung des Romans." In Nabokov, *Lolita* (*Gesammelte Werke*, vol. 8), 696–700.

———. *A Guide to Nabokov's Butterflies and Moths*. Hamburg: Dieter E. Zimmer, 2001.

INDEX